Richard Murphy Architects

The Fruitmarket Gallery, Edinburgh

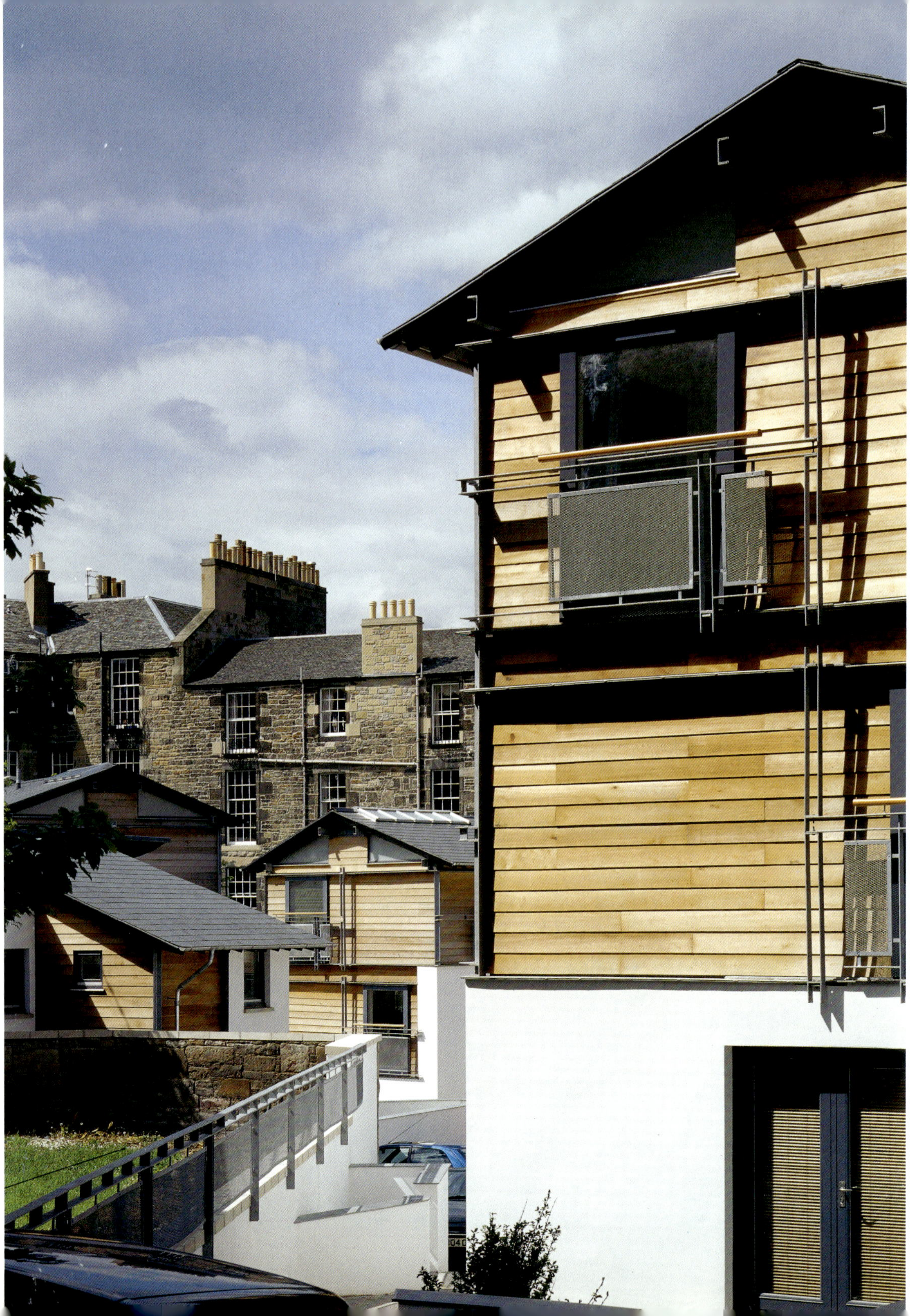

Richard Murphy Architects
Ten Years of Practice

Essay by Richard Weston

Acknowledgements

This book marks ten years of the practice of Richard Murphy Architects, ten years that would not have been possible without the enthusiastic collaboration of two groups of people: my past and current clients and those who have worked or are working at No 34 Blair Street. I have been extremely fortunate on both counts. There is a book waiting to be written called "Great Clients of the World" and undoubtedly a number of our own would feature; indeed I believe that it is no coincidence that our best work has been for our most responsive, open-minded and above all, trusting clients of which there have been many. In the same period I calculate that almost a hundred students and architects have passed through No 34. I like to think of design and its realisation as a wholly collaborative affair and I hope that the experience has been as invigorating for them as it has been for me; indeed I find it very unnatural to write of our work in the first person singular. The practice is moving to a new home at the Breakfast Mission in Old Fishmarket Close and the new conditions will permit a long overdue civilized working environment without I hope any loss of the intensity generated from what Charles McKean famously described as the 'bistro atmosphere' of No 34.

The preparation of this book would not have been possible without the forbearance of my colleagues, in particular my associates Bill Black, James Mason and Matt Bremner. The logistics of putting the book together have fallen on Matt Loader of the office and the ever patient book designer Lucy Richards. Richard Weston's essay has, I believe, recorded our work with both proper academic rigour and individual enthusiasm and my three days with Richard touring twenty-one of our buildings were a delight – even if he did remark as we parted at Edinburgh airport that he was 'Murphed out!'. Thanks are also due to John and Eileen Francis, Sue and Rod Stoneman, Rob Joiner and Patrick Webb who have each written generously of their side of the story of a creative collaboration and to Magnus Linklater for his enthusiastic overview of our activities in the world of the arts during his time as Chairman of the Scottish Arts Council.

The exhibition which this publication accompanies is a collaboration with our past client The Fruitmarket Gallery and in particular the Director Graeme Murray and Juliet Knight and George Gilliland. The film by Murray Grigor which forms an essential part of the show is the latest in a number of joint projects with a very good friend. The lot of a film maker and an architect have much in common, and Murray always ensures that we never, as he puts it, 'synchronize depressions'. As an office we invite external criticism and many of the projects featured here have benefited from the frequent and welcome visits of my mentor Isi Metzstein. I am delighted also that Charles McKean agreed to write our foreword, particularly as he had such a major role in setting up the competition for Dundee Contemporary Arts, our most ambitious project to date.

Finally, neither exhibition, film nor book would have been possible without generous support from Hillaldam Sliding Door Gear, Apotheek Van Hulten, Scottish Enterprise, Scottish Screen and Creative Edinburgh, but in particular to the extraordinary generosity of the Dunard Fund without whose intervention none of this would have happened.

Richard Murphy
Edinburgh, September 2001

Contents

6 Foreword by Charles McKean
8 **Richard Murphy, The First Decade:**
   Essay by Richard Weston

29 **House Extensions**
30 Blytheman House
32 Francis House
35 Palmer House
38 Morrison House
40 Comparative constructional sections

43 **Houses**
44 Stoneman House
48 Van Hulten House
52 Stewart House
56 Marshall House
57 MacLean House
58 Høgel House 1
62 Høgel House 2
63 Knox House
64 Gordon Houses
66 McCormack House
68 Murphy House
70 Harrison House

75 **Housing**
76 Dublin Colonies
80 Canongate
83 Graham Square
86 Old Fishmarket Close
88 Belford Road
90 Cramond

95 **Social Buildings**
96 Maggie's Centre
100 Harmeny School
104 St Andrew's University
106 Jesus College
108 Napier University
112 Inverewe Gardens Restaurant
114 Adult Learning Centre, Kirkintilloch
116 Bath Street Office Foyer
117 Edinburgh Park Office

119 **Buildings for the Arts**
120 The Fruitmarket Gallery
127 Dundee Contemporary Arts
136 Hamilton Arts Centre
138 National Gallery of Scottish Art and Design
140 Peebles Arts Centre
142 Centre for Contemporary Art and the Natural World
146 Caenarfon Creative Enterprise Centre
150 Stirling Tolbooth Arts Centre

156 **A Moment of Introspection:**
   Afterword by Richard Murphy
160 The Practice
161 Awards
162 Photography credits
163 Exhibition credits
164 Colophon

Foreword

It is a mature, small country that can easily welcome unusual success and/or innovation in its midst, and, architecturally, Scotland is still maturing. The probability is, therefore, that the publication of the projects of first ten years of the Murphy atêlier, created from their crazily overcrowded shop at the louche end of Blair Street (not that Blair!) next to the sauna, will be regarded as bumptious if not presumptuous. Yet, at the least, it might be justified by the rare concentration of awards and prizes the practice has been awarded within and without Scotland since its inception.

Nobody should be surprised at the bumptiousness, however, if they have ever attended a Murphy exhibition or building opening, when the most enthusiastic speakers proved to be the clients, or the builders, or even the sliding door manufacturer. The office is proud of its work, as are its clients and creators and fabricators. For a young architect, having passed through Murphy's is a dangerously good thing to have on a CV.

The great value of this book is that it brings together many dispersed or carefully hidden projects. Sometimes the only way of identifying a Murphy project is to look out for queues of patient people on suburban pavements waiting to visit some tiny extension or alteration his clients had made available on *Doors Open Days*. The queues, long before the current extent of his celebrity, spoke volumes about a growing reputation passed by word-of-mouth. So it is only in a volume like this that generic themes or philosophies, so carefully analysed in Richard Weston's introduction, can be observed and questioned.

There are three in particular worth emphasising: the use of light, and its accentuation by mirrors, by carefully created passages from dark into light (or its reverse); by sudden changes in volume, or by the identification and celebration of unperceived views and vistas, parts of which Weston attributes to the influence of Sir John Soane, and most obvious in the homage Murphy paid to Soane in Lord Prosser's Library. Most of his earlier buildings were small, often extending from an older, usually darker, and often gloomy-interiored house; and the move from large volumes with a fixed light source enveloped in mirk, to the brilliance of the extension was often astounding. Gordon Benson used the term 'light shock' to describe what he wanted to achieve in the Hawthornden Court of the Museum of Scotland. That is what is achieved in most Murphy projects.

The second is the strong sense of place. The normal way of avoiding challenging the planning system in Scotland is to pretend to match the sense of place by copying the materials of adjacent buildings. Not in these projects. The simplest way of proving the point is to consider how even the smallest and simplest extension is unique to that project: no question of pulling a standard scheme from a drawer. Then consider the *atêlier's* preoccupation with vistas and views – whether of Gosford House from The Fruitmarket Gallery (just slide back that east-facing window), or of Dundee Law from the café in Dundee Contemporary Arts. The flats in the Canongate provide not just a modern take on the timber galleries that adorned the tenements here during the Renaissance, but also, by breaking forward from the building line, give long linear views up that ancient route. The rural projects, equally, seek to derive form from their place even if that form is a contemporary rather than a 'traditional' one.

Perhaps the most obvious signature of a Murphy building comes from his creation of architecture from the means of making it. It is only in this book that outsiders may track from project to project the development and refinement of details, the use of materials and the developing simplicity of his approach. The architecture may derive from the needs of the project, but most projects reveal a recognisable toolkit of common motifs, common materials, and a common enjoyment of opening and closing spaces through sliding doors and lowering shutters. A principal pleasure of these buildings is that so many of them are immensely *tactile*. Yet do not be deceived. Not everything may be explained by making an artistic virtue of necessity. The industrial-seeming capitals of the columns in The Fruitmarket Gallery are new, not inherited, and some of those very businesslike-looking rivets in DCA are entirely decorative. As with the mirrors extending the clerestorey, it would be a mistake always to take a Murphy building at face value.

In one sense, the *atêlier's* record is absolutely traditional: beginning slowly with house extensions whilst tirelessly attempting to break into the sclerotic patterns of patronage through competitions. (Perhaps it is fortunate that it began ten years ago when the competitions system in Scotland was more dynamic than now). There had, inevitably, to be a competition virtual success – Inverewe Restaurant – which failed, ultimately, because of a loss of nerve by the client. It was the first of a cupboardful of unsuccessful competition entries that form the spurs of a new practice, three of which have now been constructed.

Architecture in Scotland has changed radically since Richard Murphy was an impatient Edinburgh student in the early 1980s. A number of younger practices share his fascination with materials and with lightness, and no longer opt, automatically, for the solid-walled architecture of the Scottish tradition, or the neutral curtain-wall of corporate expressionlessness. A richer language has emerged in the mainstream which, if anything, is even more firmly anchored to that sense of place, but is more inventive in how it is expressed. In any significant change like this, innovative architects – and willing clients – need courage, and benefit from pathfinders. A principal pathfinder has been the *atêlier* of Richard Murphy as this book so nicely illuminates.

Charles McKean
Professor of Scottish Architectural History
University of Dundee

Richard Murphy **The First Decade**

Richard Weston

If a birth-date for Modern Architecture were required, 1901 would be as good a candidate as any because it was then, precisely one hundred years ago, that Frank Lloyd Wright published his plans for 'A Home in a Prairie Town'. The project did not appear in an architectural magazine, but was commissioned by the far more influential *Ladies Home Journal*. And in his description Wright did not emphasise the design's novel style, but the appropriateness of its open space for 'common use and enjoyment'. This combined, he said, the functions of living room, dining room and library, and was linked to the upper floor by a large gallery: two additional bedrooms could take the latter's place, if required, but the gallery 'was a temptation because of the happy sense of variety and depth it lends to the composition of the interior'.

As modern architecture enters its second century, the pleasures of open, flowing space have yet to inform most domestic environments, and in historic settings overt expressions of modernity are still regarded with suspicion. Few places in Europe have been more zealously protected than Edinburgh's Old Town and (Georgian) New Town, and the dominance of governmental and financial institutions only adds to the city's pervasive cultural conservatism. Like a Latin carnival, the Fringe may be allowed its three weeks of officially sanctioned outrage as part of the world-renowned Festival, but the serious business of building is judged by different criteria.

When Richard Murphy set up practice in Edinburgh in 1991 it was not, therefore, an obvious or easy choice of location, but the decision was largely made for him. Apart from a spell in Richard MacCormac's office in London, he had spent most of his time in the city since completing his education there eleven years before, and in 1989 had set up the Edinburgh office of Alsop and Lyall. Two years later, after winning the competition for a restaurant at Inverewe Gardens, the London-based partnership split up and the Edinburgh office closed. The Inverewe scheme was the Edinburgh office's work and Murphy launched into independent practice with it as his first commission.

The unique sub-tropical gardens at Inverewe[1] in the remote North-West Highlands were begun in the nineteenth century and eventually, like so many Victorian ventures of their kind, passed into the care of the National Trust for Scotland. The site was adjacent to Loch Ewe and two extensive walled gardens, and the brief required a large, two hundred seat restaurant. Murphy sub-divided this into four sections, each the size of a bus party and with its own walled garden, and strung them in a gentle arc along the contours and against an existing retaining wall, which he thickened to accommodate the kitchens and a grotto-like servery. The café roof, reminiscent of the influential passive-energy Hampshire schools, was supported on steel 'trees' and consisted of a series of gently folded glazed planes, with louvres to shade the front elevation of windows, which in turn could be slid away on sunny days to transform the café into an open veranda.

Beautifully integrated with the site and, like the gardens, inventive in responding to the climate, it was a superb design. Working drawings proceeded apace until, eighteen months after winning the competition and with the contractor poised to move on site, the Trust cancelled the project. It is pointless to speculate how Murphy's career, or the still faltering trajectory of modern architecture might have been changed had Inverewe been built, but with it, one might argue, died the best hope for contemporary architecture in the Scottish Highlands, and instead of bursting on the scene with what was certain to be a widely published new building, Murphy himself had to find a way to survive on the young practice's classic diet of extensions and conversions.

The exquisitely wrought domestic projects which quickly followed brought him to national attention, but locally they were often perceived as alien and threatening. The city's financial institutions might be allowed to ring the New and Old Towns with crudely designed corporate behemoths, but the sacred conservation areas, hedged about with legislation, guarded by planning officers unaccustomed to assessing the merits of serious modern architecture, and peppered with residents quick to complain about contemporary intrusions, had been almost completely protected from visible signs of modernity. Any proposal, therefore, no matter how thoughtfully adapted to context, would have to be fought for long and hard, and the back gardens of Edinburgh became, for a while, Murphy's battleground.

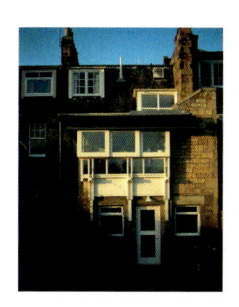

The brief for Murphy's first built project, completed in 1992, was that typical pot-boiler for solo practitioners, a back-extension to create a garden room. The house was in Inverleith Gardens[2], a mature suburb on the fringes of the New Town, and Murphy quickly realised that by building on two floors rather than one, as the client had envisaged, the addition could enjoy outstanding views. The result was not simply an extension clipped on to the rear of the house, but an integration of old and new which effected a radical reorganisation of the interior. Light was introduced through a long roof-light running down the party wall, under which a narrow 'secret staircase' descended between shelving to give direct access to the kitchen below. This, together with two voids linking the spaces, allowed conversations to be carried on between floors and created – to borrow Wright's words – a 'happy sense of variety and depth' in tune with the client's convivial lifestyle.

The project included Murphy's first version of one of modern architecture's classic devices, the corner window liberated of load-bearing duties thanks to cantilevered beams which support the wall or roof above. By bracketing the timber structure proud of the wall surface, the windows – three on the front and five on the side – could slide open and be parked completely out of sight, transforming the built-in seat into an open balcony from which to enjoy the city's celebrated skyline. The effect, as Richard MacCormac aptly noted, is like an early Renaissance painting in which the missing middle ground 'juxtaposes an interior scene with the distant silhouette of a hill or town'.

Wright's model Prairie House was a response to the needs of clients who could no longer afford servants and were beginning to break free of Victorian proprieties about the 'proper place' of women and children. Murphy's extensions were similarly designed in response to new patterns of living and intended to restructure the whole house. Like most pre-1914 middle-class dwellings, the Edinburgh properties on which he has mostly worked were arranged with 'polite' rooms at the front and serviced by staff who toiled in strictly functional kitchens and washrooms, appended to the rear or placed 'below stairs'. The street frontage and garden were elegant and formal, a public face to guard the privacy of the family; the walled space to the rear was unconsidered, more like a service yard than an outdoor room. This arrangement could hardly be less suited to today's needs, when families tend to share one big, messy space – a kind of kitchen-dining-television room with, ideally, direct access to a private garden – and disperse into separate rooms to sleep, study, entertain friends and enjoy an array of personal technology unimaginable even a decade ago.

Two years after the Inverleith Gardens project, Murphy completed another two-storey extension, in Gilmour Road[3], part of a Victorian suburb: the programme and budget were larger, and the architectural language at his command more sophisticated. A two-storey outbuilding – or 'build out' as they are known locally – was partially demolished and a small study/meditation room created in the base (the client's daughter is a Buddhist, and her parents share her interest in spirituality).

The stone base was extended in brickwork and concrete to form a narrow staircase to the kitchen, and above the masonry, bolted back to the base but projecting boldly out, is an independent steel structure, with raking diagonal struts and cantilevered corners. The roof is joined to the house by means of a glazed strip which brings in extra daylight to the former kitchen – now converted into a dining room – and the flying steelwork supports a balcony, the dramatically overhanging roof, and sliding glazed and timber panels. These dissolve both corners, transforming the interior into a belvedere with fine views over a communal garden, and beyond to the volcanic plug known as Arthur's Seat – which is

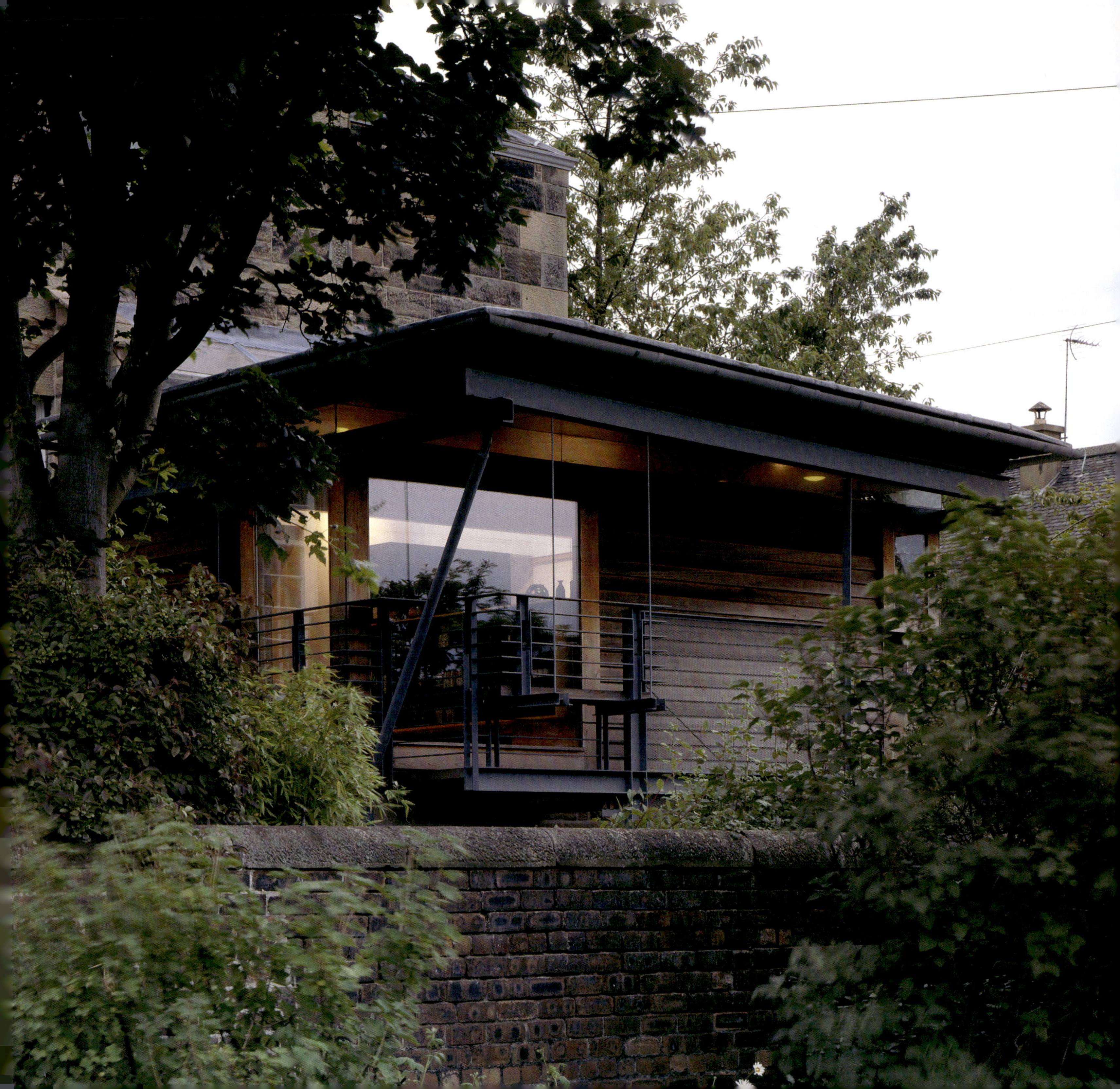

neatly framed by the small corner window above the worktops. Just as intriguing to many visitors, according to the clients, is the mystery of the sink, which hangs above a void so as not to interrupt the flow of space, and appears to be served by invisible pipes!

Both these projects bring to mind Gottfried Semper's identification of a masonry platform and carpentry roof as two – with the hearth and cladding – of the 'Four Elements of Architecture', and I am also inescapably reminded of one of the icons of modern architecture, Gerrit Rietveld's Schröder House, built in Utrecht in 1924. Both spring from masonry and, to enjoy the view, invert convention by having their living rooms at first floor level. Rietveld's interior can be reconfigured using sliding partitions, and the feeling of enclosure is similarly dissolved by opening corner windows. Like Rietveld, Murphy likes to use moving parts to transform his spaces – at Gilmour Road, when the large timber panels and full-height glazing slip away, the effect is liberating – and both delight in celebrating daily life by providing sills and shelves for display, built-in furniture, and ingeniously contrived storage: in short, by taking every opportunity to promote the art of habitation through which houses become homes.

Flexibility in accommodating changing patterns of use is central to modern architecture's most radical contribution to domestic design – the open plan – but few individuals, let alone families, feel comfortable with the total openness of the glass-enveloped spaces favoured by architects such as Mies van der Rohe: 'who', Murphy likes to ask rhetorically in lectures, 'would want to be bed-bound with 'flu in Mies's Farnsworth House[4]?' According to mood, time or season, depending on whether we wish to be sociable or alone, our houses must cater for a multitude of demands, social and psychological: we desire the open prospects of the bird's nest, but also the enclosure and refuge of the cave. Sensitive to these deep-rooted needs, Murphy responds by manipulating his sections to generate spatial variety – invariably reinforced by multiple sources of natural light through roof and walls – and by enabling the enclosure to be transformed using moving parts.

Just as the wall-panels of a traditional Japanese house appear and disappear according to season or time of day, so in a Murphy building ceilings can be hand-cranked down at night to conceal roof-lighting, large areas of glazing slide apart to dissolve corners and link house to garden, or timber panels open and close, sometimes internally, sometimes externally. A kitchen extension in Dirleton, a village outside Edinburgh, rings the changes on the sliding theme with a continuous run of seven counterweighted square windows which pivot open effortlessly to link kitchen and mother to garden and triplets.

The pleasures to be derived from such transformations can be seen in full measure in the extension designed for a consultant surgeon and his wife in Abbotsford Park[5] in Edinburgh. The washroom and kitchen appended to the rear and side of the house were demolished and replaced with a single storey kitchen/sitting room. The galley kitchen ranges along the north-facing wall and is bathed in light from the glazed strip which forms the narrower wing of an asymmetrical butterfly roof. To the south, the sitting area opens to the garden through large glazed doors which slide away out of sight, and is made more intimate by a low flat roof. The plywood-lined and lead-covered roof cantilevers dramatically out from projecting steel channels, and to compensate for the overshadowing a raking clerestorey is formed between its underside and the small flat roof. At night, the entire space can be transformed: sliding timber panels cover all the major openings and sections of ceiling can be lowered to conceal the clerestorey and roof-light: open veranda by day, wood-panelled room at night: it is unmistakably Japanese in spirit, but realised in a constructional language which is Murphy's own.

Closing down interiors in this way can be partially explained as a response to the Scottish climate, where large areas of glazing appear wasteful of energy even though they meet all the relevant regulations. They are also a means of eliminating the need for 'unarchitectural' curtains. But the prime motivation is surely the way in which they enrich the pleasures of occupying space by enabling the occupants to turn bird's nest into cave and back again –

Essay 11

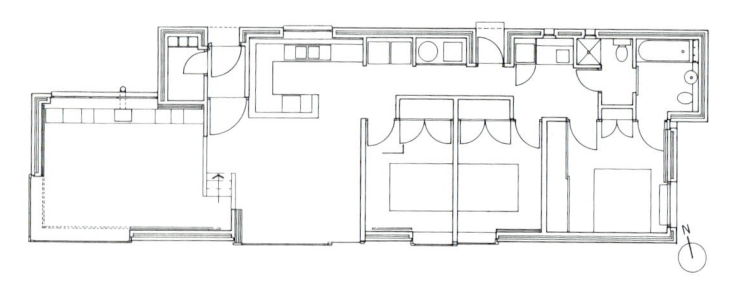

a possibility seen on a large scale in the Stewart House[6], completed in 2000 on a site north of Scotland's oil capital, Aberdeen.

The butterfly roof and linear plan with a 'thick wall' of service spaces to the north and an open, heavily glazed south-facing front echo the Abbotsford Park extension, whilst the tell-tale diagonal rods which hold down the overhanging roof give away their shared debt to one of Murphy's favourite architects, the Australian Glenn Murcutt. The section responds to the sloping terrain by stepping along the length of the plan to create a lofty lounge to the west and more intimate bedrooms to the east. The galley kitchen and dining room are placed a few steps above the living area, across which they enjoy long horizontal views, through the clerestorey and out across open farmland.

The kitchen and timber-lined corridor are filled with daylight from the continuous roof-light which links the main roof to the thick wall, and at night panelling made of identical wood to the walls can be cranked down in sections to form a horizontal ceiling. Large timber panels slide across the extensively glazed living room, giving the whole interior the ambience of a ship's cabin – a feeling perhaps enhanced by the client's choice of a darker veneer than Murphy himself proposed.

A striking feature of Murphy's early projects is the consistency and quality of their craftsmanship. This is not the result, as might be supposed, of unusually generous budgets, but of the kind of collaboration between architect and builder which has become all too rare. The domestic-scale projects in Edinburgh were all undertaken by the same builder, Steve Evans. His background – apprenticeship as a carpenter followed by a degree in sociology as a mature student at Edinburgh University – is, to say the least, unusual, as was his response to Lord Cameron and the committee of the Edinburgh New Town Conservation Society when called down from the work to give his programme for the conversion of their premises. Not used to such demands on a Murphy project, he recalled the words of Mussolini and declared to the bemused circle of worthies: 'Our programme is to govern!'

Evans was introduced to Murphy when he needed retrospective approval for alterations to his flat, following the decision to start his own business. He had already undertaken some work for Marian Blytheman at Inverleith Gardens and when she asked if he knew of any architects 'with some imagination', he returned the favour by introducing her to Murphy. The contracts which followed fly in the face of orthodoxy. None of the jobs was subject to competitive tender, because Murphy knew he could get a fair and better price for his clients by negotiation, and with a guarantee of the quality he expected. Evans, in turn, learnt how to build modern architecture. Producing the accuracy which eliminates second-fix work demands became second nature.

When Murphy was unsure how best to achieve what he wanted most economically, Evans could be relied on to suggest a solution. At Abbotsford Park, for example, the shutter to the roof-light over the kitchen is counterweighted by a simple but ingenious system of four weights which successively come to rest inside the studwork, so as to avoid its crashing closed at high speed, and the triangular shutter over the gable-end clerestorey has an elegantly modernist pull-cord which Evans found on a seventy-year-old WC cistern. At Dirleton, the counterweighted tops to the pivoting windows are made of scaffold poles filled with lead, and the pivot-pins were set slightly off-centre to allow for adjustments. The benefits of such collaboration are far-reaching. Not only did it reduce the amount of detailed drawings required from job to job, but the availability of a builder who relishes the challenge of high-quality modern architecture helps to support the emergence of other work. There is already talk of a 'School of Murphy' in Edinburgh, and his office has spawned several younger practices who are beginning to do interesting work on their own – and, not surprisingly, turning to Evans to build for them.

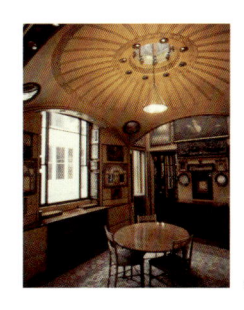

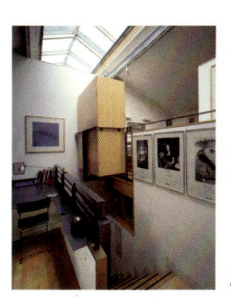

Although, as I have suggested, the Schröder House[7] might appear to be a primer for Murphy's fascination with a planar vocabulary heightened by moving parts and disappearing corners, he has never been conscious of it as an inspiration – and, unlike some architects, he is more than ready to acknowledge the creative debts of which he is most aware: to the Italian Carlo Scarpa and to, arguably, the most original of English architects, Sir John Soane, whose house-turned-museum in Lincoln's Inn Fields he considers 'the most modern building in London'. 'Modern' is an intriguing term to apply to Soane, not least because the rediscovery of his work as a stimulus for contemporary design owes much to the American architect Robert Venturi, whose 1966 book *Complexity and Contradiction in Architecture* was both a catalyst for the happily short-lived episode of stylistic Post Modernism and a significant contribution to that more searching and far-reaching re-evaluation of the discipline which stressed continuity with, rather than rupture from, the past.

What Venturi especially valued in Soane was his ability to create and play with ambiguity, to make spaces that are, as Venturi puts it, 'both rectangular and curvilinear, and domed and vaulted', or which 'enrich the sense of enclosure and light' by juxtaposing different elements to create 'detached spatial layers'. He loved the partition of suspended arches which is 'meaningless structurally yet meaningful spatially' – forbidden fruit to orthodox modernists – and which 'defines rooms at once open and closed'. For Venturi, and later for many others, the Museum became a primer in spatial and optical delights: light sliding in mysteriously from hidden sources to illuminate walls and permeate the interior; intricately layered spaces; ceilings which appear to float; mirrors everywhere – the tiny Breakfast Room[8] alone has more than a hundred – to multiply the light, dissolve boundaries and re-present the surroundings in miniature; and walls which thicken to house objects, delaminate into planes and slots of space, or contain wall-sized panels which swing open – in Soane's case, to reveal successive layers of paintings.

American Post Modernists, who rejected the spatial continuity of modern architecture and designed buildings as if they were made of nothing more substantial than chipboard, could emulate these effects all too literally. For Murphy, who retains a love of continuity and believes in tectonic rigour, the possibilities had to be abstracted and absorbed as part of a distinctively modern way of making buildings. You can detect Soane's influence in the intricate interlocking of different spaces and levels – so vividly achieved, and so difficult to photograph, in the tiny extension in Inverleith Gardens – and in the way light is deployed to entice people along what Le Corbusier called the 'promenade architecturale' through a building: wall-planes are illuminated by hidden sources of daylight, or corners sliced open to entice with light from a distance and allow unexpected views close up.

Murphy's most obvious direct debt to Soane is his love of mirrors. In the Stewart House, placed at high level, they extend the apparent length of the corridor; in the house he now occupies in Royal Terrace Mews[9] they expand the tiny upper floor laterally so convincingly that most people do not notice the trick until it is pointed out; and in the extension in Dirleton they line the wall below a continuous strip of roof-glazing to help bounce more light into the space. Although Soane never had occasion to slide strips of mirror into the junction between lead cladding and irregular stone walls, as Murphy does in Gilmour Road, one suspects he would enjoy the dissolution by light and reflection of the kind of gap architects normally consign discreetly to the shadows.

Soane's influence is pervasive in Murphy's work, but the only project in which it self-evidently informs many of the strategic decisions is a beautiful apartment in Edinburgh's Moray Place[10], the twelve-sided centre-piece of one of the New Town's finest estates. Designed for Patrick and Mary Harrison, the former a distinguished retired Secretary of the Royal Institute of British Architects (a post which, in keeping with our corporate times, is now designated 'Chief Executive'), it occupies the old Billiards Room, Butler's Pantry and assorted minor service spaces below, which project from the rear of the grand house above.

14 Essay

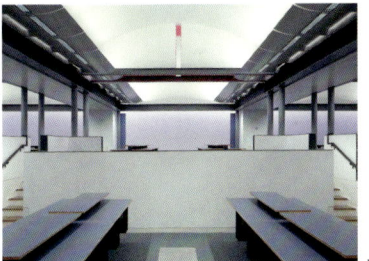

The apartment has, in effect, only two proper windows, both to the rear, and typically for the New Town you enter a full storey below pavement level from a sunken light-well. Murphy opted to emphasise rather than disguise the subterranean quality by threading a long, dark, print-lined corridor through the interior. You pass under a series of overtly Soanian open lintels, which act as display shelves, and your passage is made more mysterious by occasional mirrors which extend the vista or introduce an unexpected flash of light. Finally, after turning left and right, you are drawn forward by top-lit walls – the source, naturally, hidden from view – and can then enter laterally into the kitchen, dining and living rooms. All three sit below a barrel-vaulted roof and ceiling which floats symmetrically, like one of Soane's celebrated saucer-domes, between flanking bands of circulation. Framed by planes of light, it directs your attention out to fine views over what were once Lord Moray's pleasure grounds – the living room is set two steps below the kitchen and dining areas to enable the whole volume to participate in the spectacle[11]. Just as compelling is the view of the apartment at night. Framed by stone and glowing with a gentle, warm light, it is the epitome of the refuge, a persuasive argument for the cave, not the tectonic framework of Laugier's Primitive Hut, as the primordial model for architecture.

The need to house and display the Harrisons' substantial library and collection of glasses, ceramics and other artefacts gave Murphy ample excuses to layer and compartment the space without fully dividing it – and, almost inevitably, to indulge his love of mirrors. Openings in some of the hollow 'thick walls', for example, allow views through, whilst others are filled with mirrors and, you suddenly realise, only appear to do so. As we have come to expect, the apartment can also be radically transformed. On warm days the sturdy, timber-framed glazed doors disappear into the thickness of the apparently solid external wall, from which, at night, sliding wooden panels emerge to act as internal shutters. And, as in the Stewart House, high-level shutters can be cranked down to seal the perimeter roof-lights: in a phrase which cannot be bettered, Mary Harrison describes the night-time transformation as being 'like living in a cigar box'.

The spatial idea developed in the Harrisons' flat is re-deployed on a grand scale to create a new computing centre for Edinburgh's Napier University[12]. The accommodation replaces heavy engineering workshops and the 50 by 40 metres space is framed on all four sides by windowless walls. Murphy has structured this large volume with a tartan grid of steel columns which alternates broad, barrel-vaulted bays with narrower, flat-roofed service zones. Four changes in floor level which place the computers on a gentle hillside perpendicular to the vaults, low partitions, and the square clusters of columns combine to articulate the overall space into twenty workplaces with twenty-five students in each.

The obvious precedent is Louis Kahn's Kimbell Art Museum[13], but whereas pictures demand light, computer screens are averse to it. And so, unlike the Kimbell, the vaults are not split to allow in light, but cut vertically down their gables. Between the plastered vaults are vaults of glass with red painted sides cut with a slot to admit subdued slivers of red sunlight to animate the space. Ambient light, true to the spirit of Soane, enters indirectly, reflected down from the edges of the vaults and through continuous roof-lights along two opposed perimeter walls. Like an artificial sky floating between planes of light, the roof will form a striated canopy to unify the space: still under construction when I saw it, the finished interior promises to combine grandeur with intimacy – a striking and humane contrast to the latter-day mills in which so many now toil in front of VDU's.

If Soane's influence, overt or covert, can be detected in almost everything Murphy has designed, the same is certainly true of Carlo Scarpa. Little known outside Italy until after his death in 1978, Scarpa was soon widely acclaimed for his mastery of materials and detail, seen most successfully in his transformation of historic buildings in ways which respected the old whilst remaining unashamedly modern in expression. His abiding inspirations were the work of Frank Lloyd Wright, the De Stijl movement, and that most pervasive of inspirations in the West for much of the last century, the traditional architecture of Japan.

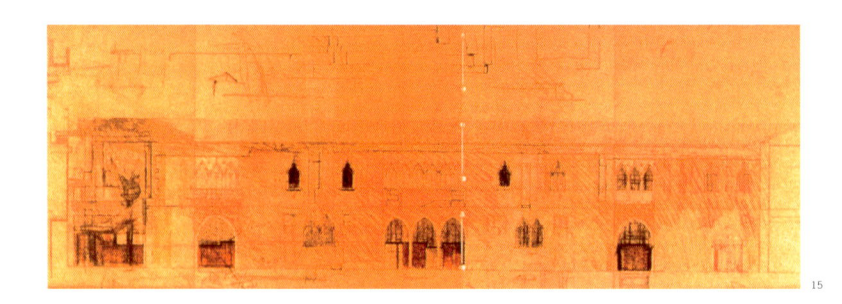

By the mid 1980s Scarpa was becoming something of a publishing industry, but Murphy discovered his work early, in 1982 and almost by chance, as part of a break from Giancarlo de Carlo's celebrated Summer Schools in Urbino.

The encounter with Scarpa's masterpiece, the Castelvecchio Museum[14] in Verona, proved unforgettable, and Murphy was lucky enough to be there when it was showing an exhibition of Scarpa's palimpsest-like drawings in which lines and thoughts are layered even more densely than materials in the finished work. Scarpa's approach to historic buildings struck a particular chord because at the time Murphy was working in Edinburgh for Simpson and Brown, a practice noted for their conservation work. Convinced that constructing 'fake history' – common practice in Britain then and now – was fundamentally misconceived, he found in Scarpa confirmation of William Morris's observation that 'all continuity of history means is, after all, perpetual change'. Four years later, and by then a lecturer at Edinburgh University, Murphy returned with students to survey the Museum room by room, detail by detail. In 1990 he published the resulting drawings in a book on the Castelvecchio which provided the first complete record of Scarpa's work: it was a lasting contribution to scholarship, but more important for Murphy was the liberating effect on his own work.

For Scarpa, as for Morris, past and present should be integrated as part of a continuous unfolding of ideas and habitation, expressed in different yet complementary formal languages and materials. For Murphy, faced with the challenge of extending and adapting old buildings in one of the best preserved cities in Britain, the lessons were clear. The new work must be resolutely modern, but rather than demolish the old completely it could be artificially 'ruined' and then integrated into the whole as one of several actual or implied temporal, constructional and spatial layers.

The consequences of this approach can be seen in projects as diverse in scale as the house extensions and a large public building like Dundee Contemporary Arts. Several of the domestic projects involved partial demolition of an existing outbuilding, and where they did not – or total removal was more economic – Murphy opted to build a masonry base to tie the new work back to the old house and to provide a springboard for the superstructure of sliding planes and floating roof. At The Fruitmarket Gallery, situated in the Old Town conservation area and completed in 1993, he had the opportunity to explore this approach on a larger scale. His model was the courtyard elevation of the Castelvecchio on which Scarpa retained the diverse original openings, but sealed them using an orthogonal glazing system whose members were deliberately placed out of synchrony with the existing structure. The cumulative effect was to suggest the presence of a continuous new screen behind the façade, and thereby hint at the extent of the changes within, whilst preserving the old fabric largely intact[15].

Faced with the need to effect a major transformation on a modest budget, Murphy kept the perimeter walls of the old market, cut out large voids where required, and then filled and overlaid both old and new openings with planes of varying permeability[16]. These range from lead-clad panels – which seem to slide sideways out of the wall, or vertically down from it – through expanded metal and translucent rectangles of glass-block or sand-blasted glass, to large areas of clear glazing[17]. And whereas Scarpa's planes merely appear to slip and slide behind the wall-plane, Murphy responded to the need to lift large art-works directly into the first-floor gallery by deploying a sliding full-height glazed screen in front of a hoist. Framed and glimpsed from outside, the lifting device hovers tantalisingly between industrial relic and abstract sculpture, and when required the frame slides away – in an echo of the security screen below – to free the hoist to rotate out ready for action.

16 Essay

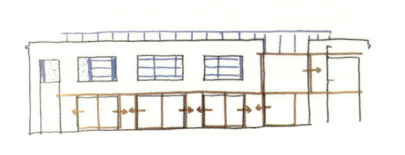

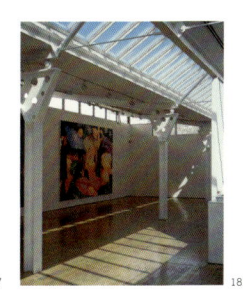

Predictably, The Fruitmarket Gallery's roof-lighting system challenges orthodoxy. Filtered and sanitised, there is little that is natural about the 'natural light' which is allowed to enter most galleries, but lacking the budget to afford a 'proper' system, Murphy opted for something reminiscent of a north-light factory roof which, reflected either side of the ridge, also faces south, flooding the gallery with light and – heaven forefend! – banding the floor with sunshine. The contrast with the mausoleum-like interiors of many of our latter-day temples to modern art could hardly be greater, and for most exhibitions poses no problems; when it does, the offending glass is simply whitewashed like a greenhouse in summer. This challenge to the almost ubiquitous conventions of the introverted White-Box gallery is reinforced by ringing the upper floor with a clerestorey which frames slices of Edinburgh – distant skyline to the north, fragments of Edwardian architecture to the south, de-familiarising the familiar and suggesting that engagement between city and art which ought to be any such institution's lifeblood[18].

Two years later, in 1995, ideas developed in the gallery were applied in the conversion of a small, run-down building in Royal Terrace Mews[19] into a house. The key to Murphy's strategy was turning the interior upside down: the suspended floor was lowered and what had been a low hayloft became a split-level, loft-like living-sleeping space; below, the originally much taller ground floor – made for coach and horses – provided an integral garage (a planning requirement), and intimate entrance and kitchen/dining space. Light floods in through a continuous ridge-light, permeating down to the ground floor via the staircase and through a slot behind the sleeping platform. Externally, the changes are disclosed in an elegant, planar composition: the new floor is visible and supported by a steel beam which also acts as the track for the sliding garage door, glass blocks light the lobby, and above the beam two glazed openings are placed either side of a 'hanging' lead panel – behind which, internally, lurk sliding timber shutters to close the openings at night. Seen from the street by day these openings could be mistaken for a clerestorey, but inside are discovered to be at floor level, giving the sensation of floating above ground.

The following year a detached nineteenth-century stable provided the starting point for a larger-scale conversion to create 'Maggie's Centre'[20] in the grounds of Edinburgh's Western General Hospital. The brief was the inspiration of Maggie Keswick Jencks, landscape architect and wife of the distinguished critic Charles Jencks, and arose from her own experience fighting cancer, a battle she lost in 1995. The idea was to provide a place where those diagnosed with cancer could have access to information, counselling and a range of help ignored by orthodox medicine – yoga and massage, nutrition and beauty therapy. The atmosphere was to be domestic, not institutional, and the brief called for as much flexible space as could be provided within the given walls.

Murphy's response to the limited headroom was to carve out a double-height, top-lit entrance space from which – on axis with the door – a staircase sets off between two cushioned alcoves. Then, as in a much grander country house, the stair divides and two symmetrical flights depart in opposite directions. They do not reunite in a moment of Classical closure, but continue on their separate ways to serve two counselling/therapy rooms. Lined with bookshelves and furnished with habitable quarter-landings, the staircase is singular yet homely, like a giant piece of furniture inserted into the space – a favourite idea of Murphy's former employer, Richard MacCormac. It organises the whole composition and bears exactly the same relationship to the existing building as the fly-away structures of the domestic extensions – part of the 'furnishing' by which masonry is rendered habitable.

Externally, Maggie's Centre was given the same planar treatment as the mews house and The Fruitmarket Gallery. Four years later, when he was asked to extend it, Murphy took the opportunity to extrude, in true Scarpa manner, a new lead roof from under the existing slated one. The result is a delight, like pulling out a giant drawer, and more successful to my eyes than the shallow S-shaped roof deployed on the larger, single-storey extension at the opposite corner. The chosen roof-form neatly side-stepped the anticipated demand from conservation-minded planners for a bulky pitched roof to match the existing, but that profile has become so familiar as to border on cliché, and unlike conventional forms does not appear sufficiently obvious to assume the status of a modern vernacular.

Opposite and a few properties along from his house in Royal Terrace Mews, Murphy is working on an almost identical property. The basic strategy is the same, but the differences reflect experience gained from living with his own design. The roof-light has been halved in area, and will run down only the south-facing side of the ridge: Murphy has found that the earlier version admits too much light, and reducing it symmetrically either side of the ridge would not admit sufficient low winter sun. The kitchen has moved upstairs and will now overlook a ground floor living room – a more convivial arrangement for entertaining than being cut off in the downstairs kitchen.

In both The Fruitmarket Gallery and mews houses Murphy was working with old but architecturally undistinguished buildings which did not demand the rigorous conservation standards required when converting historic structures. In Stirling, in the shadow of one of Scotland's most celebrated castles, he won the chance to transform a building of real architectural merit[21]. Originally a seventeenth-century Town House, it was later doubled in size and gained an impressive tower to become the court house and jail. The court sat at the centre of a U-shaped plan above extensive vaults, and was flanked by a multi-storey wing of masonry-vaulted cells running right up to the roof. More recently it has been used as a somewhat ramshackle youth centre, with a 100-seat theatre in the former courtroom.

The commission was secured following a limited competition and, doubtless emboldened by Scarpa's example at the Castelvecchio, Murphy was the only one to propose smashing through into the old courtyard to provide the required 200-seat auditorium: the new construction, clad in lead externally, will emerge through a vast, steel-framed opening to ride like a giant backpack on the old building. Large sliding panels enable the theatre to be sub-divided to re-create the original proportions of the restored courthouse. Nearing completion at the time of writing, the project promises many delights. Not least will be a dramatic promenade up a steel stair threaded through a 'tower of light' between the backpack and the old building, and a rich repertoire of Scarpa-inspired moments. New treads are to be laid over the dangerously worn treads of an old stone staircase and the resolution of tricky, sometimes violent, collisions of old and new, steel and masonry, offers manifold opportunities for enjoying complexities and contradictions in detail.

The widespread fascination with Scarpa's work went hand in hand with growing interest in understanding sites and cities historically, as places layered through time and possessing a physical 'memory'. Like Venturi's *Complexity and Contradiction*, a key text of this other, far more searching aspect of post-modernism was also published in 1966 – Aldo Rossi's *The Architecture of the City*. Its impact on the Anglo-Saxon world only began in earnest in the 1980s, following the 1982 publication of an English translation, and although Rossi's ideas were in many ways alien to the British empirical tradition, his Continental style of thought was to pervade the way architects think about cities.

Consider, for example, Murphy's Dublin Colonies[22] housing. The site occupies part of the former Village of Broughton and is an aberration in Edinburgh's New Town. The village was supposed to have been demolished long ago to make way for orderly Georgian terraces, but it somehow survived to became a symbol of resistance to gentrification, only to fall into a slow but terminal decline. Rather than extend the geometric discipline of the surroundings, Murphy decided to build over the footprints of the old buildings. The new accommodation – twenty-six flats and six houses, all privately owned – also rejects the dominant residential form of the New Town, the tenement block with its common internal stair. Instead, Murphy opted for external access. The results might appear to be merely a picturesque exercise in townscape, but to those who know – or to anyone who takes the trouble to investigate – their size and configuration memorialise a unique episode in

Edinburgh's history, transforming the white render and Hertzberger-inspired stairs and balconies into emblems of dissent amidst the New Town's decorous propriety.

At 112 Canongate[23], a corner site on Edinburgh Old Town's famous Royal Mile, a project for a housing association offers a different response to an historic context. Won in competition in 1992, but not built until six years later, the five-storey building contains nine flats and a shop, and rises as high as possible without the expense of a lift. Believing that the people who climb the most steps should be rewarded with the best views, Murphy responded to the 'projections and crazy roofs' of the frontages shown on historic prints of medieval buildings along the Royal Mile by jettying out the top flat and cladding it with timber. An unashamedly Romantic move in striking contrast to the Presbyterian asperity of the rear elevation, it is the kind of picturesque gesture which can easily be seen as a sop to woolly-minded conservationists who have no grasp of the rigours which make for real architecture. But for those lucky enough to enjoy the raking views up and down the Royal Mile, the opportunity to step outside the building line must be a daily delight.

Establishing continuity with the past also motivated the design of the Stoneman House[24] at Killeenaran, south of Galway city in a beautiful rural part of Ireland. Driving along the narrow roads Murphy noted that the old houses were typically sited in a shallow depression and screened by fieldstone walls, and as a result seemed to be 'all roof', and to merge with the land. The rapidly proliferating new houses, in ghastly contrast, were conspicuously detached, often on high ground, and swept away the old walls. Determined to build in response to, but without mindlessly aping, the vernacular, Murphy designed a two-storey house with a lower floor of high stone walls which locked into the traditional field pattern. In constructional terms, the stone acts as rain-screen cladding, and the timber-boarded first floor, rather than mastering the masonry in the familiar way, appears to slide out from behind it. Above, the profiled metal roof echoes the farmers' barns as surely as its rounded ridge suggests a debt to Glenn Murcutt[25].

Internally, the accommodation is divided between children's bedrooms and a family dining room and kitchen on the ground floor, and the master bedroom suite and a large sitting room above – the latter has a corner window to frame a superb view unfolding across a narrow road, over a stony beach to the hills of Clare, and finally out to the Atlantic Ocean. An unusual request from the client drew a predictable response from Murphy: Mr Stoneman wished to sit in the bath with a drink and still be able to conduct a conversation with family and visitors below! A sliding wooden screen, openable whilst immersed to preserve his modesty, was duly provided, and a corresponding device in the sitting room enables almost the entire house to be united into a continuous space.

The plan of the Stoneman House developed from the earlier Van Hulten House, designed in 1995 for a couple with two young children on a site in The Netherlands surrounded on three sides by water. Murphy organised the rooms around a double-height void, across which the master bedroom was intended to span like a bridge, with sliding shutters to be opened during the day to re-establish spatial continuity. The client, uneasy with such openness, opted to make one of the walls solid, a minor compromise which could take its place in the ongoing story of modern architects' determination to unify all the spaces of a house into a continuous 'spatial organism', as the architectural jargon has it. This began, as we have seen, with Wright, but for Murphy it is inescapably linked to childhood memories of American sit-coms such as *I Love Lucy*, in which an idealised family life was lived out in a single big room – so different from British experience at the time where, even in the smallest terraced houses, Victorian propriety was still echoed in the social and physical compartmentation of rooms.

Wright's motives, as we have already noted, were as much social as aesthetic, but it has become customary in recent architectural criticism to concentrate largely on the visual and formal aspects of buildings – the handling of space and light, the manipulation of form and structure, the juxtaposition and detailing of materials. In work of high ambition these may be explained as the outward and visible signs of an inward and theoretical position, but such criticism is apt to downplay what, almost half a century ago, the historian and curator of the Soane Museum, Sir John Summerson, argued is the defining characteristic of modern architecture: "the programme as the source of unity is, so far as I can see, the only new principle involved in modern architecture". The programme embraces the sizes and inter-relationships of spaces and an understanding of the patterns of use the building is to house, and its implications are generally distilled into what architects like to call the 'diagram' for the building – an organising idea whose ramifications are as much social as spatial.

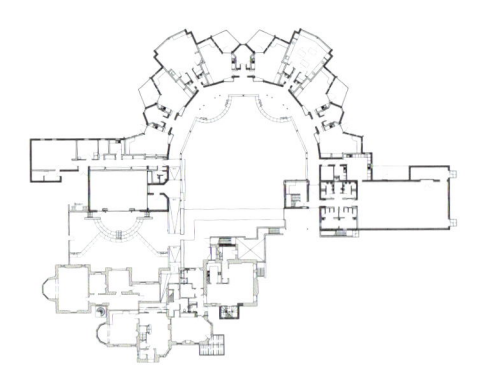

Getting the diagram right is the architect's most fundamental task, because no amount of finesse in construction or formal composition can redeem a misconceived plan. It is therefore ironic that it is precisely this skill which architects are now asked to deploy at considerable speed, and for little or no remuneration, in that increasingly ubiquitous system of exploitation known as 'invited competitions' or 'competitive interviews'. Happily, Murphy has repeatedly proved at a variety of scales and levels of complexity that he has an almost uncanny knack for getting the basic organisation right.

As we noted in discussing his first house extension, the client expected a single storey addition, but was delighted when he spotted the views that would open up from first floor level. In Glasgow, in competition with several well-established practices for the design of a new entrance and foyer to brighten up a call centre occupying a depressing 1960s office block, he was the only one to observe that the existing lift descended below the current raised entry level, enabling him to put in a gentle ramp down from the pavement to avoid the long and cumbersome internal ramps which the others needed to provide wheelchair access; and at the Stirling Arts Centre, the bold idea of extending the auditorium out over the courtyard provided the key to liberating the internal planning. In retrospect, such decisions are apt to appear so obviously right that it is easy to assume they were self-evident.

The transformation of Harmeny School[26] illustrates how vital 'getting the diagram right' can be to the life of an organisation. The School is run by a charity and caters for seriously disturbed children aged between eight and twelve years. They are referred to it from all over Scotland by local authorities who have exhausted other ways of coping with them, and are taught in groups of six or seven by two teachers. They need constant supervision and total security, and the brief included a 'crash room' in which, *in extremis*, they could be confined. The school occupied a disparate collection of buildings scattered around an old house modified early in the twentieth century by Sir Robert Lorimer, who moved the entrance from the south to the north elevation. The atmosphere was depressingly institutional and the brief prepared for the competitive interview called for new teaching accommodation to replace a prefabricated shed, and two new residential houses.

The school expected the architects to propose detached new buildings, which all duly did – except for Murphy who, instead of offering an instant solution criticised the brief, with its call for what he believed were far too many single-function rooms, and suggested they embark on a review of their entire accommodation before deciding what was needed. The Trustees and the Head Teacher saw the logic of Murphy's approach and the reorganisation which emerged was radical. It reversed Lorimer's inversion of the main entrance, and disposed the classrooms as a semi-circular crescent behind what is again the back of the building. Flanked by the music room and sports hall, the classrooms and two specialist teaching spaces for science and art are accessed off a covered way, sunken slightly below a gently sloping lawn, as if to invoke memories of the evolution of academic environments from the ecclesiastical cloister.

The assembly/music room and a small outdoor amphitheatre are placed on axis with the house, and the rest of the accommodation ranged in relaxed symmetry. Classrooms are paired to share an office/observation room and framed by a shallow gable: symmetry is reinforced by the central door placed behind a single column, and then released in the

20 Essay

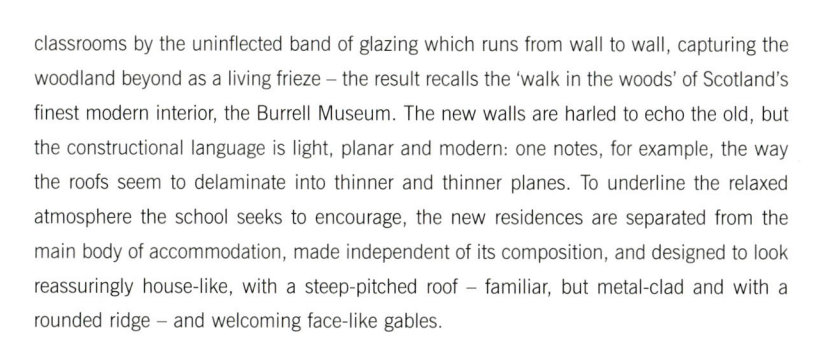

classrooms by the uninflected band of glazing which runs from wall to wall, capturing the woodland beyond as a living frieze – the result recalls the 'walk in the woods' of Scotland's finest modern interior, the Burrell Museum. The new walls are harled to echo the old, but the constructional language is light, planar and modern: one notes, for example, the way the roofs seem to delaminate into thinner and thinner planes. To underline the relaxed atmosphere the school seeks to encourage, the new residences are separated from the main body of accommodation, made independent of its composition, and designed to look reassuringly house-like, with a steep-pitched roof – familiar, but metal-clad and with a rounded ridge – and welcoming face-like gables.

Buildings cannot solve social or behavioural problems, but nor – as it is fashionable to suppose – are they entirely independent of them. At Harmeny, the most important architectural move was the creation of the courtyard, which acts as a secure break-out space into which the children can be allowed to retreat when they feel the need to be alone: this single but vital decision, according to the Head Teacher, has helped to transform the school's life. The children adapted quickly to their new surroundings and the teachers have noted significant improvements in their behaviour, the most obvious sign of which is the decline in minor damage. As the school takes possession of its environment, the staff and children are planning gardens to the rear of the classrooms and new planting to help to anchor the buildings and circulation routes into the site. Murphy is keen to work with them and understandably nervous about the visual quality of what will result, and says he is learning to 'loosen up a little' about such inevitable changes. Every architect has to come to terms with such anxieties, but only memorials to the dead can claim the right to remain frozen in time: architecture necessarily changes with the life it frames.

Programmatic concerns are equally evident in a housing association project at Graham Square[27] in Glasgow, opposite the former Meat Market and on a site occupied by the totally derelict Market Hotel. The design sprang from Murphy's experience living in Edinburgh in what was known locally as a 'Colony House'. What appeared to be a conventional row of two-storey houses was in fact a double-fronted block of two rows of back-to-back flats: one side was rendered convivial and neighbourly by people sitting on the platforms of their external stairs, whilst on the other, which was served by internal tenement staircases, the residents never seemed to get to know their neighbours. With this in mind, Murphy decided to demolish the most dilapidated central section of the hotel and make a new courtyard with external stairs to two groups of flats in the converted sections of the hotel building to either side. Sheltered by a grand, symmetrical glass canopy from which uplighters wash the walls with light at night, the effect is unashamedly theatrical and hotel-like. The arrangement has proved popular with residents: they liken it to a Mediterranean house, and the well-cared-for courtyard has become the sociable meeting place Murphy intended.

The full range of ideas we have explored are encountered at Dundee Contemporary Arts[28], Murphy's largest public building to date. The commission was won in 1996, in competition with other leading Scottish architects and a major talent from south of the border, London-based David Chipperfield. Having missed out on the oil boom that brought wealth to Aberdeen, Dundee decided to try the kind of arts-led regeneration which was proving so successful elsewhere in Europe. The brief was complex, combining as it did the typical arts requirements – two cinemas, galleries, meeting rooms, activity rooms for children, and a café-bar – with a printmakers' workshop, accommodation for the local authority's Arts and Heritage Department, and facilities owned by the University of Dundee – laboratories, offices, studio, and a flat for a visiting artist. The L-shaped site has only a ten-metre frontage to Perth Road, and is sandwiched between the neo-Gothic Roman Catholic cathedral, which is built almost to the street frontage, and a stolid detached villa, set back in its own garden and occupied by the Clydesdale Bank. To the rear, the site broadens and drops some ten metres down to a car park, across which, from higher up, the River Tay can be seen beyond a waterfront blighted by roads.

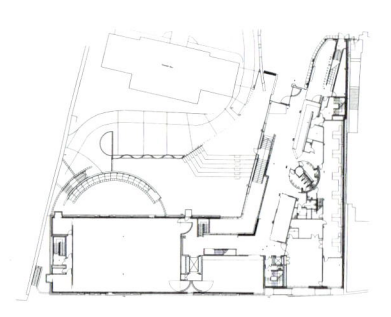

Murphy's diagram for the organisation developed from two key decisions: the main entrance must face the city, not the car park; and the café-bar must become the hub of the building. Denied the opportunity of presenting an impressive frontage to the street, Murphy opted to tempt in passers-by by poking out a cheeky, prow-like nose just beyond the cathedral: aligned on Tay Street, the road opposite, it marks the start of a memorable architectural promenade and is jauntily cantilevered into view and fully glazed to hint at the delights in store. As you approach the entrance, past an enticing view into the shop, a solid timber door slides magically open to reveal the street-like foyer: top- and side-lit, the walls seem invitingly brighter than the outdoors you leave behind.

Directly ahead are the galleries, their bright white walls framed by timber-panelled sliding doors which stand, open and darker, in the shade of a mezzanine floor. Inside the first gallery, open corners were intended to draw you across the space: to the right is the entrance to the second, much larger gallery, and to the left was a tall corner window placed to frame a view out to the Tay. I say 'was' because the director did not welcome this intrusion of the real world into the hermetic interior of his white box, and has boarded it over.

The galleries use essentially the same roofing system as that in The Fruitmarket Gallery, albeit with rather more sophisticated means of controlling, when required, unwanted sunlight. Seeing Richard Wentworth's bent-wood sculptures spread out across the vast, sun-banded floor, ought to make anyone question the widespread insistence on sunless, sepulchral light for displaying most contemporary art. Keen to break down the boxiness of the space by floating the roof on clerestorey glazing, Murphy solved the problem of being able to black out the glazing when required by playing one of his favourite tricks: what appear, inside and out, to be windows are in fact double-sided mirrors. The deception is so convincing that visitors to the The Fruitmarket Gallery who know Dundee and are therefore alert to such games, often persuade themselves that a perfectly genuine clerestorey is actually a mirror . . .

The café is reached via a broad stair which runs directly down from the main entrance into a double-height volume flooded with light from a fully glazed re-entrant corner which, it almost goes without saying, can be slid back to link interior to courtyard. Terraced with giant steps, this doubles as an outdoor amphitheatre for readings from the 'poet's pulpit' above, and is also overlooked by a glazed bay off the main gallery which turns visitors into performers. Murphy's determination to create a sociable meeting place in climatically challenged Dundee is reminiscent of Alvar Aalto's efforts to recreate the delights of Italian piazzas in his native Finland. The bar is tucked just around the corner from the café, and both recede from the inside-outside 'town square' beneath a low, black-painted tangle of exposed structure and services whose casual, seemingly unfinished quality is in striking contrast to the layered and lovingly detailed balustrades above – to the nautically minded, it might recall the feeling of descending below decks into the boiler-room.

The café-bar is placed at the hub of the organisation, and gives direct access to the cinemas and printing area, helping to make it a meeting-place both for visitors and for the diverse people and organisations who occupy the building. Its pivotal role brings to mind the Victoria and Albert Museum's controversial advertising slogan of a few years ago – 'Ace café with museum attached' – and is in striking contrast to Chipperfield's proposal, which placed the café on the roof, as a reflective space to enjoy views out rather than to act as a social condenser for activity within. The V&A was accused of 'dumbing down', but making the café-bar the social heart of the Dundee building is vital to its success, both in widening access to the Centre and in helping it, in turn, to become a catalyst for urban regeneration. Almost never empty, it positively teems with life in the evenings and at weekends, providing Dundee with a genuinely public interior. New restaurants and other establishments have already opened nearby and the air of optimism about this formerly run-down part of the city is palpable.

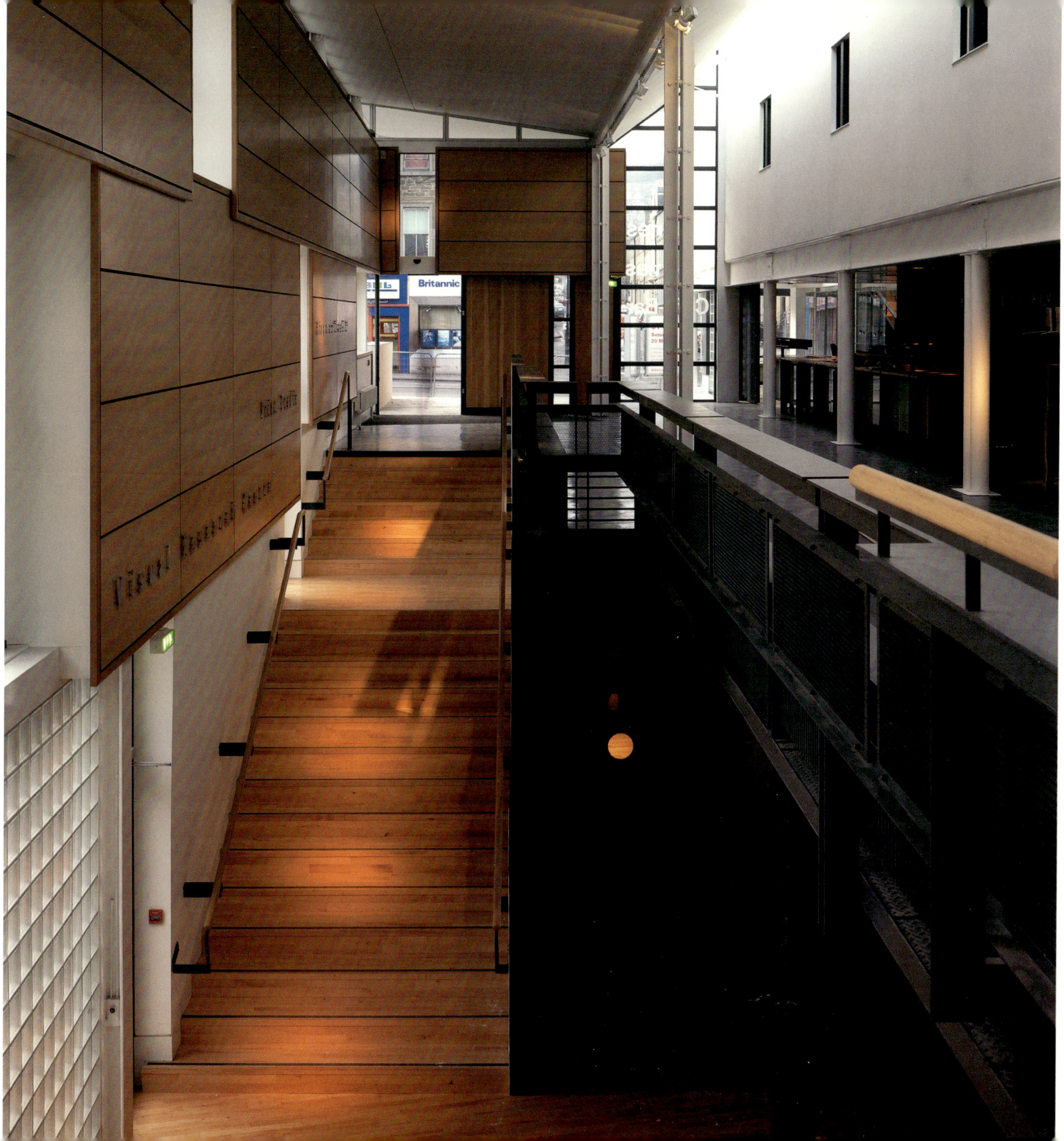
Britannic

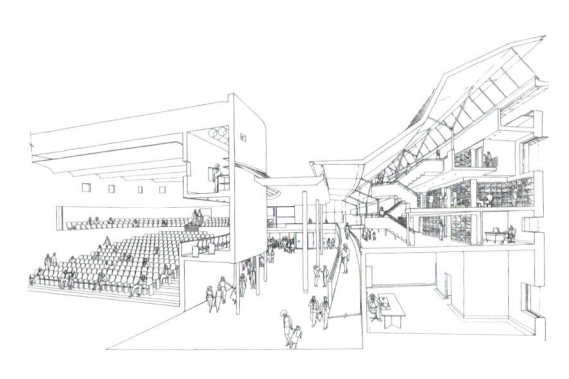

The requirement in the brief to re-use the large brick warehouse which occupied much of the site effectively turned the Dundee building into a large-scale essay in combining new and old of which Murphy was a proven master. The roof and interior have been removed, the walls partially 'ruined', and the pre-patinated copper on the new walls used to repair the gaps between brickwork, clerestorey and eaves, and – in an echo of Scarpa's implied screen at the Castelvecchio – to fill, wholly or partially, redundant openings. The approach works brilliantly on the courtyard elevation, where the old brickwork is dominant and the openings relatively few, but to the rear proves more problematic. Frame almost any part of this large elevation with a camera and you capture a beguiling image of a beautifully crafted fragment, but as a whole the collage-like composition, in which neither new nor old is sufficiently dominant, lacks the strength to command the car park and traffic-engineered wasteland beyond.

Internally, however, layering is deployed to great effect. Timber panels float in front of walls to slip and slide, along and down, across areas of glazing, blurring distinctions between solid and void. The debt to Scarpa is clear, but you are also reminded of the wainscoting traditionally employed to inhabit masonry walls, and of Gottfried Semper's celebration of cladding as a fundamental 'Element of Architecture'. Scarpa-inspired, too, are elegant structural details like the pairs of circular columns which sit either side of plated and bolted junctions between steel I-beams, and the stepped walls which screen the secondary staircase back up from the café to gallery level.

Soane's ghost is present here too, most overtly, perhaps, in the narrow slots – like tiny lancet windows – introduced behind the bar to allow drinkers and passers-by to catch tantalising glimpses of the silver screen in the main cinema behind. They bring to mind the secret openings through which Soane, unseen, could supervise his unruly pupils, but sadly what seemed here an innocent enough way to drum up business and add gaiety to life, fell foul of a double bind. Glimpses of X-rated material were fleetingly offered to general view and, in the other direction, very occasionally, a tiny ray of sunlight flickered across part of the screen. Louis Kahn, who believed that 'a slice of the sun' should enter every room, and that even a cinema needs natural light to show how dark it is, would doubtless have approved. The Centre's management, however, took a different view, and the slots are now covered. Similarly, another cinematically voyeuristic moment in the building has also succumbed: people entering up the stairs from the car park pass, Hitchcock-like and in full view of the waiting audience, in front of a window below the projection screen – over which, of course, a shutter used to slide when the film began.

A first major commission places enormous demands on any architect, especially those, like Murphy, who delight in detail. The necessity of re-using an old building left him open to the criticism often levelled at Carlo Scarpa that he needed the crutch of an existing fabric as a foil to his own ideas. Any doubts on this score, however, are dispelled by subsequent competition projects such as that for a large, new-build Arts Centre in Hamilton[29], south of Glasgow. Characteristically – and properly – Murphy began by questioning the brief, which called for the library, theatre and public meeting room (which he christened the 'Town Room') to be combined in a single building. He opted, instead, to give each element its own identity and then link them, as if really part of a traditional urban composition, by a paved, piazza-like foyer with multiple entrances. The library was conceived as a gently curved wall of books forming the long side of the internal piazza, and crowned by a folded-plate roof which cascaded down from slender steel 'trees' and then cantilevered out over a ramp to the foyer below.

The remaining sides were framed by the orthogonal stage and back-stage accommodation of the theatre, a smaller wall of studios, and the Town Room. The studios and Town Room were both placed at first floor level, with exhibition space below the former and a café and WC's under the Town Room. This palazzo-like volume projected into the town's new square – part of a master plan for the area – and opened onto it through giant sliding doors, transforming the interior into a public stage. To confirm the debt to Italian townscape, the auditorium of the theatre was accommodated in a semi-circular drum, undercut by the rake of the seats and projected out into the space like a giant apse – much as Aalto had done, in 1924, in the Workers' Club in Jyväskylä, where the foyer is also a fictive piazzetta. Sadly Murphy will not get to build this impressive project: the competition was won by a scheme which placed the library on top of precisely the kind of introverted large-lump building he was determined to avoid.

Although Richard Murphy's work clearly belongs to the evolving tradition of a radical modern architecture, he has shown no inclination to follow fashion by exploring the extremes of abstraction and aesthetic reduction favoured by the European mainstream. And whilst the works of Soane and Scarpa may be the inspiration for many of the most distinctive features of his work, it is surely to Frank Lloyd Wright that he owes the deepest, if largely unconscious, debt. Like Wright, Murphy delights in clear, expressive construction, in the qualities of materials, and above all in responding to the life for which a building is a framework and foil. Such concerns might be thought to define the practical art of architecture, but in our increasingly media-dominated age, in which image so often counts for more than substance, they seem far from many architects' minds.

At the domestic scale, Murphy creates richly articulated spaces[30] where others would be content to offer stylish rooms, and at the public scale, he believes that form-making should always be subservient to place-making. As a result, his interiors are marvellously habitable, responsive to the movement of the sun, time of day or change of season, and as accessible to the layman as to architectural cognoscenti – his private clients consistently report how even sceptical friends are won over by hitherto unknown pleasures of space and light. Wright was always at pains to point out that photographs could not convey the qualities of the deep, horizontal spaces of his Prairie Houses, and having visited almost all Murphy's completed buildings I know that they, too, must be appreciated in reality rather than in the pages of a magazine – unlike many of today's designer buildings, whose delights are captured on film before being corroded by life.

Although many of his projects are small, Murphy's work seems to me the most distinctive, sustained contribution to the art of architecture produced in Scotland during the 1990s. But in architecture, talent alone is no guarantee of professional success. The great nineteenth century American, H. H. Richardson, summed up this dilemma perfectly when he was asked after a lecture what he thought was the architect's most important skill. His audience was doubtless expecting learned thoughts on the relative importance of composition or construction, plan or elevation, but Richardson replied in three words: getting the job.

In architecture, rather more than in most professions, 'getting the job' is a difficult and uncertain art, and it will be fascinating to see how Murphy's career develops. As an Englishman abroad working in a Scotland increasingly conscious of its national identity, one suspects that he does not have ready access to the most influential social networks. Nor is his the kind of work to which the conservative financial institutions that dominate Edinburgh are naturally drawn. Given the longstanding rivalry between the two cities, being Edinburgh-based also makes it harder to win work in commercially more vigorous Glasgow, and in Scotland even the most adventurous developers have yet to show an appreciation of, let alone appetite for, the economic as well as social value which innovative design can add to an imaginatively conceived project.

The obstacles facing anyone seeking to realise modern architecture in Edinburgh are perfectly illustrated by the fate of what should have been the culmination of the series of mews houses, for a site in Circus Lane[31] behind the New Town's Royal Circus. The plan is beautifully packed like a jigsaw around a spiral stair, and the elevations extend the planar language so successfully developed in Royal Terrace Mews. On the contextually crucial street frontage steel beams, glass blocks, narrow bands of clear glazing, vertical and horizontal larch boarding, and close-spaced timber mullions skip asymmetrically back and forth within the shallow zone defined by the thickness of the masonry return-ends, whilst to the rear, symmetry is asserted so that, as with many a grand country house, the garden front is more imposing than the entrance.

Murphy's apt observation in the planning submission that the densely layered street frontage 'takes its inspiration from traditional Japanese houses, in particular, the slightly mysterious quality that they present towards the street, whilst opening completely to the rear'[32] prompted a member of The Architectural Heritage Society to object that 'the house may be perfectly fine for the Pacific Rim, but we're part of the Celtic Fringe'. To most outsiders it appears to be a model for how to integrate modern architecture into an historic area, but after more than seven months of deliberation, and despite a recommendation for approval from the city's professional planning officers, the project was refused Planning Permission on the grounds that it is 'too modern' for the area. In such decisions, as so often in Britain, the unelected and unrepresentative members of organisations like Historic Scotland – stocked, so often, with failed architects and fellow-travelling busy-bodies – are allowed to exercise power without responsibility.

Beyond these all too familiar local difficulties Murphy faces, like most medium-sized practices, the challenge of a world increasingly ruled by accountants. With the UK government determined to drive down costs through its woeful Public Finance Initiative, schools, health and other public buildings are increasingly being procured in job lots from large, commercial practices, making it doubly difficult to secure the kinds of commission for which his talents are ideally suited. Can we hope that the Scottish Parliament will realise the economic as well as cultural value of architecture – so amply demonstrated in Dublin and many Continental cities – and in this, as in the matter of student fees, assert its authority by defying yet another damaging policy emanating from London? In Richard Murphy and other emerging younger practices, Scotland has a new generation of architects with the potential to make an international impact: what they need is the enlightened public patronage which is becoming increasingly hard to find south of Hadrian's Wall.

In this less than encouraging climate it may not be altogether surprising that since completing Dundee Contemporary Arts – a triumph for the city and widely respected as a considerable architectural achievement – Murphy has secured only one new commission for a public building – for an arts centre in Caernarvon in North Wales. Such hiatuses are not unusual in architecture however, even amongst the most gifted practitioners, and Murphy has already demonstrated sufficient skill in finding work that it can only be a matter of time before other communities and, with luck, enlightened developers, present him with the larger challenges his abilities should now command.

In 1908, seven years after launching his revolutionary 'Home in a Prairie Town', Frank Lloyd Wright looked back on the first phase of his career and observed that, 'as for the future, the work shall grow more truly simple; more expressive with fewer lines; fewer forms; more articulate with less labour; more plastic; more fluent, although more coherent; more organic'. Like most architects of talent, Richard Murphy's first decade in independent practice has been marked by an abundance of ideas and an unrelenting joy in the practical business of making buildings. Beyond 'getting the job', doing more with less has almost always been the architect's greatest skill and a sign of growing maturity. Murphy's recent projects suggest that a process of distillation akin to that which Wright prescribed for himself has begun: the results promise to be every bit as fascinating as the buildings and projects documented here.

Richard Murphy Architects
Projects

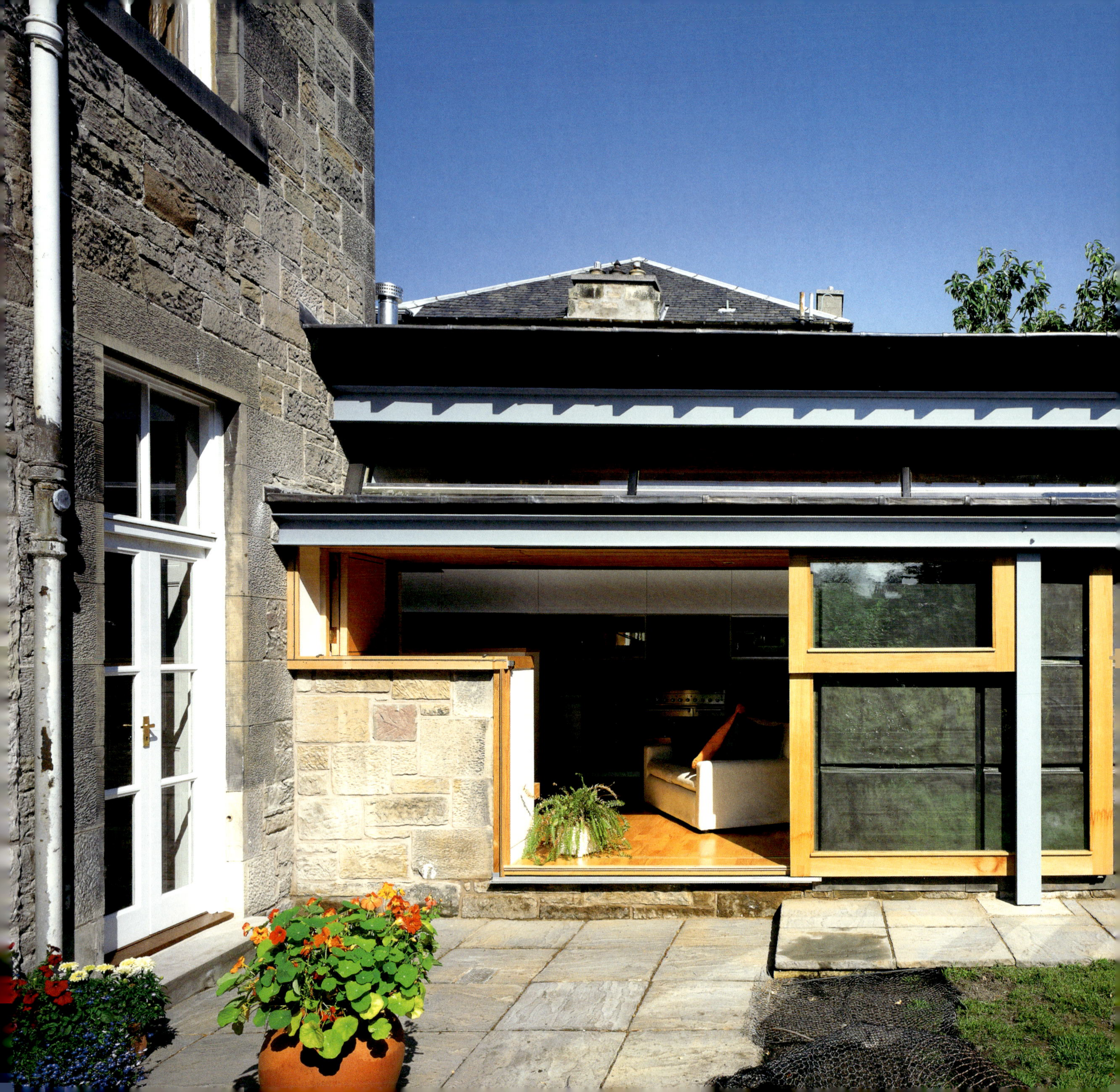

Four House Extensions

These four house extensions are representative of a number designed by the practice in its first few years, and despite their modest size they have been extensively published and have won many awards. They all deal with the familiar dissonance between a Victorian/Edwardian lifestyle and its equivalent today. Then, there was a maid in a scullery at the back, the rear garden was for drying clothes and the major rooms were placed at the front. Now family life revolves around the kitchen and in the pleasures of the back garden. Celebrating this, and dissolving the division between outside and inside, are the preoccupations of these projects, together with the idea of building demonstrably new and different constructions in or on deliberately 'ruined' former stone build-outs.

There are many similarities: they all employ expressed steel frames, have 'disappearing' sliding corner windows, add to thick stone walls with thin overlapping planar elements, and introduce top light from mostly hidden sources. Indeed, without either our clients or ourselves realising it at the time, these little projects became the testing-ground for architectural, constructional and social ideas employed on a much greater scale in later work.

Blytheman House Inverleith Gardens, Edinburgh

Completed 1991

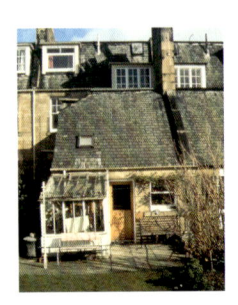

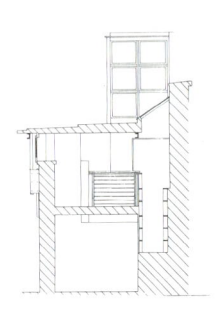

The most common small project an architect can be asked to design is a garden room. In this instance the site is the rear of an Edwardian terraced house and we were able to persuade our client not to place it in the garden at all – but rather where a bathroom had been above the kitchen in order to see an extraordinary panorama of Edinburgh available only from this height.

The extremely limited space was amplified by incorporating into it the thickness of the stone walls. A window seat occupies the plan of one wall and is constructed out of 'stick on stick' timber construction, cantilevered and expressed out from its base.

A steel structure was attached to the exterior and this supports an overhanging lead roof leaving the south and west walls free to accommodate a system of sliding windows. The windows can be slid back on the exterior so that from inside they seem to disappear – and the room can consequently be transformed into a deep veranda.

Light is brought deep into the plan by a generous roof light running along the party wall and underneath is placed a 'secret staircase' for quick access to the kitchen below. This, together with voids between the two spaces, allows a conversation to be continued between the upstairs and downstairs. The wall to the existing staircase is cut to allow constant contact between this space and the new room, and above a much larger staircase window was constructed to throw light deep into the plan of the existing house, through which it is now possible to see the distant Edinburgh Castle.

House Extensions 31

Francis House Gilmour Road, Edinburgh

Completed 1994

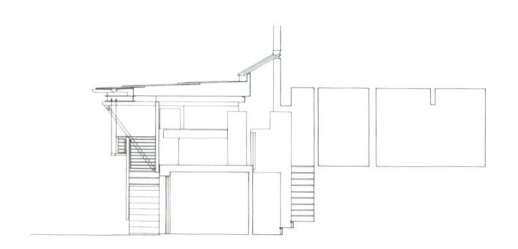

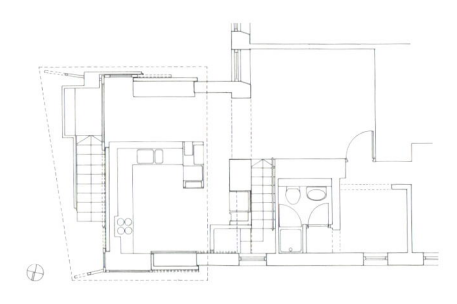

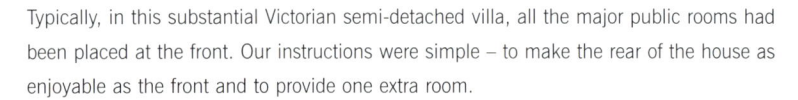

Typically, in this substantial Victorian semi-detached villa, all the major public rooms had been placed at the front. Our instructions were simple – to make the rear of the house as enjoyable as the front and to provide one extra room.

The former kitchen at the rear was compromised by a utility 'build-out' sitting on a plinth which accommodated the fall on the site from front to back. We concluded that this build-out should be 'semi-demolished', the plinth excavated to form a study with a new kitchen built above it. An expressed external flying steel structure allows a lead roof to float free of the walls which in turn consist of western red cedar panels 'offered up' to the exterior stone work and two 'disappearing corners' of glazed doors and windows respectively. From the latter is revealed a view of Edinburgh's mountain, 'Arthur's Seat', while the former gives access to a balcony and seat hanging from the new structure and a staircase connecting to the garden below. Contrary to popular belief, the Edinburgh climate allows for alfresco breakfasting for a significant number of days in the year!

To compensate for light excluded by the overhanging roof a new roof light joins the extension to the existing building and the former kitchen was converted into a dining room. A garden formed around the idea of a dry pebble river was also part of the same commission.

House Extensions 33

John and Eileen Francis write . . .

"We describe it as 'the Murphy Experience', the moment in 1993 when we realised what architects had to do to create buildings of the highest quality. Initially we made the mistake of thinking of our architect as a draughtsman rather than as a professional – someone who would realise our ideas as building plans. After the first meeting we found to our pleasure that talking with an architect can be a transformative experience as words and sketches produced more than we expected.

This architect was able to empathise with clients, mobilise their thinking about the way they live, and encourage the taking of directions which would make the whole house feel different. Together we would develop a set of new spaces where we could welcome people, produce food for them and share conversation.

We talked about Japanese design and the recent experience of our daughter living in Japan, of tree houses and needing a view in a city where the houses were often built to hide the view. We reflected on the way people lived in the Edwardian period which produced houses with grand fronts and unimaginative backs. When this talk was realised in pictures it would show a re-discovered view of Arthur's Seat, a space full of light where inside and outside seemed connected. The design would hinge on the concept of the cornerless room revealed by sliding doors – a delight in summer and a promise in winter.

Is it too extravagant to describe these revelations as a spiritual experience? The description will probably amuse people because, of course, we had the usual problems of designs which are difficult to build, problems that have to be solved to the satisfaction of architect, builder and client, compromises that had to be made. However, in those first few weeks Richard had created a bond of trust between client and architect which carried us through the difficult periods. We felt his commitment and his vision, wanted him to succeed – and remember he was not yet an award-winning architect to us, this was his third architectural project, the Blythman extension had just been completed when we began, and The Fruitmarket Gallery was in the process of completion.

When our project was completed we then experienced a secondary phase of development which we enjoyed as much as the first. The lectures, the visits, the media interest and the articles in architectural journals which were inspired by the new space were a surprise to us. We had visits from distinguished architects and judges commissioned by award-giving bodies, we listened and contributed to their conversations about the space and hopefully inspired new clients with our enthusiasm. Our message to the students who visited was that technical brilliance is only half the story. If you want to be an excellent architect, communication is the key. Find clients who can access your architectural vision and learn to share it."

Palmer House Abbotsford Park, Edinburgh

Completed 1996

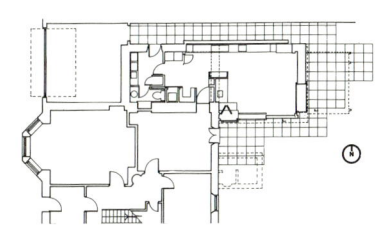

The relationship between this large Victorian semi-detached house and its rear garden was unfortunate with no direct route between the two. A utility room divided the elevation while the kitchen had been added onto the side elevation. We were asked to make sense of the rear of the house by providing a formal dining room, which it lacked, and a large family kitchen. Our solution was to demolish the existing kitchen and to replace it with a much larger extension incorporating a linear kitchen work-top along the north wall (but lit by a south facing roof light) which can serve both formal and informal dining areas equally. The remainder of the space incorporates at the garden end a hearth/TV area, family dining area and a pantry, utility, WC.

The expressed steel construction allows most of the walls to be free of a load-bearing function – one corner opens out to the garden with a south elevation opening to a new patio. In addition to the windows 'disappearing' as seen when open from the inside, the room can also be completely closed down by an internal system of insulated timber shutters. Insulated sections of the ceiling can similarly be winched down to seal off the clerestorey and kitchen rooflight. In this way the skin of the building appears to have three manifestations – totally open, totally opaque and transparent – responding both to changing climate and, more subtly, to the changing psychological responses that the seasons provoke. Externally the roof continues to form a shaded terrace with all roof drainage using a hanging chain. The north wall is in lead offered up to the stonework at either end with small windows created by the discontinuities between the two materials.

House Extensions 35

36 House Extensions

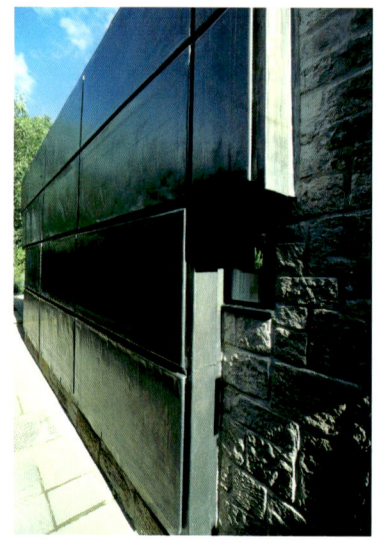

House Extensions 37

Morrison House Dirleton, East Lothian

Completed 1998

Our clients own a pleasant 19th century house with an extensive back garden in the village of Dirleton, East Lothian. Life for them was transformed with the arrival of triplets in 1996, and we were contacted shortly afterwards to deal with the architectural consequences of this domestic event.

Our solution in this case has been to semi-demolish the previous build-out at the rear and to place in it a nursery at the garden end, and a kitchen in the central section, connecting to the previous kitchen within the main body of the house which is now converted into a dining area. The house in effect has not been extended but simply rationalised to provide more efficient use of the space and to place next to the garden those rooms which will benefit by their location there.

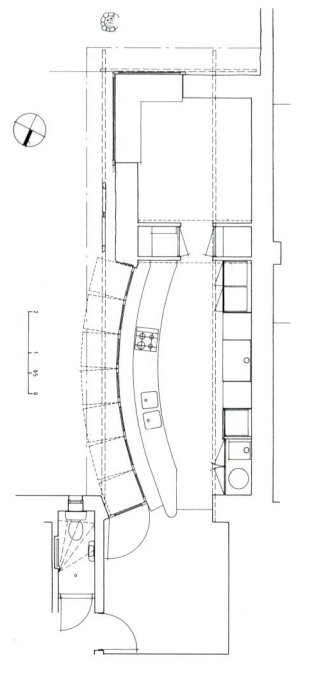

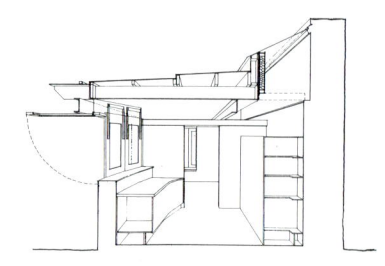

38 House Extensions

Since the kitchen is the place in which most families spend their lives, we have made the kitchen itself into a 'console' which faces on to the garden, with the work-surface area arranged in a gentle curve, looking on to the garden. To the rear of the kitchen is the Aga and all the storage units and equipment etc, and above is an east facing rooflight reflecting light from a high level mirror back into the room. The chief feature of the kitchen are the windows which are on horizontal pivots with counterweights so that all the windows are capable of being counterweighted up into a horizontal position, allowing the kitchen to be completely open to the garden; indeed the idea is that cooking and preparation of food can take place as if in the garden. The kitchen extends directly into the dining area, which now gives access directly on to the garden. At the garden end of the kitchen is a nursery with a corner window seat dug into the gently rising ground. This corner window seat becomes part of the garden when the windows are slid back with no corner structure at this point.

Comparative constructional sections

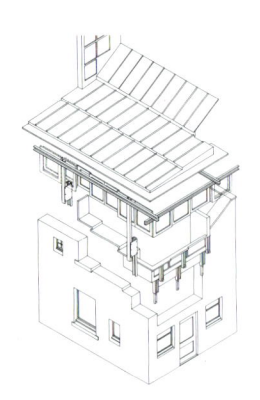

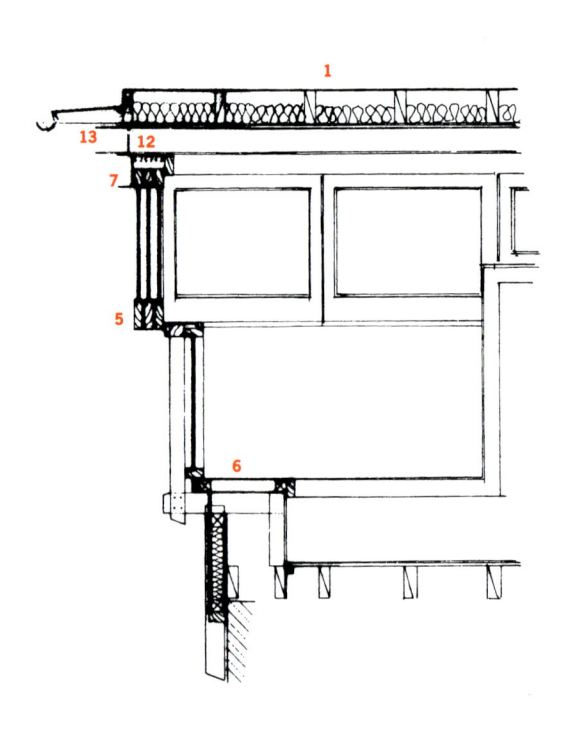

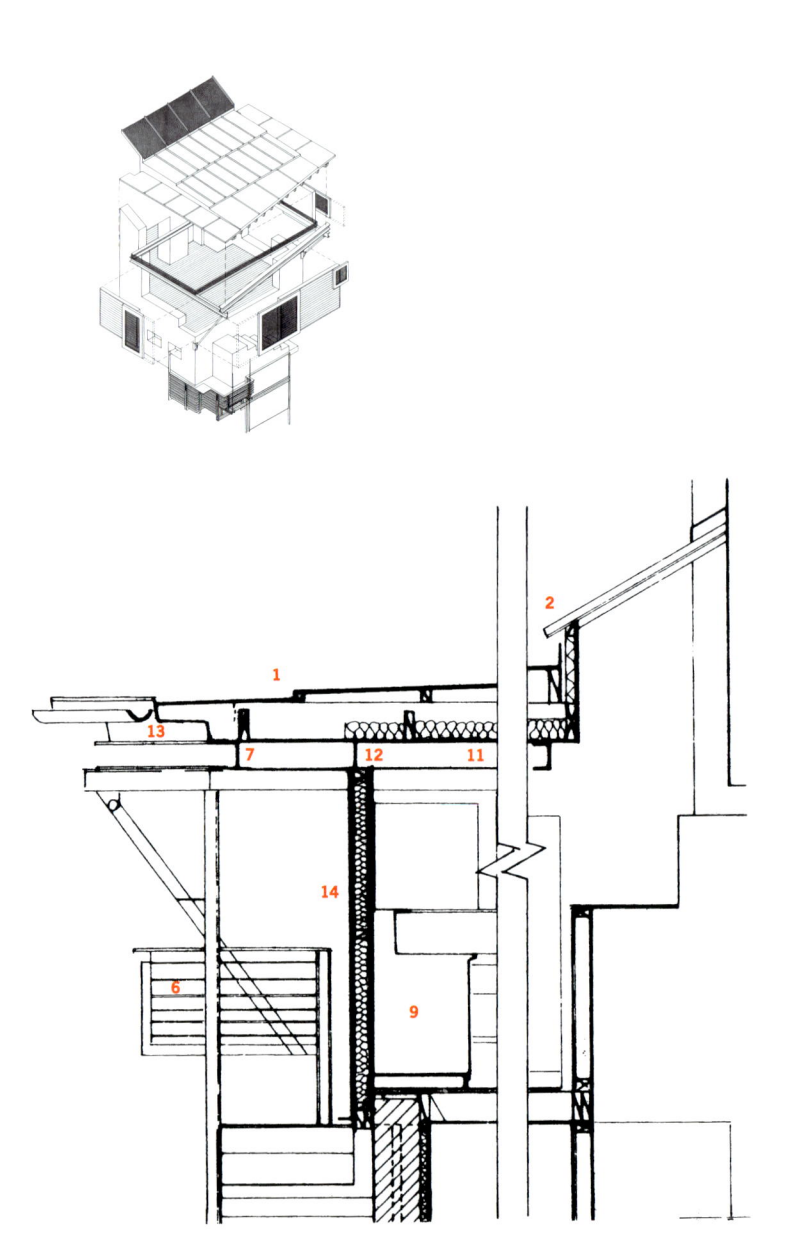

40 House Extensions

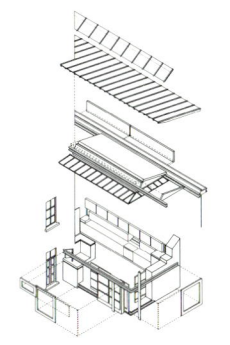

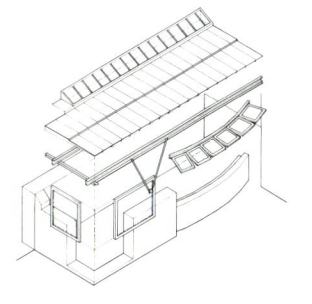

1	Lead and plywood
2	Double glazing
3	Plywood insulated ceiling shutter
4	Plywood insulated wall shutter
5	Softwood sliding double glazed windows
6	Seat
7	Rolled steel joist
8	Counterweighted pivoting softwood windows
9	Kitchen
10	Mirror
11	Decorative plywood soffit
12	Single glazed frameless glazing
13	Stained softwood rafters
14	Western red cedar boarding
15	Vertical lead panelling

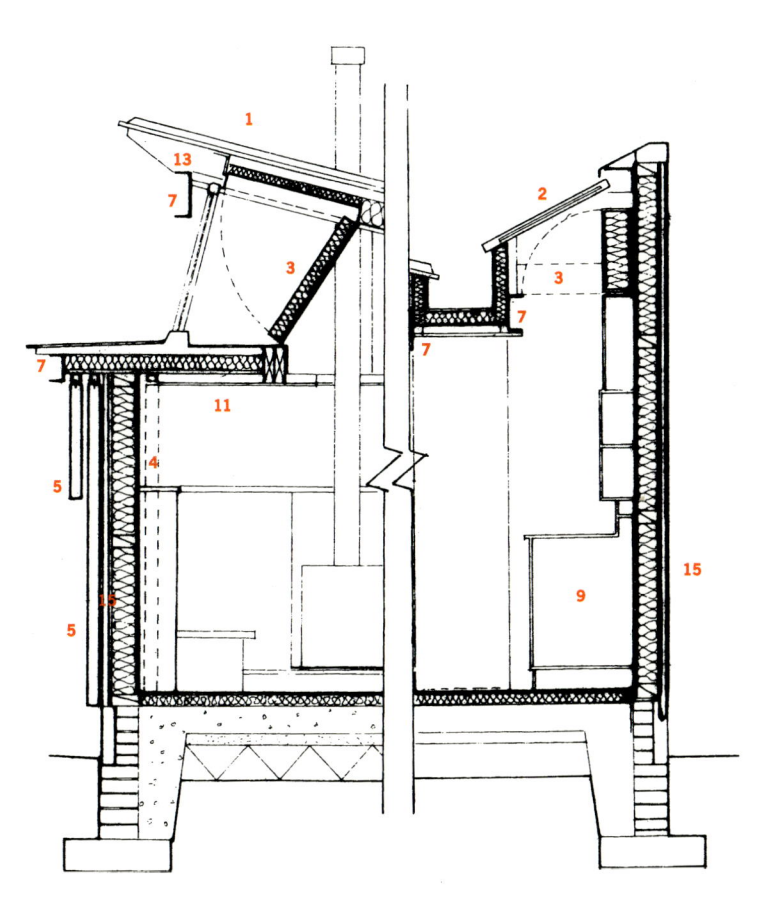

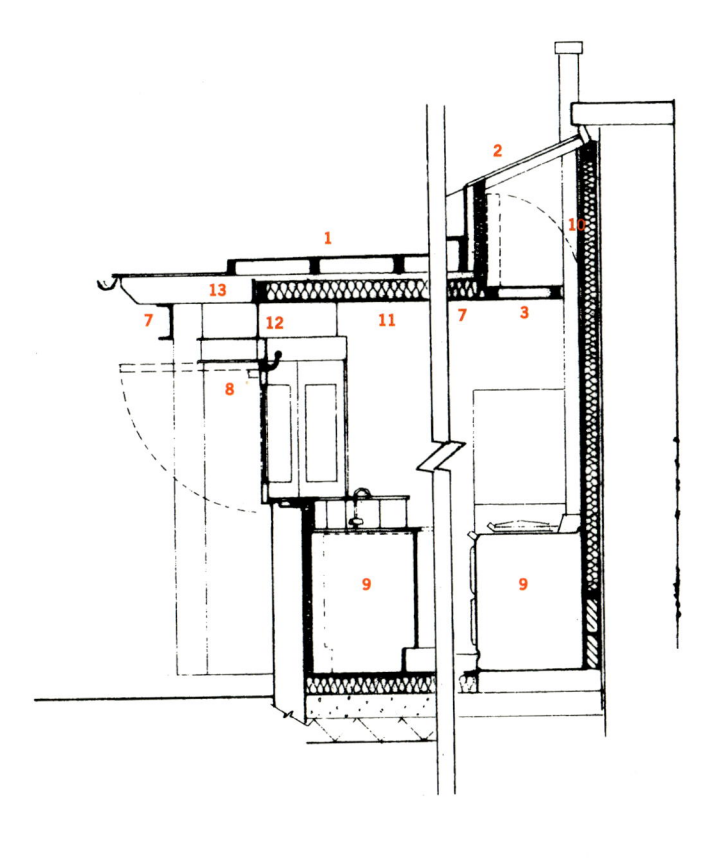

House Extensions 41

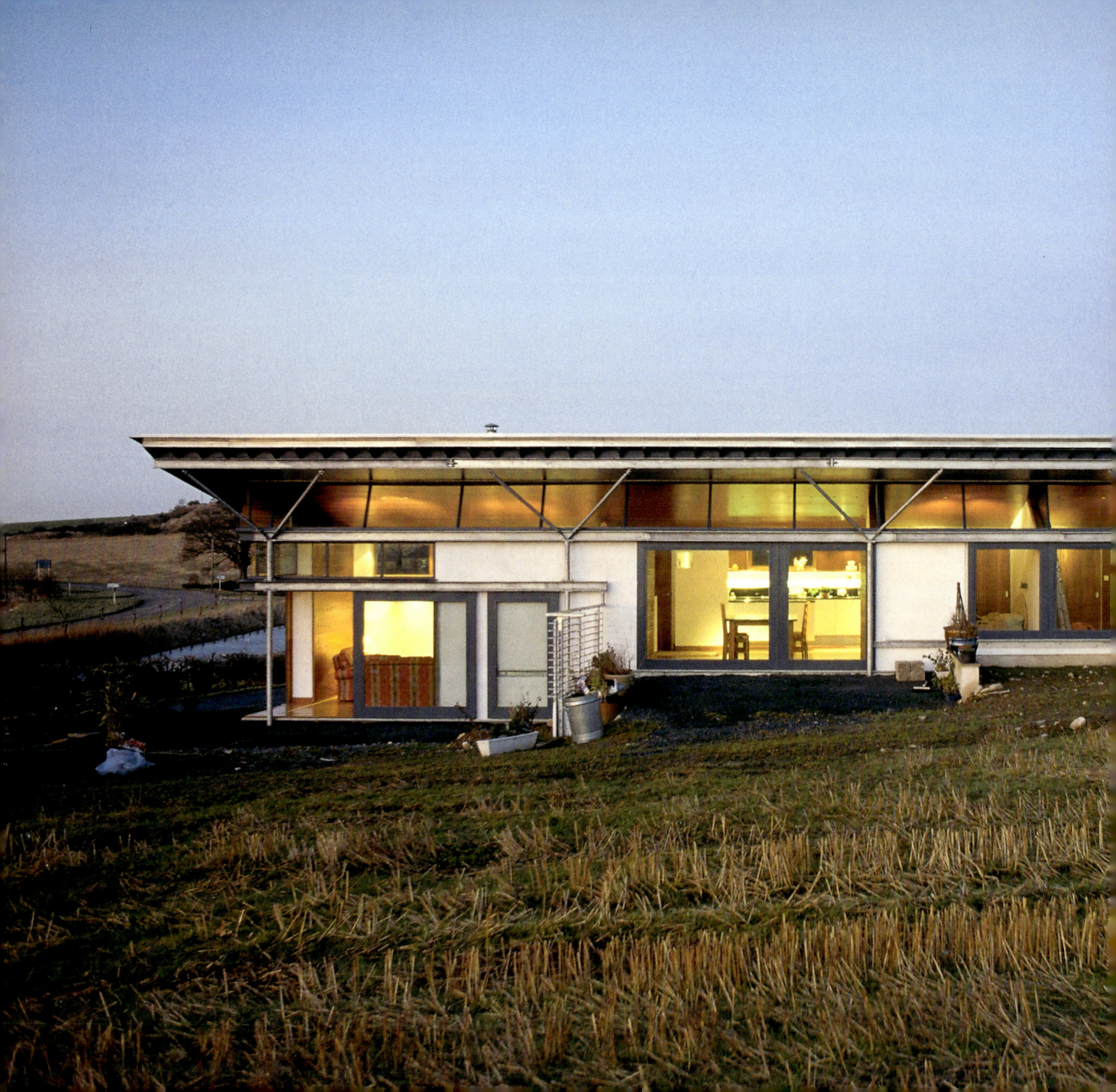

Twelve Houses

The contexts of these twelve designs could not have been more diverse: Irish, Dutch and Aberdeenshire landscapes, mature Edinburgh gardens or an Old Town Close, with a number of reinhabitations of former mews buildings and sites, and the reworking of a traditional Lothians farmsteading. All, however, exhibit three common threads: the idea of working in a new way but *with* a landscape or urban type; the celebration of domestic life with cooking and eating at the centre of all plans; and an interest in the transformation of the external skin between day and night or winter and summer.

In this last respect the Dutch architect Aldo Van Eyck stated that every house needs to be both bird's-nest and cave, to accomodate both the extrovert and introvert sides of the human psyche, and whilst normally this might be served by different rooms, we have tried to achieve this transformation in the one space by diverse systems of moving window shutters. It is no coincidence that three of the new-build projects in Scotland utilise broadly the same section when responding to the huge variation of the angle of the sun and internal insulated kinetic elements balance the vast difference in hours of daylight of the Scottish latitudes.

In general new constructions follow the simple single-section 'long house' idea, whilst the mews projects (zealous conservation-minded officials permitting) attempt to demonstrate how a building-type built for horses can be transformed for human inhabitation (mostly by turning it upside down and letting in the light). Only at Bakehouse Close, with a very restricted site area, has the idea of a tower house been attempted with all the resonance that this model evokes of its unique Scottish precedent.

Stoneman House Killeenaran, Co. Galway, Ireland

Completed 1997

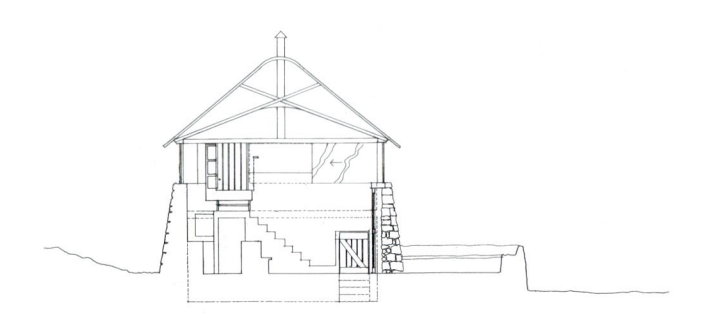

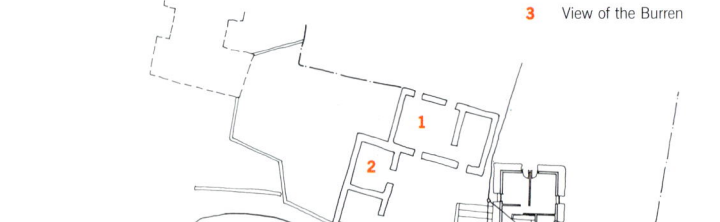

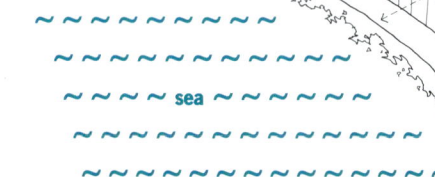

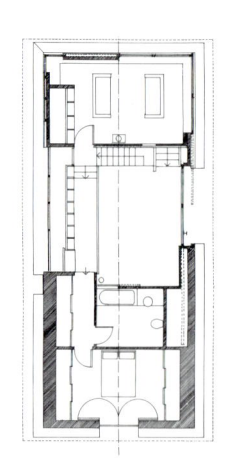

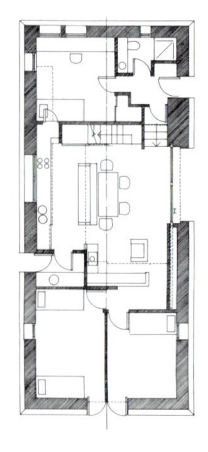

1 Former cottage
2 Outhouses
3 View of the Burren

Much of the Irish landscape has been devastated in recent years by indiscriminate bungalow development. This house, situated approximately three metres from Brandy Harbour, an inlet of Galway Bay on the west coast, could be read as a retrospective essay in what might have been: an attempt to understand the materials of the Irish countryside, and also the form of the traditional architecture, whilst at the same time making a contemporary response to both landscape and lifestyle.

Traditionally Irish cottages[1] are dominated by their roof, while internally a large central space extends up to the roof, opening onto smaller spaces at either end, a model which to our mind is peculiarly appropriate once again to contemporary family life.

44 Houses

Externally, therefore, we have adopted a simple rectilinear form with the first floor spaces partially enveloped within a roof formed of mill-finished aluminium, like the galvanised steel of local barns, and with a curved roof apex distantly reminiscent of thatch. The structure of rafters supported on 'scissor trusses' results in a gently curving internal vault finished in plywood. The landscape of undulating drystone walls is gathered up at ground floor level to form a battered rain-screen to the insulation, placed externally around a block work construction. Between the drystone walls and the aluminium roof is cedar boarding and sliding windows.

Internally, entrance is made at a slightly lower level where there is also a study/guest bedroom. A large family room dominates the centre with sliding glazed doors opening direct to a terrace looking to Brandy Harbour. Connected by sliding panels at first floor is a living room with disappearing corner windows to view the sea, whilst at the other end, reached by a bridge, is the master bedroom, which looks north to a further view of the sea. Unusually the bathroom is also connected to the main space with a sliding panel to allow conversation between a bather and others in the kitchen below or the living space across. The ruin of a previous house will form a walled garden and a re-roofed barn completes an informal enclosure with the new house.

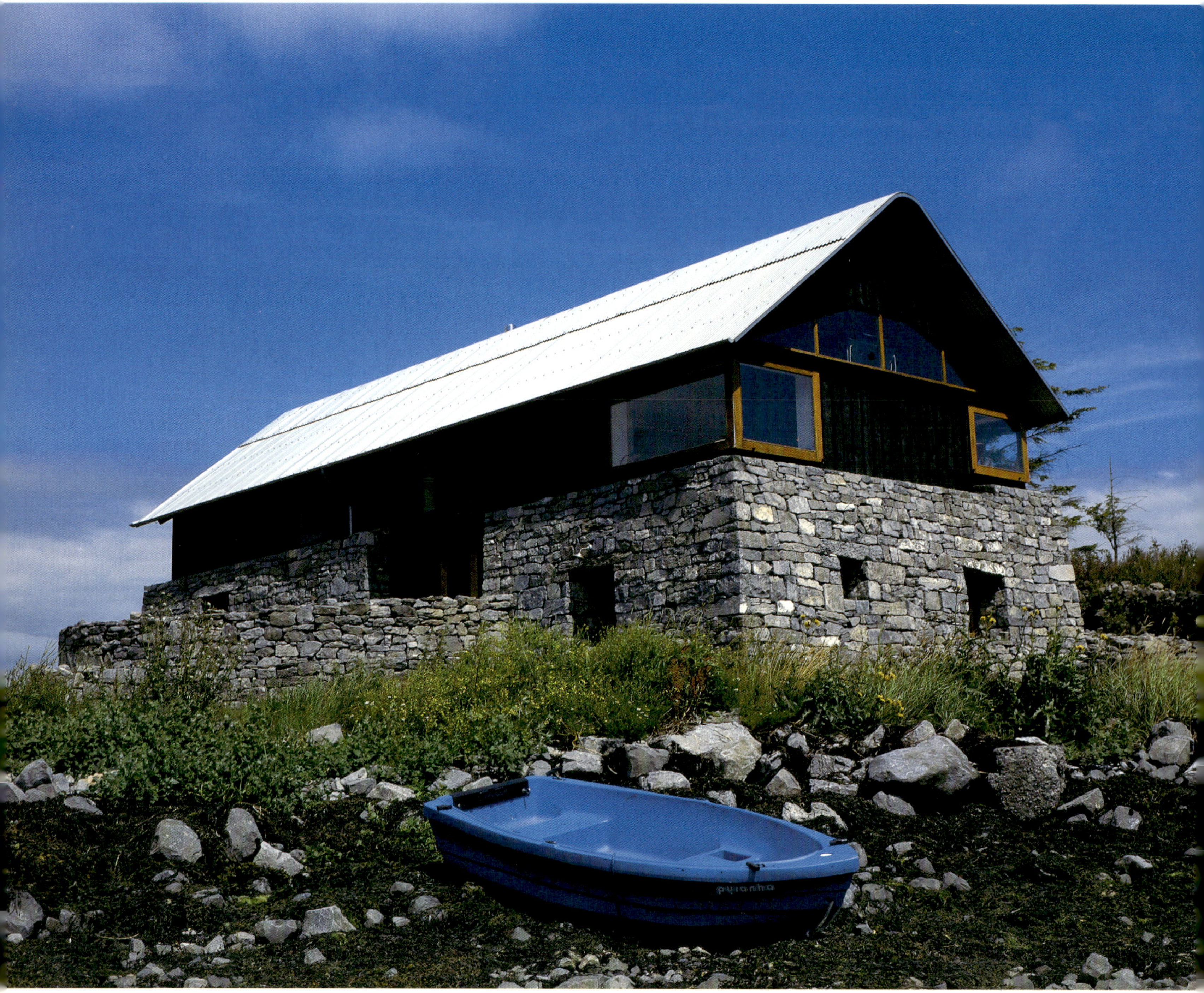
pyranha

Rod Stoneman writes . . .

"Finding myself in a place and at a time where I was coming to build a house late in the day . . . My father was a builder, so how could I not embrace the risk involved in an innovative design? Call it brave or call it reckless – that's always a matter of how it turns out in the end.

Meeting the architect and his practice it seemed to be exactly the same as the precarious economy of independent film production. Small entrepreneurial companies operating on short cycles of production followed by the insecurity of micro-operations sustaining themselves through erratic one-off commissions. I also recognised the hauteur of the auteur, the 'keep out' signs put out to protect creative work; there was the ominous and apocryphal tale of Lutyens' responding to a Yorkshire millionaire client "I hear what you say . . ." and then ignoring him completely. There has to be a proper autonomy for the work of the architect, whilst being attentive enough to assert one's own peculiar tastes and desires. It's clear that it is indeed the architect who is designing the house and not the 'client' – although we have to live in it and that gives one some purchase, literally. In this instance the interchange was inflected by geography – the house was virtually built by fax. It was a slow but exhilarating experience of seeing a building made inch by inch. Watching a habitable space take form. Of course one would make some adjustments for the next one – there needs to be a bigger utility room to function, we should be wary of an electronic toilet and we should have thought through the audio insulation of different spaces more in advance. The strength of this drystone walled house is in the relation of the vernacular to the modern. In its response to location and culture it is an implicit critique of bad taste, lazy planning, and the collusive, venal structures that underwrite them, that continues to damage the landscapes in the west of Ireland.

The change from the land to the sea is the most exciting place to be. The landscape finds its own patterns and the house settles into it – "Touch this earth lightly" in Australian architect Glenn Murcutt's words. But then there is the quotidian reality of how we live in the house: movement between areas, shifting sight lines, the subtle relationships between spaces, the transition and articulation of light – the house offers an enhanced movement through everyday life. Also, with three young boys and a menagerie of ducks, hens, dogs and stick insects there is the constant flux and commotion, the tenderness and mayhem of la famille.

This house is a polemic against the facile formulaic transpositions of sleazy bungalow bliss; it stands as a challenge to the current confused mediocrity. Frankly, it is also more interesting than the expensive one-off bungalows my father built for the local bourgeoisie in Torquay, Devon; indeed perhaps the whole project has an oedipal dimension for me. I would like to think that the house projects a kind of art for all – it has a militant intelligence and intrepid aesthetic that one could conceive of for culture as a whole . . . As Oscar Wilde wrote, "A map of the world that does not include Utopia is not worth even glancing at . . ."."

Sue Clarke writes . . .

"In Galway for the film festival, film-maker Murray Grigor sat in the kitchen of our rented house in the West of Ireland and said he knew just the man to design the house we wanted to build. Richard Murphy came and stayed with us a few times while we walked the land and looked at possible sites. He designed the basic idea of our house sitting at our kitchen table surrounded by children, dogs and plates of home-made biscuits. He understood the way that we live, focused around the kitchen, and had also seen the central living space of a neighbour's traditional Irish cottage. We had a choice of two builders, brothers, and took them both off to Edinburgh on a daytrip to visit Richard and see some of the other work he had done. It was inspiring for all of us, and in the end it was Declan Kilmartin, the younger brother, who rose to the challenge and took on the house.

The construction was different to anything he had done before, single blockwork, delta lining and a rain batter of drystone walling to form the outer core, plus a steel beam girdling the entire house and supporting the corrugated aluminium roof structure. After a few pints of Guinness and a lashing of oysters in a local pub, Richard was quite confident that Declan could undertake the job without the need for a project architect, so we did it all by fax.

I was redesignated 'Clarke' of the Works, running in and out of Galway with trailerloads of building supplies, and being the oddjob person. Being so involved with the day-to-day progress of the house I feel that I know it all, from the skeletal core to its outer skin; balancing on noggin boards to paint the walls before the floors went down, and spending a blissful Mother's Day, in overalls, with soft rain coming down outside, staining all the window and door frames before they were fitted into the house.

For a short time there was some doubt about the avant-garde nature of the roof, but a resolute stand from architect and apprentice builder won over the fearful party. It still gives us great joy, when walking up to the house, or viewing from the water, to see the roof reflecting the sky above and sometimes becoming almost invisible, like a floating cloud above the house.

The house has some wonderful spaces, opening and closing off from each other with sliding screens, depending on sociability. It feels like living in a ship sometimes, with the bridge connecting rooms on the upper floor, and the upstairs windows jutting out to sea. It blends into the landscape, harmoniously – passers by sometimes think we built a house from within the shell of an old drystone barn. The verdict from our children's friends, when visiting for the first time is that our house is "cool". No better compliment than that!"

Van Hulten House Joure, Friesland, Netherlands

Completed 1998. Garden design, Klaas Noordhuis.

Our site sits on the outer edge of a suburban housing development which itself sits on the edge of this small Friesland town. The site is a flat rectangle which projects on three sides into a small lake beyond which is a park and then the open countryside of the polder.

Looking for forms in the Dutch landscape, we became conscious of the traditional combined farms and farmhouse – great single section buildings – and in the somewhat dislocated environment of a housing estate we elected to emulate these forms with a simple building of an extruded section: a barrel-vaulted space with two side sections.

The house is arranged on the site to give the maximum private garden, and is organised internally with a children's zone near the entrance and a parents' zone towards the lake. At the centre, as a meeting place between parents and children, is a double-height family kitchen/dining room which can open directly to the garden.

This is a noisy place packed with the daily life of the family, and it is in contrast to the quieter living room, linked by sliding screens and fronting both the lake and garden. Above it is a mezzanine study with its own external stair access (not yet constructed) to the garden. The construction is timber frame clad in western red cedar with a mill-finished aluminium roof.

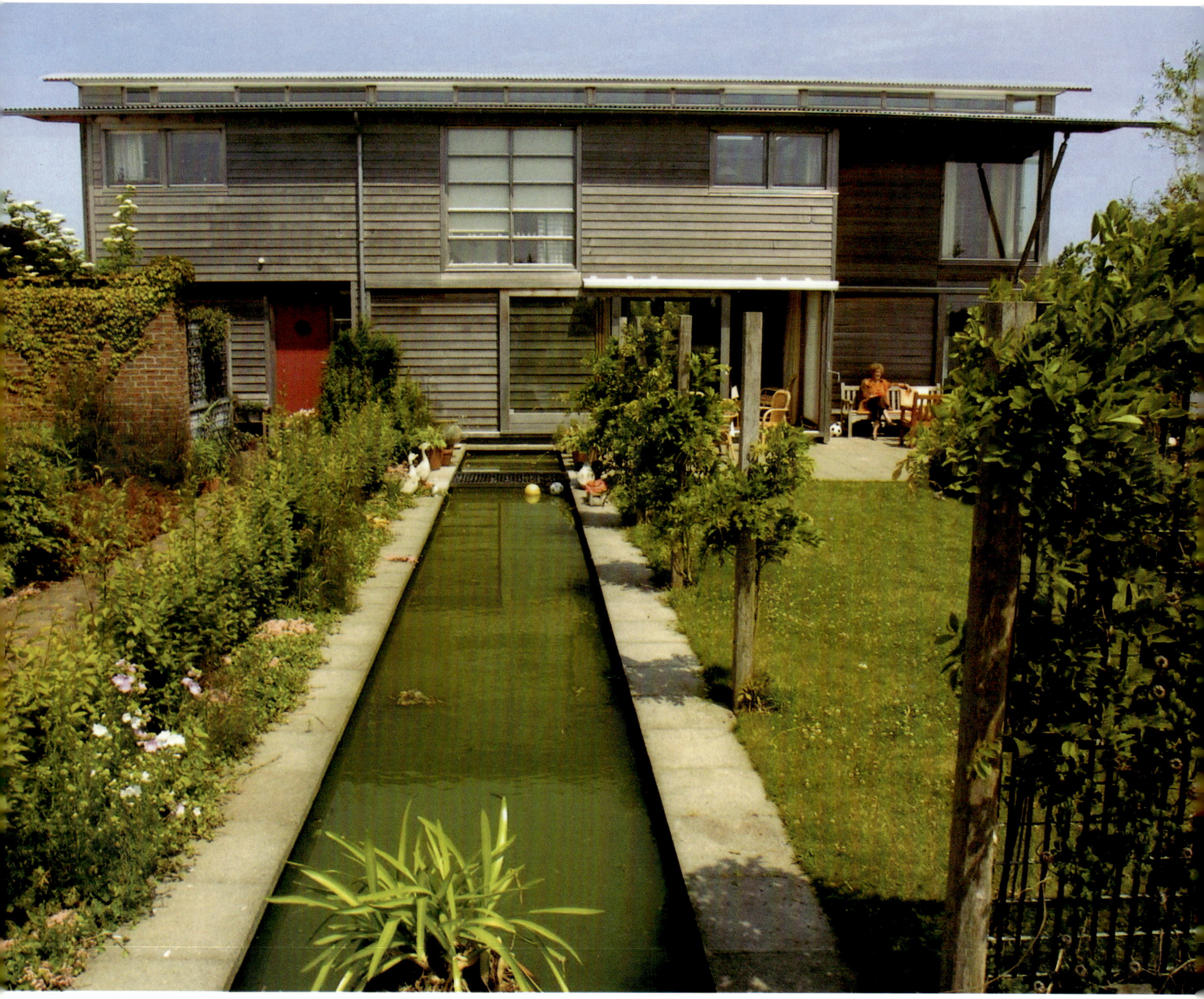

50 Houses

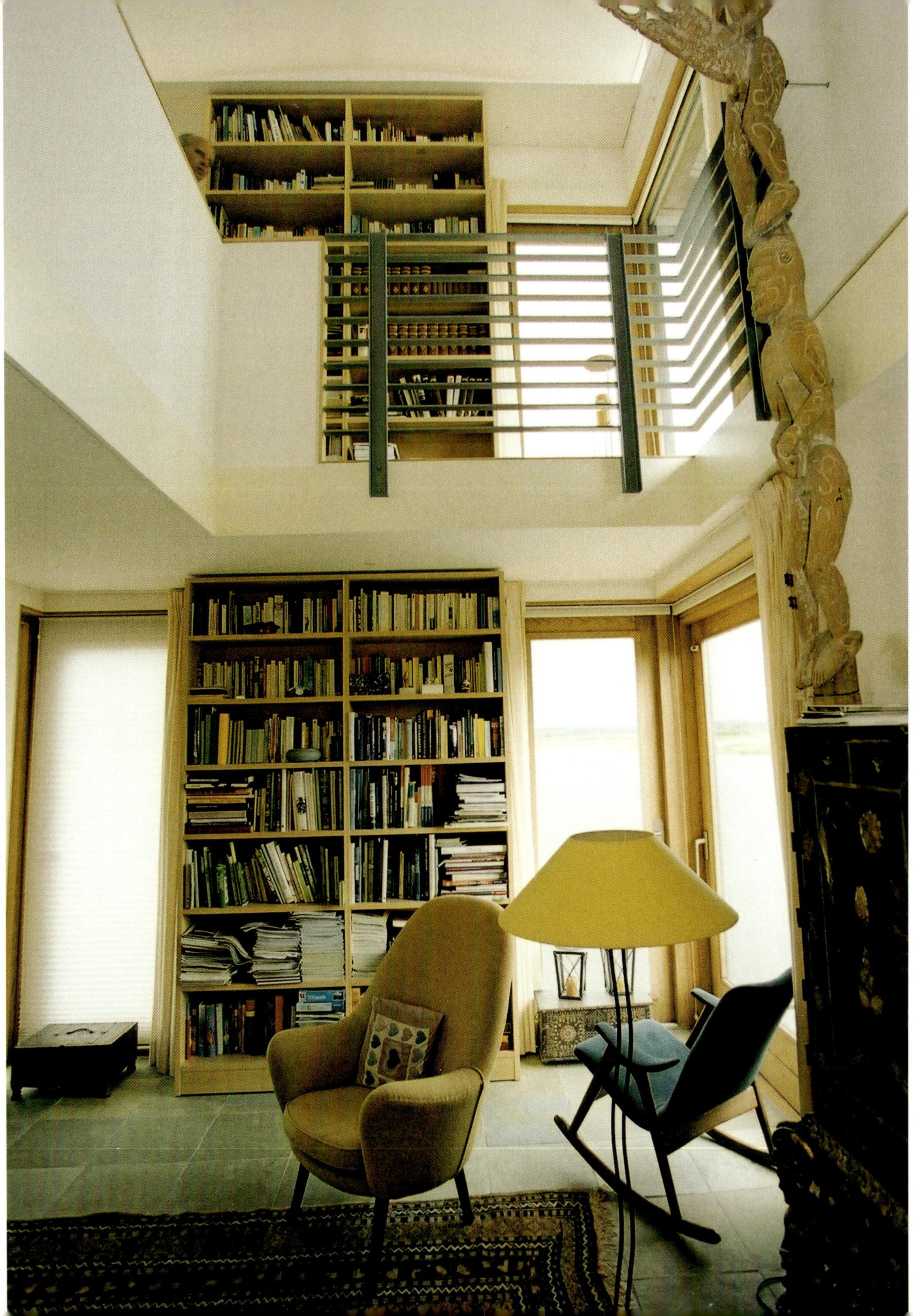

Stewart House Milldale, Aberdeenshire

Completed 2000

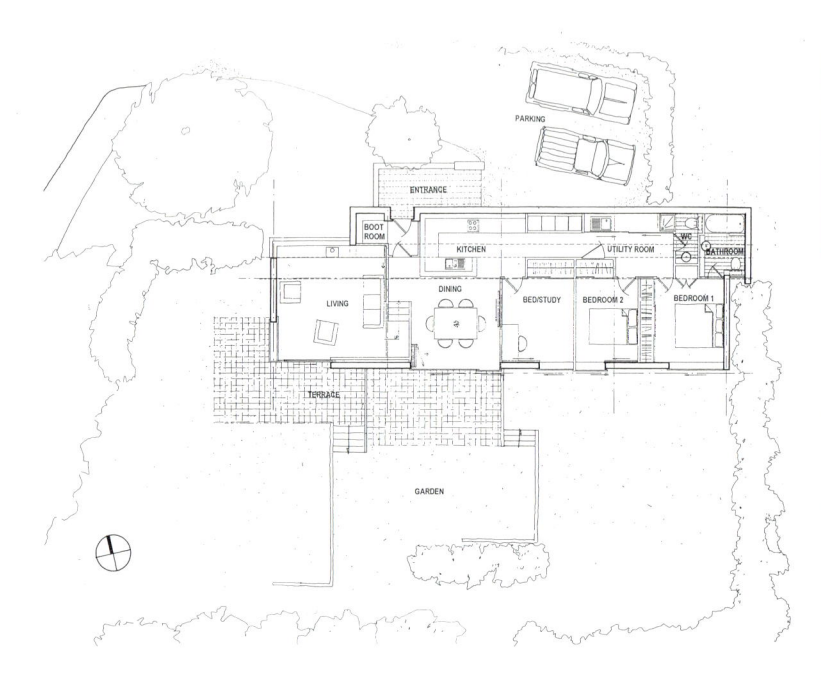

The plot is at the southern end of a crescent of detached bungalows forming the hamlet of Milldale. There is a small bank of trees between the plot and the adjacent main road, and the ground rises slowly from west to east. The locale is an unspectacular but pleasing open landscape of gently rolling farmland with a long view to the south.

In inspiration there is an undoubted debt to Glenn Murcutt, but then the Highland corrugated-iron[1] vernacular has an uncanny similarity to its Australian counterpart. Our project shows a linear design, single storey, on an east-west orientation. This indicates a termination of the development of the hamlet of Milldale and presents a virtually blank wall to the north, or semi-public side of the house. It is pierced only by entrance doors and some very small windows. The extent of the house is only evident from the south elevation, which is largely glazed, with the whole design being orientated to maximise passive solar gain: the angle of the roof admitting maximum low winter light but providing shade in the height of summer.

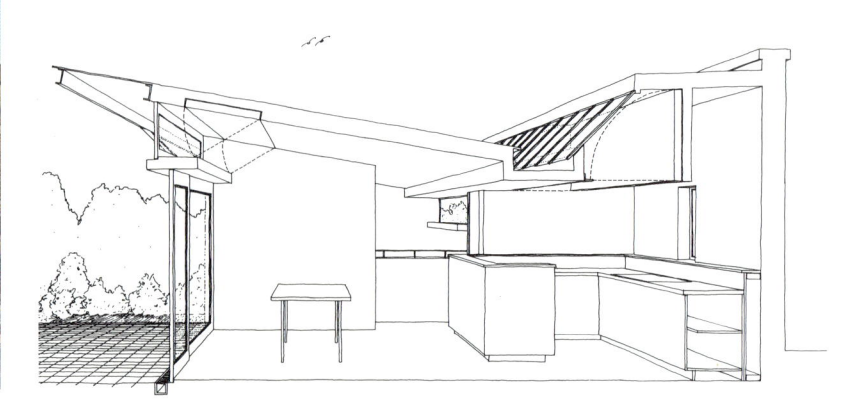

52 Houses

Houses 53

Internally, the layout of the house consists of a kitchen/dining area at the centre, with bedrooms to the east and a living room at a lower level to the west, capturing the afternoon and evening sunlight. The section of the house shows a glazed south elevation and also a long ridge of south facing glazed roof lights to bring in sunlight along the northern edge of the main part of the plan. Integral to the design of the house are insulated shutters to all the windows and roof lights to minimise heat loss in the winter and at night time so that a large proportion of the skin of the building can vary its insulating and solar gain qualities depending on external conditions.

The materials of the house are dry-dash blockwork externally, with clear-stained timber window frames on the south elevation, and a tern-coated steel roof. The structure is a hybrid: a galvanised steel frame to the south for the open facade and load bearing blockwork internally and to the north elevation. Extensive landscaping is proposed along the southern boundary of the site with a series of stepped gardens adjacent to the living room, kitchen/dining room, and bedrooms respectively.

Houses 55

Marshall House Ravleston, Edinburgh

Completion 2002

The acute dearth of building plots within Edinburgh convinced our clients to purchase a 1960s house and demolish it for the sake of the substantial garden. Our design develops the idea of the monopitch back-lit section first tried at Abbotsford Park and later developed at Milldale in Aberdeenshire. The plot is rectangular, falls three metres from one end to the other, and is surrounded by a substantial coniferous hedge. From an upper level it is possible to see Edinburgh Castle to the east.

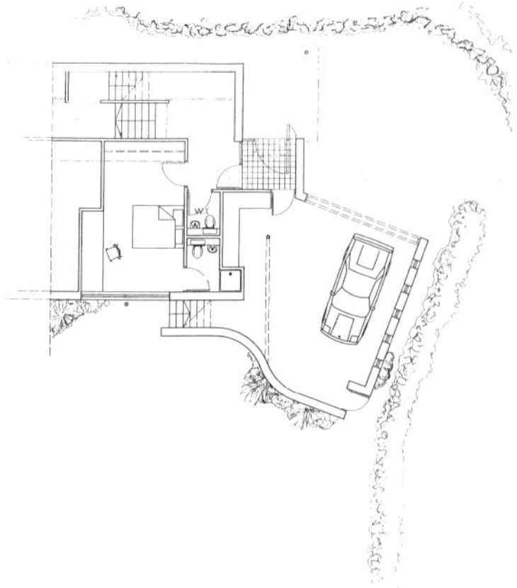

Our design maximises the garden area and south-facing characteristics by placing accommodation along the whole of the north edge of the site. At the heart of the house, the kitchen/dining areas occupy a 1.5 storey space in the middle of a section which develops from single storey bedrooms to the west, to a living room and terrace placed above a garage to the east. From the terrace it will be possible to view the Castle. Top-lit circulation is placed along the northern edge of the plan and acts as a 'background of light' to each of the main spaces. All windows, clerestories and roof lighting are fully shuttered and the structure is a hybrid of steel frame and load-bearing brick.

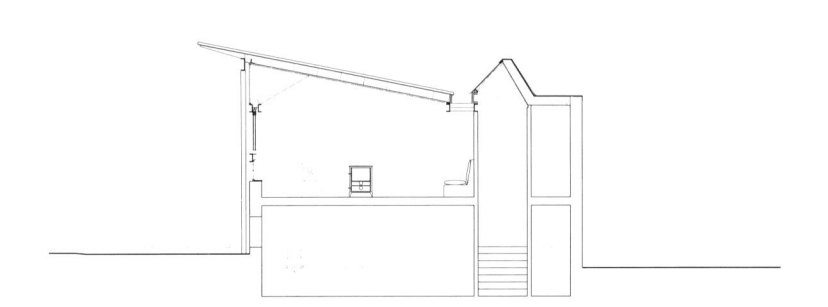

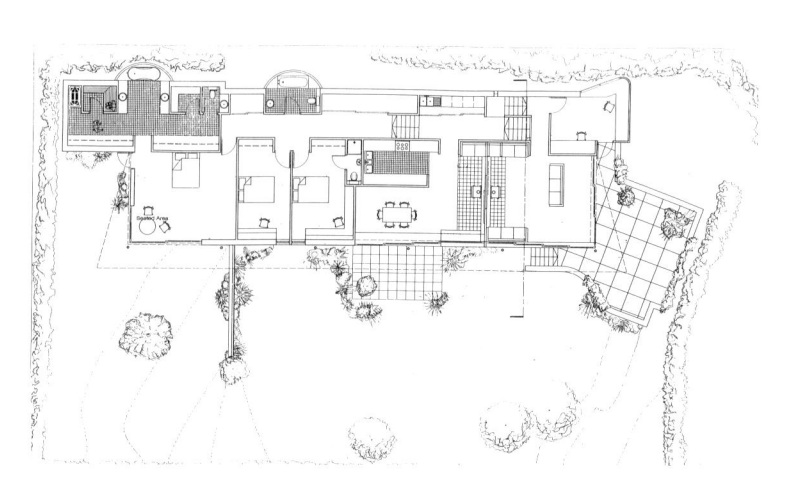

MacLean House Barnton, Edinburgh

Limited competition 1995

The practice was selected with two others for the highly unusual opportunity of building a large prestigious family house (complete with 'granny house') on a large site, with a view of the Forth and an extensive mature garden in the most exclusive residential road in Edinburgh. Even more unusual was the client's determination to demolish a substantial Edwardian property in order to create the site.

The design utilises the monopitch/back lit section (first used at Abbotsford Park and later developed at Milldale and Ravelston) so that all major rooms face south. The section of the house gradually deepens with the fall on the site, from children's accommodation at one end through the kitchen and living room to the master bedroom set in the branches of trees above a guest room at the western end. The two social spaces in the centre open completely to the landscape and, although at slightly different levels, also to each other.

Entrance is from a courtyard to the north partially defined by a separate 'granny house' being a two bedroomed scaled down version of the main house. It has its own address and front door and also faces south to its own walled garden across which is found the children's nursery.

None of the architects selected won the competition and a house was built instead to the designs of the architect who advised the clients on the judging of the competition.

Høgel House 1 Royal Terrace Mews, Edinburgh
Completed 1995

This former 1820s stable and hayloft, unlike many Edinburgh mews properties, had not yet been converted to residential use when we were commissioned to convert it into a one bedroom flat for rent. Our conversion is meant to express the idea of a new house found within the repaired shell of the existing stable so that the history of the building is expressed, particularly on the front facade.

To obtain planning permission a garage was required so the majority of living accommodation is found at first floor level. To accommodate this the original first floor level was lowered, and this is expressed on the front elevation in a steel channel which also forms the runner for the garage door. The asymmetrical planar language of the new architecture finds expression in panels of glass blocks and lead on this façade, the latter appearing to form an inner skin behind the stone but in reality dressed into either shadow gaps or mirrors.

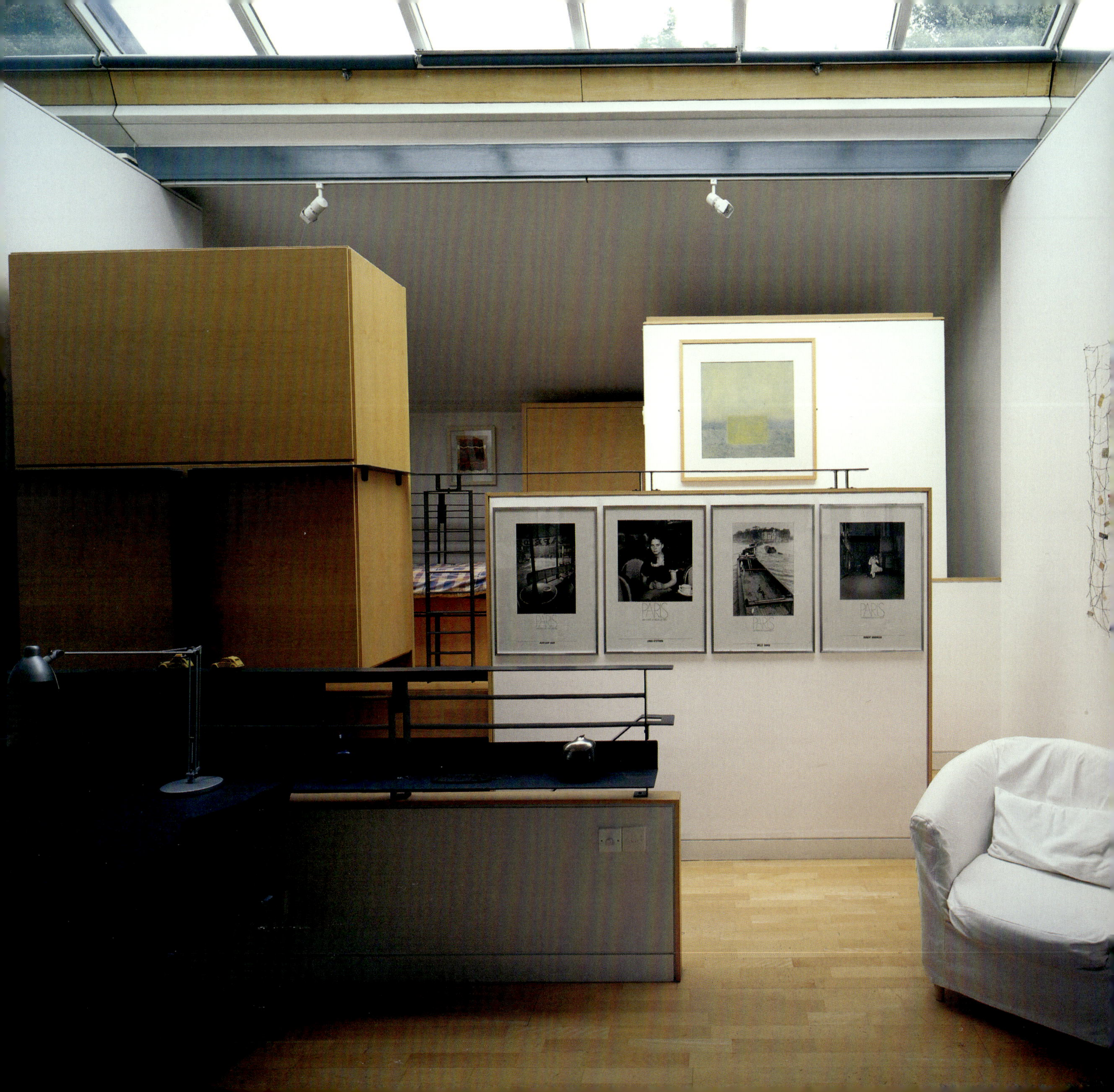
PARIS
PARIS
PARIS
PARIS

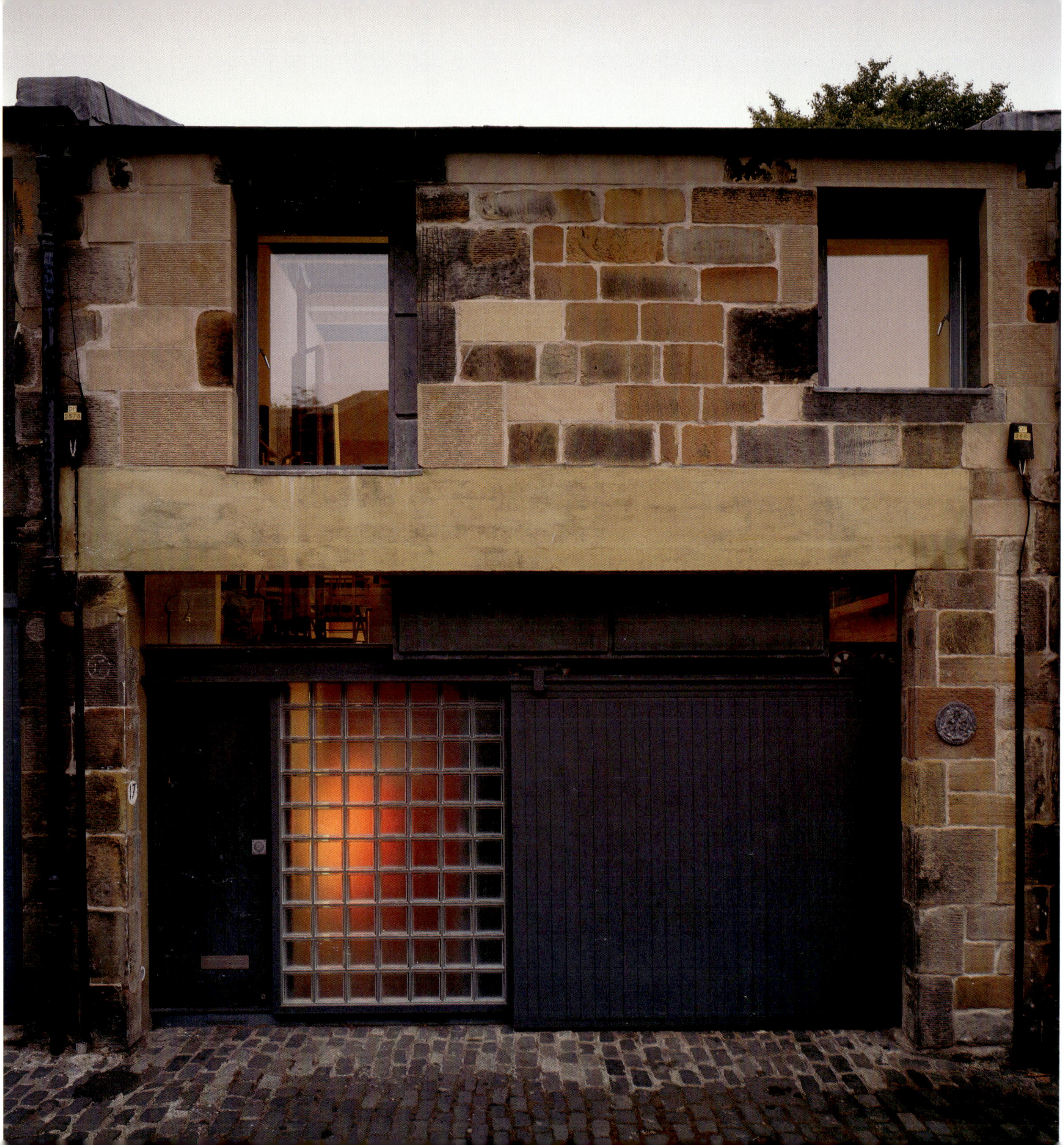

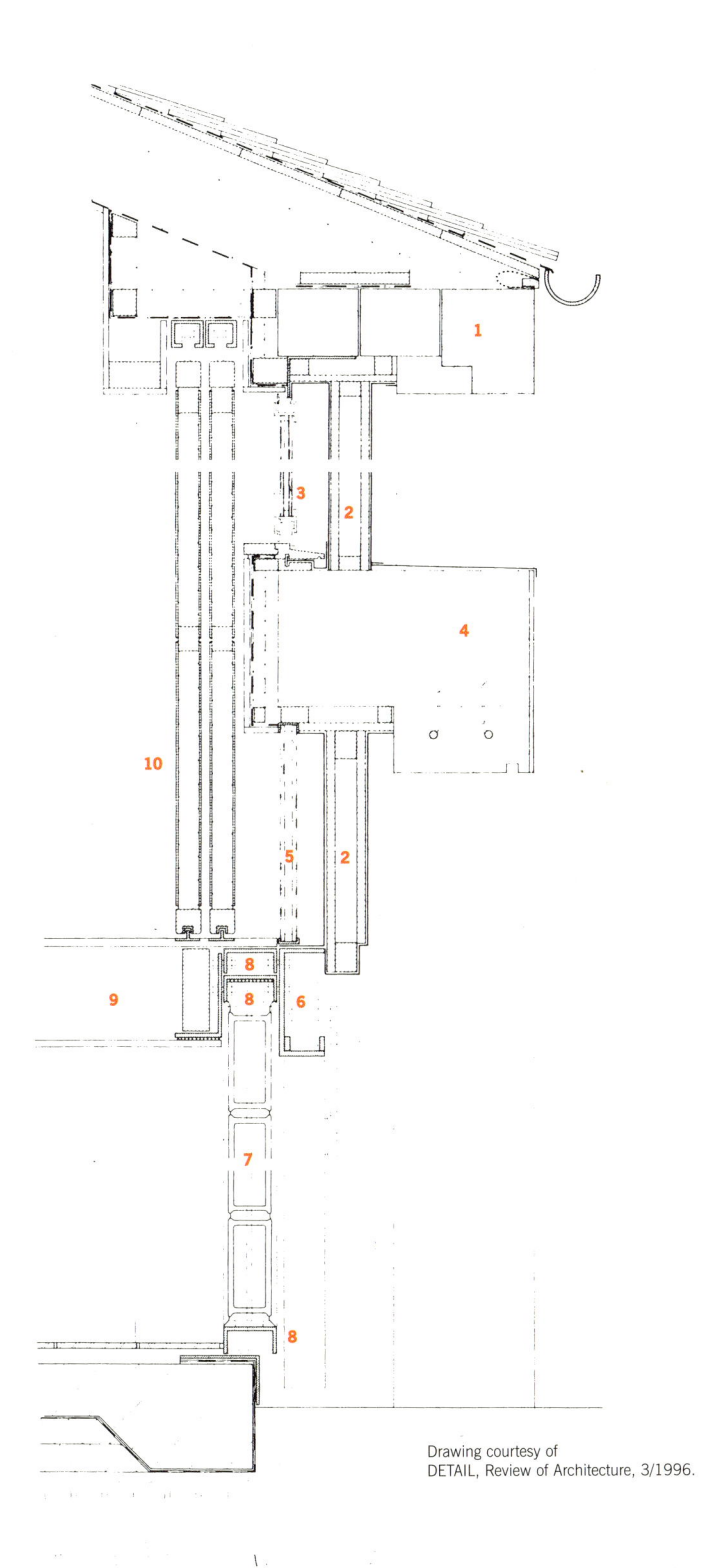

1	Existing lintel to upper window
2	Lead covered plywood panel
3	Steel window frame
4	1960s concrete lintel
5	Double glazing
6	Steel channel & garage door wheel runner
7	Glass block
8	Steel channel
9	First floor timber joists
10	Plywood insulated sliding panels

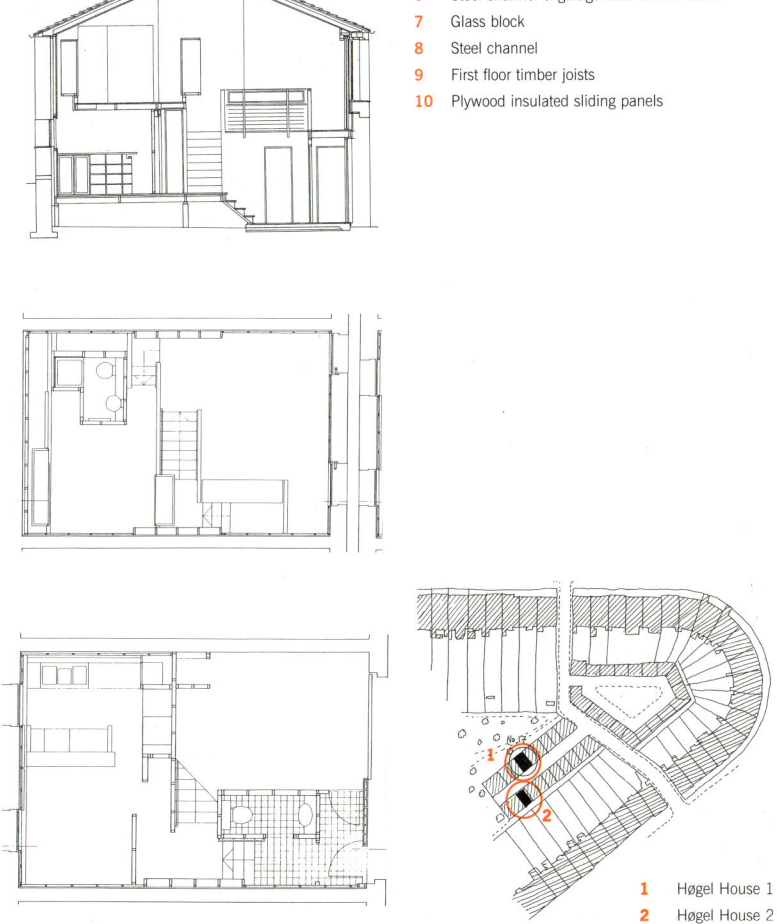

1	Høgel House 1
2	Høgel House 2

Drawing courtesy of
DETAIL, Review of Architecture, 3/1996.

Internally the lead masks two panels which close the whole front façade at night. The flat is a continuous space, culminating in a bedroom, with functions distributed around the path of the sun which is admitted through a dramatic ridge roof light. This single act brings all the necessary extra light into the property while still maintaining the integrity of the uninterrupted slate roofs. Internally mirrors are placed under the ridge to extend the space laterally and to throw light around the room in opposition to the path of the sun. Much of the furniture, including wardrobes, desk and even the bed were designed as part of the commission.

Houses 61

Høgel House 2 Regent Terrace Mews, Edinburgh

Completion 2002

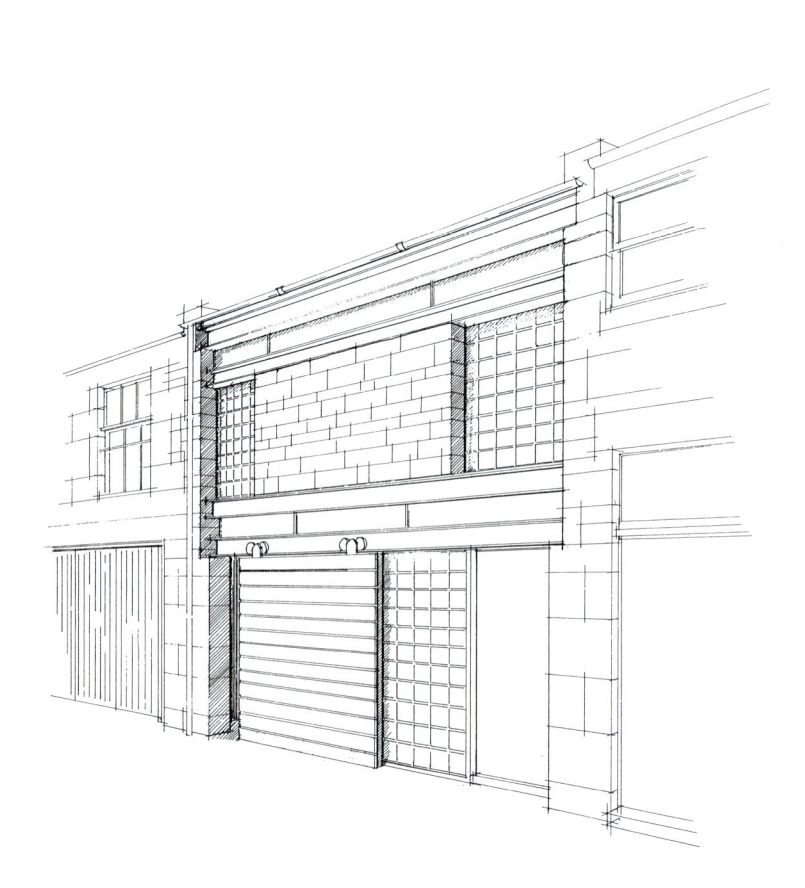

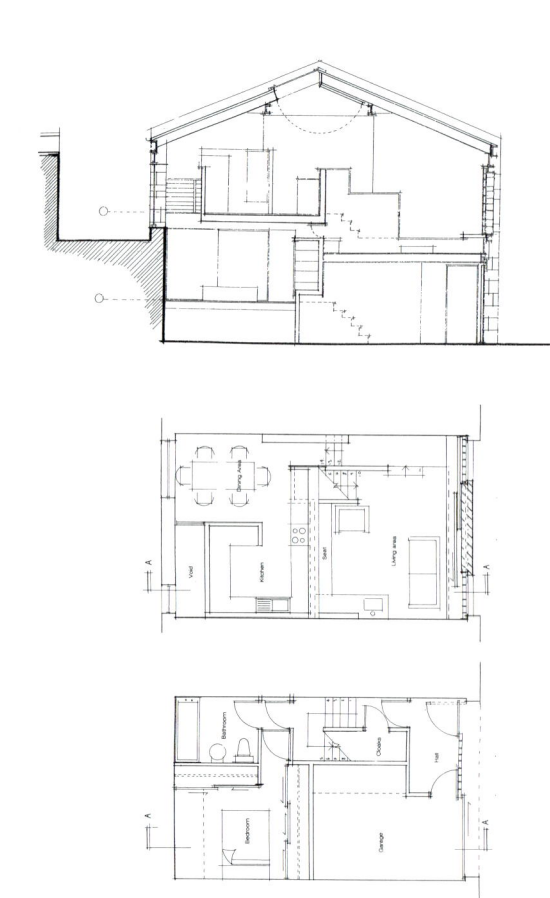

Eight years after the commission for the conversion of 17 Royal Terrace Mews the same client returned with an almost identical project on the opposite side of the street. Although this time not derelict, the existing building was in poor repair so that virtual complete demolition could again be contemplated.

The street façade plays similar games of layering, although the initial proposal of a screen of glass blocks was modified by planning department insistence on a substantial panel of stone at first floor. Views out through horizontal slot windows are controlled and limited to the street and up to the sky to avoid privacy infringements with houses across the lane.

Richard Murphy moved into No 17 in 1996 and the experience has led to variations on the inside at No 10. This time the kitchen/dining area is placed above the bedroom and the ridge light has been substituted with a south-facing rooflight, complete with pivoting timber shutter for night-time use. The multi-level section remains along with many unexpected connections between the spaces.

Knox House Circus Lane, Edinburgh

As yet unrealised

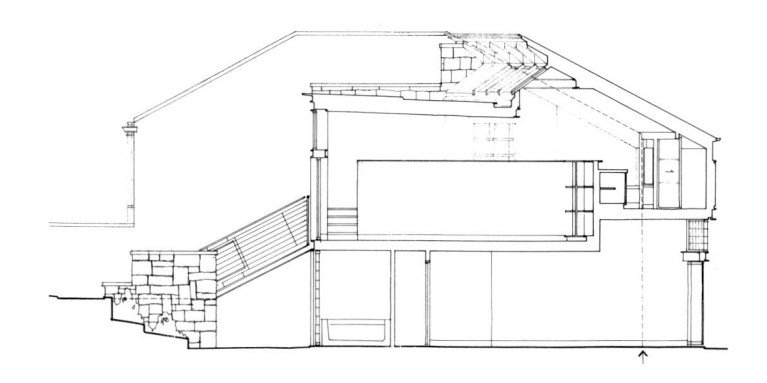

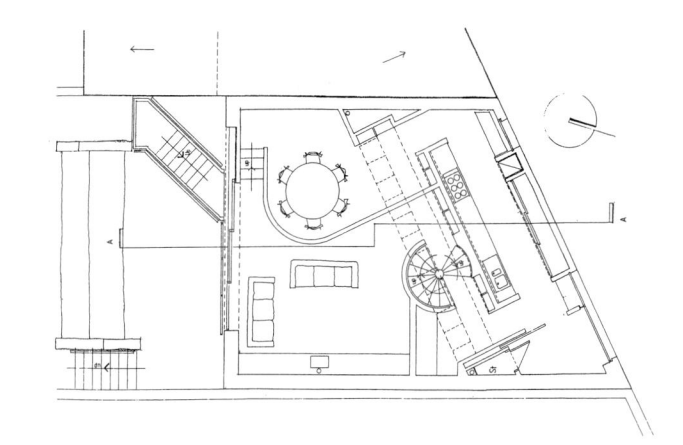

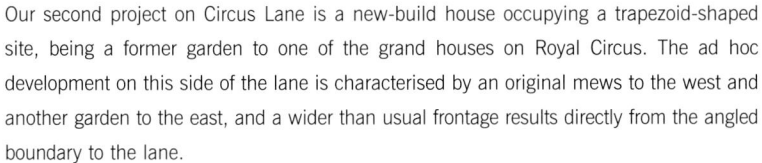

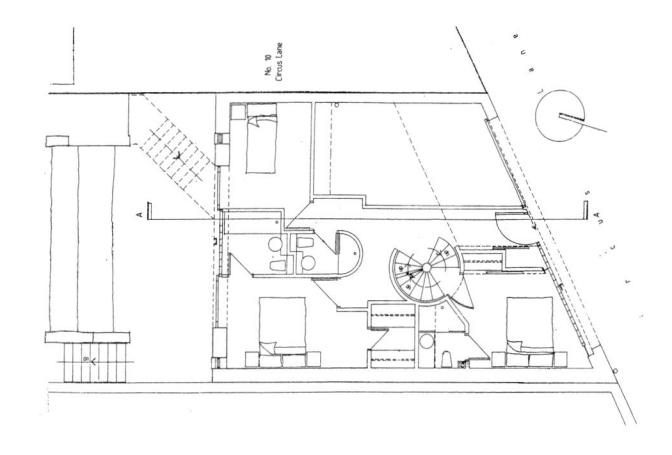

Our second project on Circus Lane is a new-build house occupying a trapezoid-shaped site, being a former garden to one of the grand houses on Royal Circus. The ad hoc development on this side of the lane is characterised by an original mews to the west and another garden to the east, and a wider than usual frontage results directly from the angled boundary to the lane.

The design places the bedrooms with the garage on the lower floor and a single space for kitchen, living and dining on the upper floor. A slope on the site ensures that the garden is equidistant between the two. The kitchen is placed as a galley along the Mews elevation looking down to the living area and is lit by a roof light where the slated roof to the lane meets a flat lead roof to the rear.

The façade continues the 'back to front' tradition where mews elevations are relatively ad hoc compared to the formality of the garden façade as viewed from the big house. Both façades are of steel, glass and timber overlapping planes framed by rubble stone walls, the front being asssymetrical and informal whilst the garden elevation has the formality of an expressed piano nobile.

Internally a spiral stair, placed under the light, visits all four levels (there is also a small semi-basement), and articulates the transition between the front and back geometries of the plan.

Gordon Houses Circus Lane, Edinburgh

Completed 2001

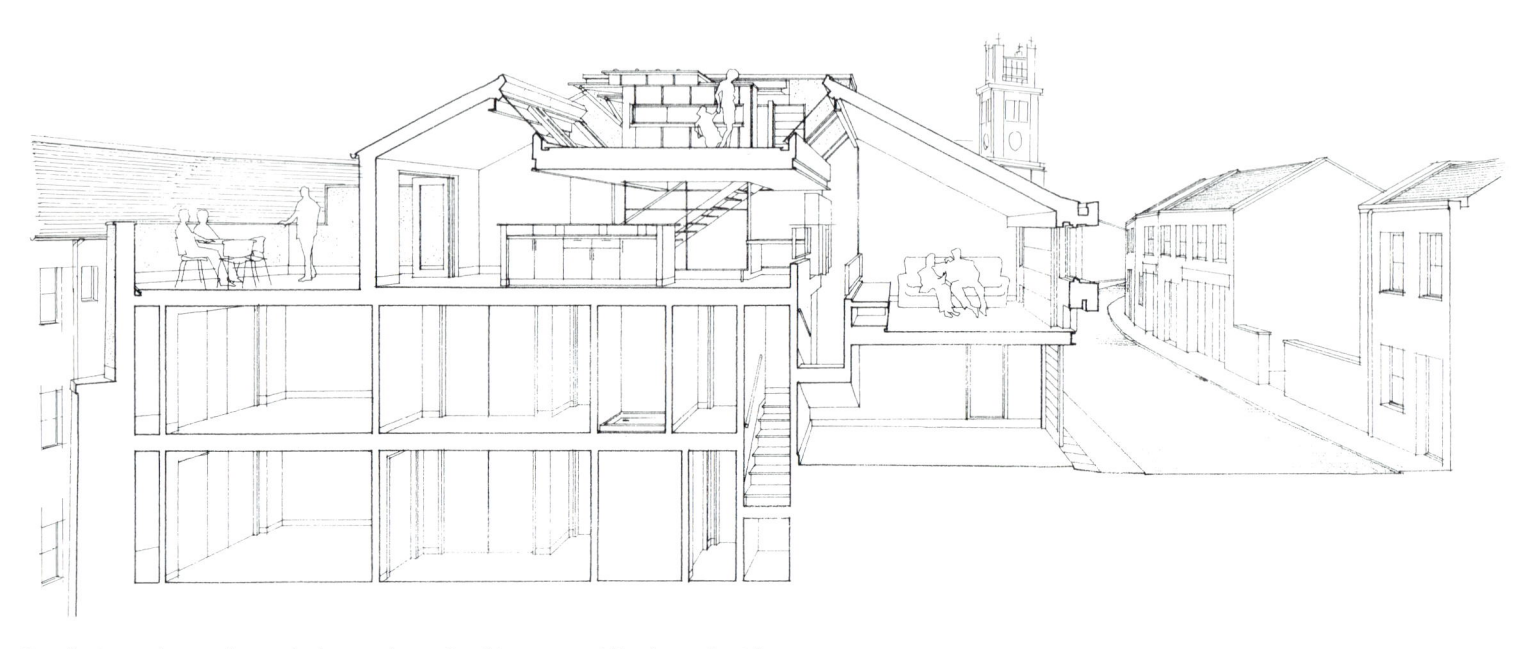

Our client owned a warehouse-shed occupying a site of two mews widths (approximately five metres each) but of an unusual depth of 15 meters and had, as we discovered during site investigations, the possibility that made-up ground at the rear of the site could be excavated to form a basement level.

The consequence of this unusual site configuration is that what appear as small houses to the lane mask substantial properties internally. The façade follows the idea first built at No 17 Royal Terrace Mews of expressing a major ground floor and minor upper floor in stone, juxtaposed externally with a revealed internal lining of lead, glass block and timber which reverses the relationship.

Internally the houses are 'upside down' with bedrooms on the ground and lower floors, lit by a lightwell to the north, leaving the upper floor as a continuous space of living kitchen and dining room in a stepped section flowing onto an external terrace to the rear.

Slate pitches to north and south are separated from a flat roof in the centre by two generous roof lights. A stair and rolling roof hatch gives access to the roof to make a second and spectacular roof terrace to each house; thus a narrow site develops unexpectedly into two four-storey, four-bedroomed houses with substantial and unexpected external areas.

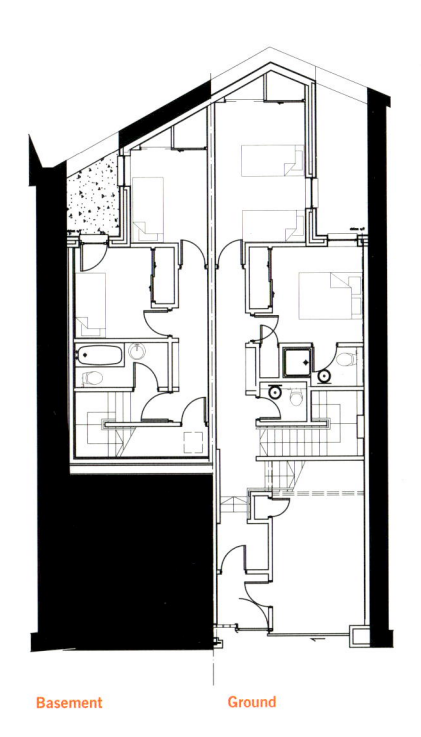

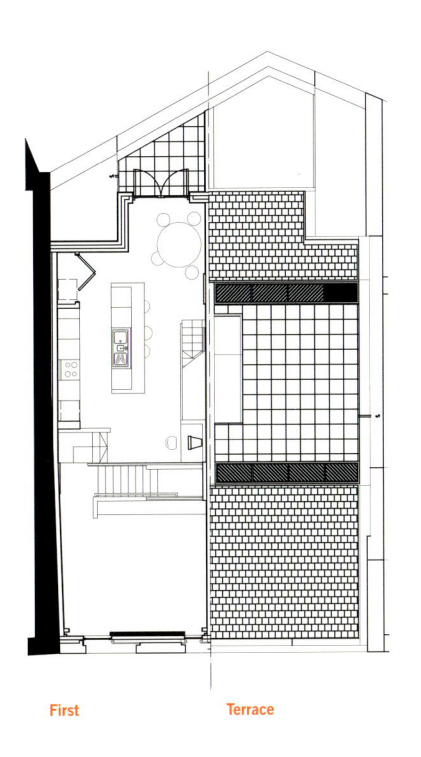

Basement   **Ground**   **First**   **Terrace**

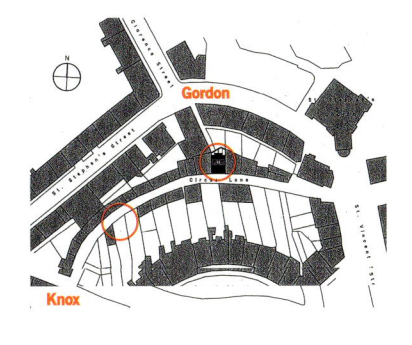

Gordon

Knox

Houses 65

McCormack House Broomhill, West Lothian

Completed 2001

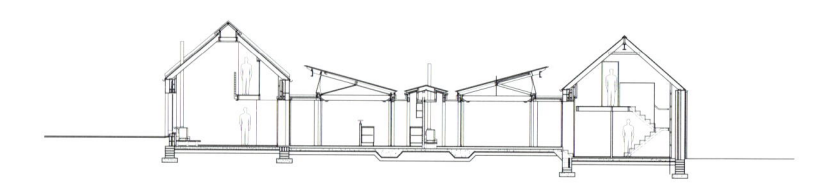

The derelict farmsteading at Broomhill, West Calder, dates from 1791 (we think) from a carved lintel found in the farmhouse. It is a typical Lothian steading building being single storey stone construction and having the original farmhouse in the centre, facing south, with two wings of farm buildings on either side forming an informal courtyard. The steading had been derelict for some time and, for safety reasons, had had all its roof timbers removed.

Our proposals describe a project for the partial inhabitation of the two wings of the steading, the partial demolition of the remains of the original farmhouse, and the construction of a new pavilion building linking the two former steading wings. The strategy of the design is to place within the remains of the steading the cellular rooms of a large family house; these being generally the bedrooms and service accommodation. In this way we can use the existing window openings (supplemented by ridge roof glazing) and avoid making major new openings in the stone walls. The kitchen/dining area and the living room were placed in a glazed pavilion between the two original wings.

To the west are children's and guest accommodation; to the east, parent's rooms and a gym. The winged roof of the pavilion springs from a top-lit spine wall housing kitchen and inglenook fireplace. Both the living room and kitchen are fully shuttered and can connect directly to exterior spaces, both north and south, by sliding/folding windows. The form of the new building bears a superficial resemblance to the profile of a microlight, a passion of both the client and his extended family, and now the architect.

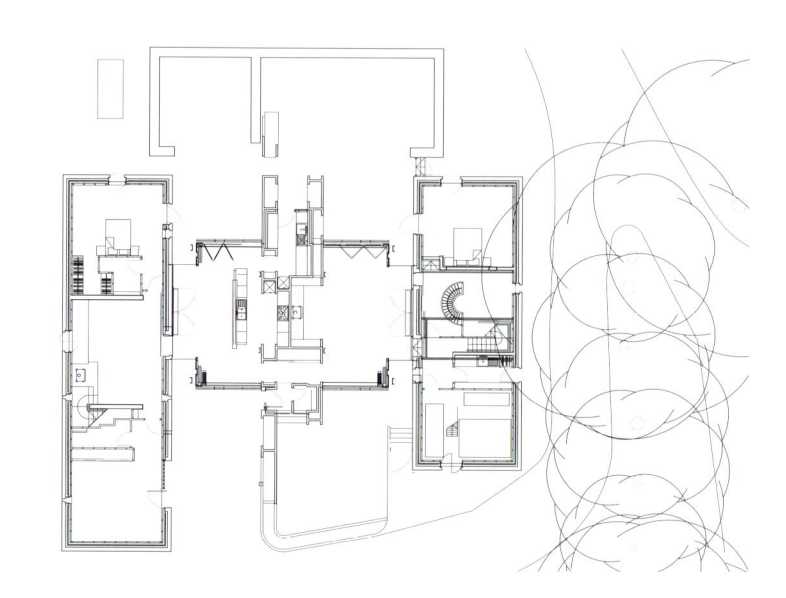

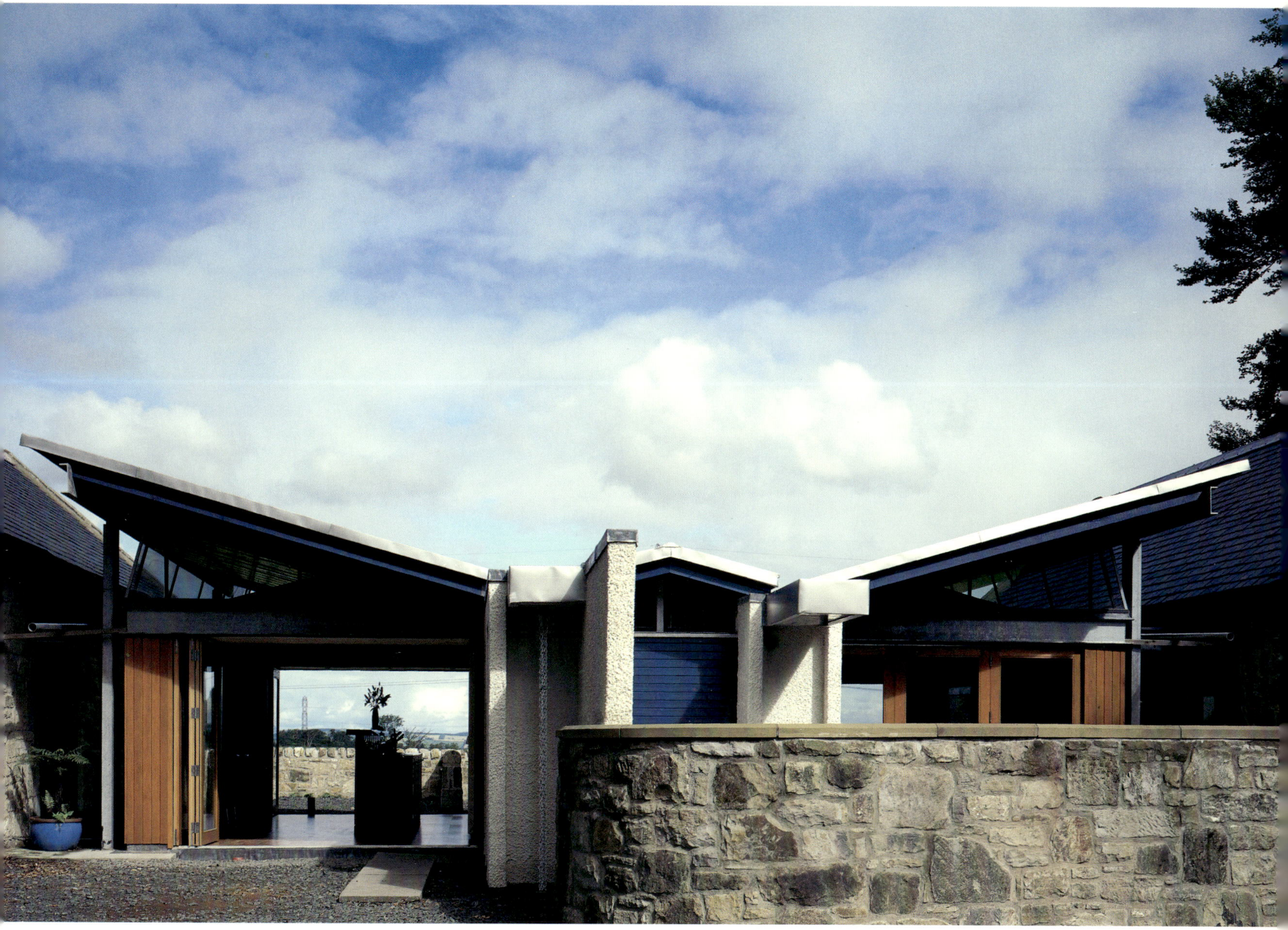

Murphy House Bakehouse Close, Edinburgh

As yet unrealised

As part of the Holyrood Brewery redevelopment the practice completed the renovation of a former warehouse in the (reopened) Bakehouse Close for Frank Spratt Developments as offices for himself and accommodation for the Royal Fine Art Commission for Scotland. The close itself is one of the oldest and most picturesque in the Canongate but peters out immediately opposite the development. An opportunity was spotted to build a house with a tiny footprint of 50 sq m against the crow-stepped gable of the Edinburgh Museum to the north and along a high boundary to Scottish and Newcastle's remaining brewery to the west.

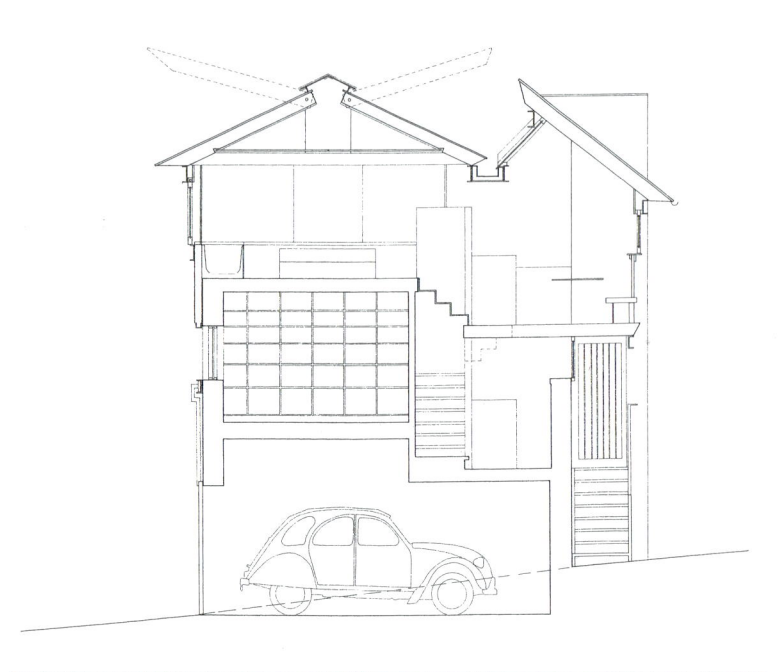

The house, consisting of two bedrooms, study, garage and living kitchen and diningroom, follows the medieval tradition of having a heavy masonry base with lightweight cantilevered externally expressed volumes above. The plan spirals through 'third' levels with the entrance being a reinterpretation of traditional external staircases to the north at an upper level. The plan places major spaces to the south with the living room occupying the most substantial volume and commanding a 'gunsight view' of Salisbury Crags with kitchen and diningroom on the north side, lit by a south roof light. The dining room occupies a cantilevered room above the entrance stair and the vertical journey culminates in the main bedroom also containing a cantilevered shower room and a secret bath concealed under a window seat.

Fenestration (all internally shuttered) opens the major rooms to the outside with windows placed on the outside of the walls so that they disappear when open, and with corner windows which similarly seem to dissolve when open. A ridge roof light is shuttered by two hinged ceiling panels, combining to form a flat soffit at night. Finally in the spirit of a highly kinetic design the aluminium roof hinges about the ridge powered by hydraulic rams to open living area and main bedroom to the brevity of the Scottish summer!

The construction of the house has been prevented so far by the adjacent brewery who refused to waive a legal right of refusal on a three metre boundary strip they do not own but over which they can veto others building.

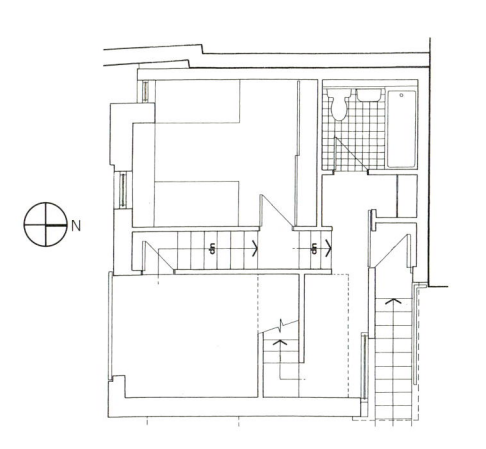

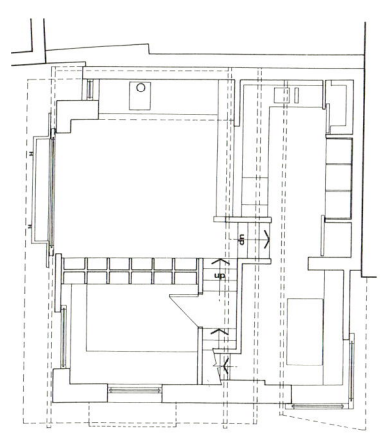

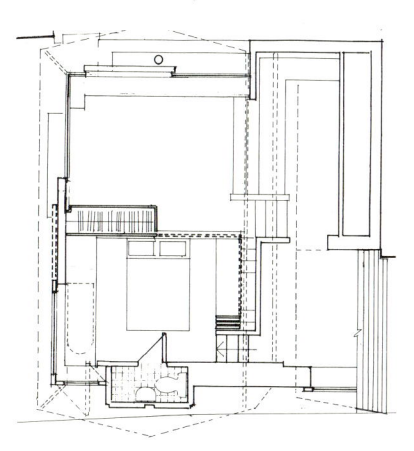

Harrison House Moray Place, Edinburgh

Completed 2000

The grand houses in this most prestigious of Edinburgh circuses have mostly been subdivided into apartments. Our clients bought part of an already subdivided basement with most of the flat housed within a single storey, flat roofed extension to the rear of the tenement connected to the street via a long umbilical corridor under the tenement itself. The bulk of the flat consisted of the former billiard room, and a variety of ramshackle kitchen facilities from the time of the grand house. The kitchen rooms were very poorly lit and the roof leaked, so we persuaded our clients to completely rebuild this section of their flat, converting the former billiard room into a master bedroom.

The site is spectacular in the sense that it has both its own private garden and a stunning view to the west, across the Water of Leith and Lord Moray's pleasure gardens, a private garden for local residents.

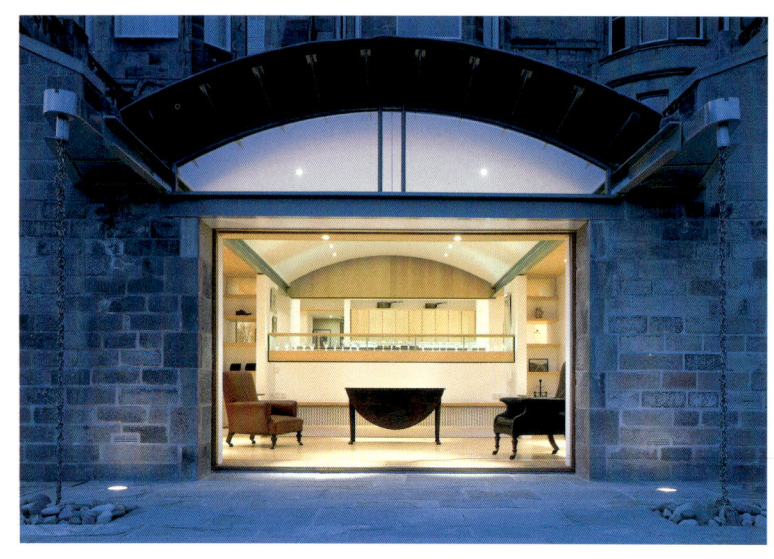

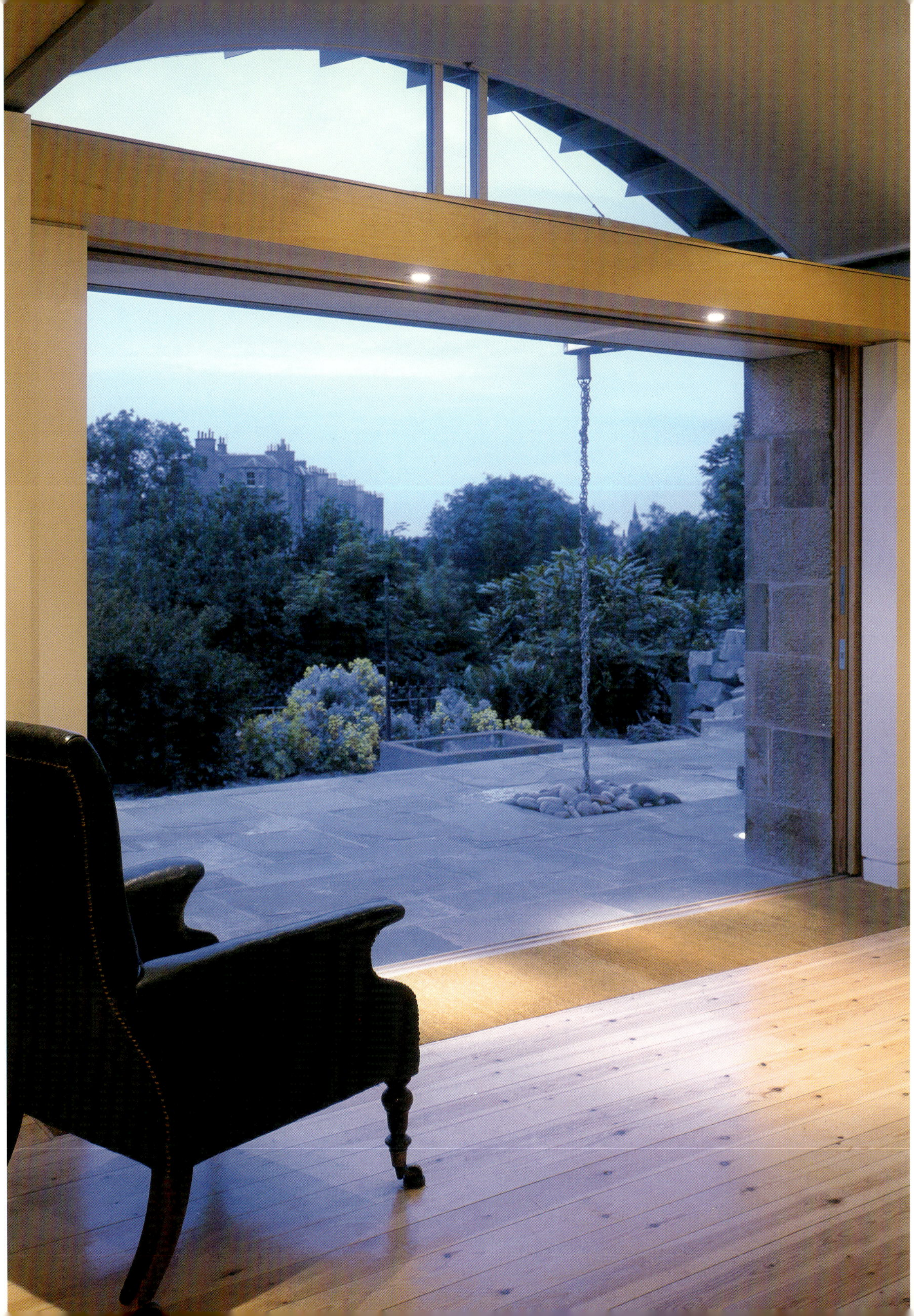

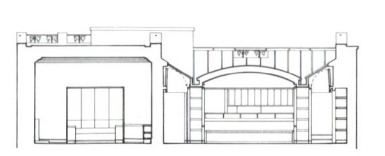

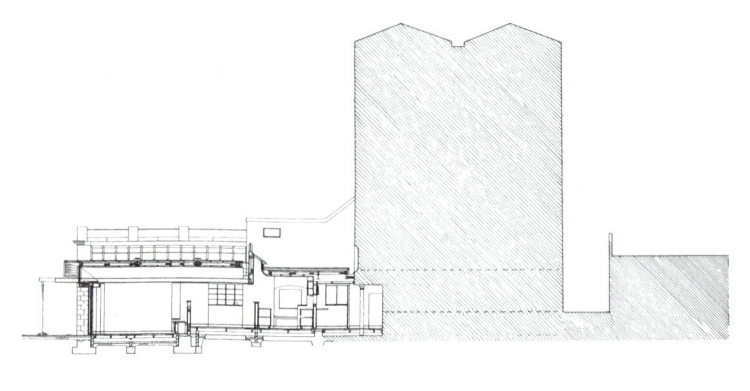

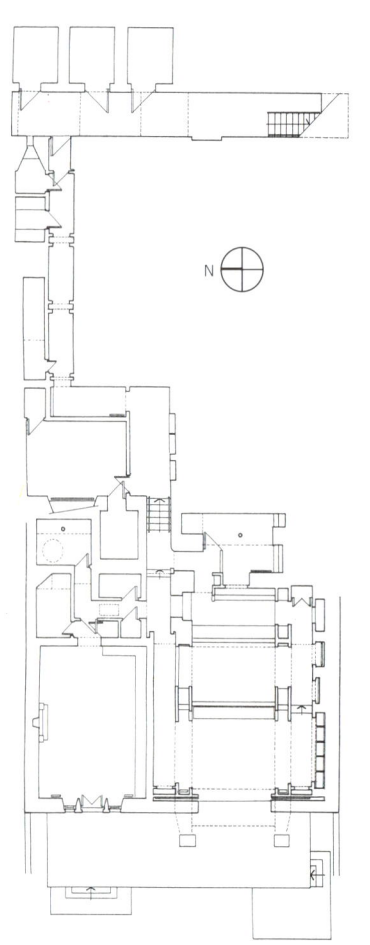

Our proposal placed a barrel-vaulted space focusing on this view, with light admitted on either side of the barrel-vault via long roof lights which also define the circulation within the main space. The vault covers interconnecting spaces of living room and, at a slightly higher level, dining area and kitchen, with a study in the innards of the flat underneath the original tenement. All these spaces look out through a window to the garden and a spectacular vista beyond. The window consists of sliding doors which disappear within the wall thickness, so that whole space can open out into the garden in the summertime. Both the doors and the roof lights have shutters which close the entire space off at night or in the winter. The effect of light is reminiscent of, and inspired by, the Sir John Soane Museum in London.

Houses 73

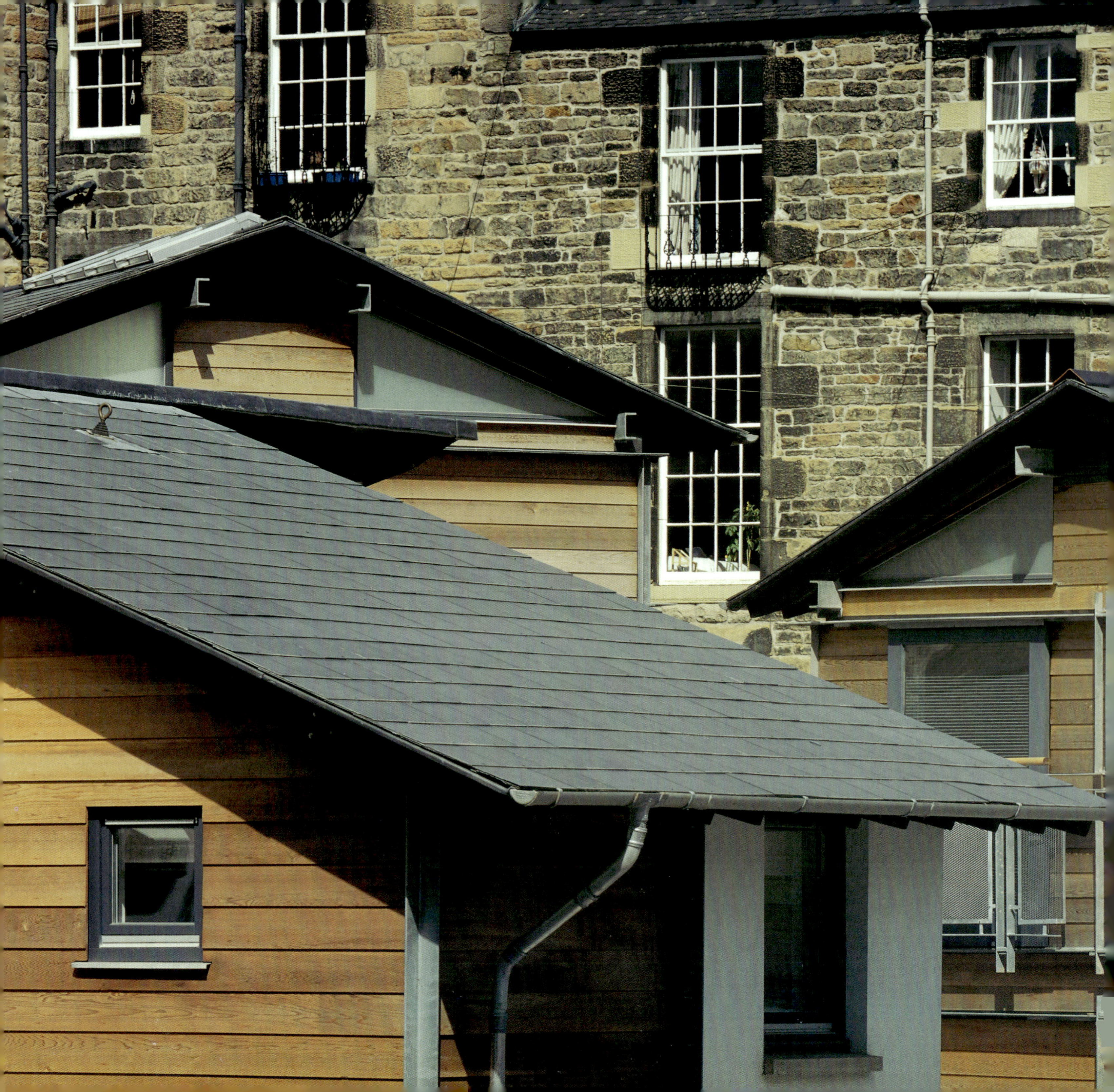

Six Housing Projects

The story of post-war British housing has not been glorious. In the private sector we have seen the abandonment of the promise of the Garden City idea, and instead there has been an uncontrolled proliferation of suburban nowhere-land and a descent into stylisic kitsch. In the public sector there have been all-too-well publicised sociological and constructional disasters resulting from over-inventive architectural form. Both tendencies have been anti-urban in spirit and have drained the city of its inhabitants. The architect today, approaching the subject of housing, understandably does so with some caution and humility.

Luckily there is a resurgence of enthusiasm for living in the city. All the projects illustrated approach their context in a relatively conservative way – they may be modern to look at and to live in but their form is generated from a reworking of the pattern of building already found in the surrounding area. Where space allows – at Dublin Street and Graham Square – an effort has been made to deliberately foster a sense of community by the device of celebrating residents' comings and goings through the reinvention of the external staircase.

The one non-urban project, at Cramond, is perhaps the most potent. It is rare to get the chance to impact on suburban design, and here we are proposing the abolition of the front garden, the clustering of houses around shared courtyards, and the fashioning of public space into walled lanes or, as in the case of the apartments, shared walled gardens. If successful the implications of this project could be far-reaching.

Housing 75

Dublin Colonies Edinburgh

Completed 1999, for Buredi Ltd

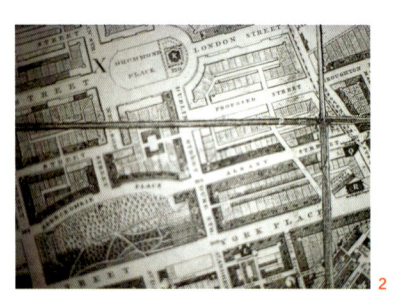

1 1747
2 1817
3 1851
4 Print of a house in Broughton Village
5 Ramsay Garden external stair, Edinburgh Old Town

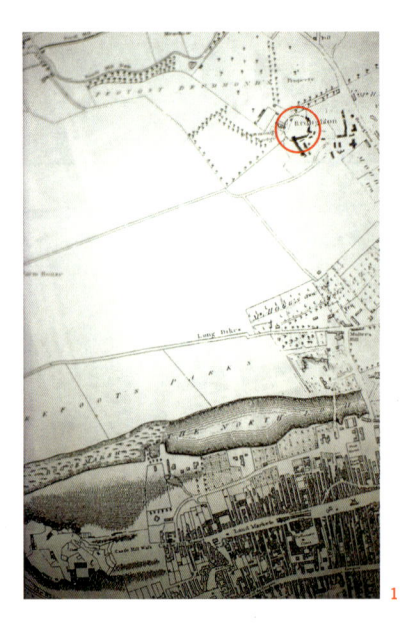

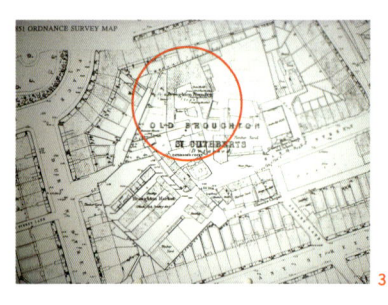

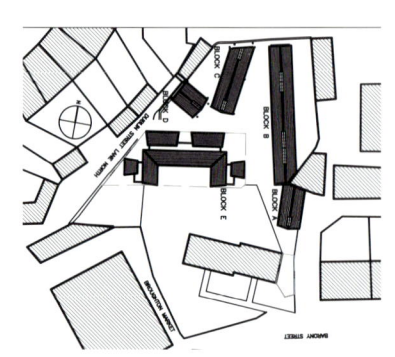

This project won a limited competition in 1994 but was not constructed until 1999. The starting point for the design of this housing project was the realisation that the site is one of the very few examples of a land-use pattern in the Georgian New Town that predates the New Town's construction. The buildings that existed on the site were of indeterminate age, but their footprints could be traced back to the partially destroyed Broughton Village, which, as can be seen from the succession of maps, originally sat in countryside. It had been scheduled for total elimination, but eventually found itself encircled by New Town tenements. There is therefore an almost archaeological significance to the site and although it was impossible to save or reuse the existing buildings, we elected to preserve broadly their footprints and also, to a degree, the spirit of an organically planned village. In this sense we designed the antithesis of the formal and hierarchical New Town pattern.

76 Housing

Our project consists of a walled precinct of houses arranged in two three storey 'ranges' corresponding to previous buildings. The vehicle and pedestrian entries of the precinct are both marked by three storey gate houses. Most of the project is for one and two bedroom flats except for six family houses on the south side.

In the spirit of reinterpreting the medieval, all apartments are reached by external staircases. The living rooms of the top floor flats are placed under the section of the roof with ridge light glazing. All the elevations are freely composed and include timber panels (a memory of the former timber yard nearby) and the spaces between the buildings develop in an informal manner.

78 Housing

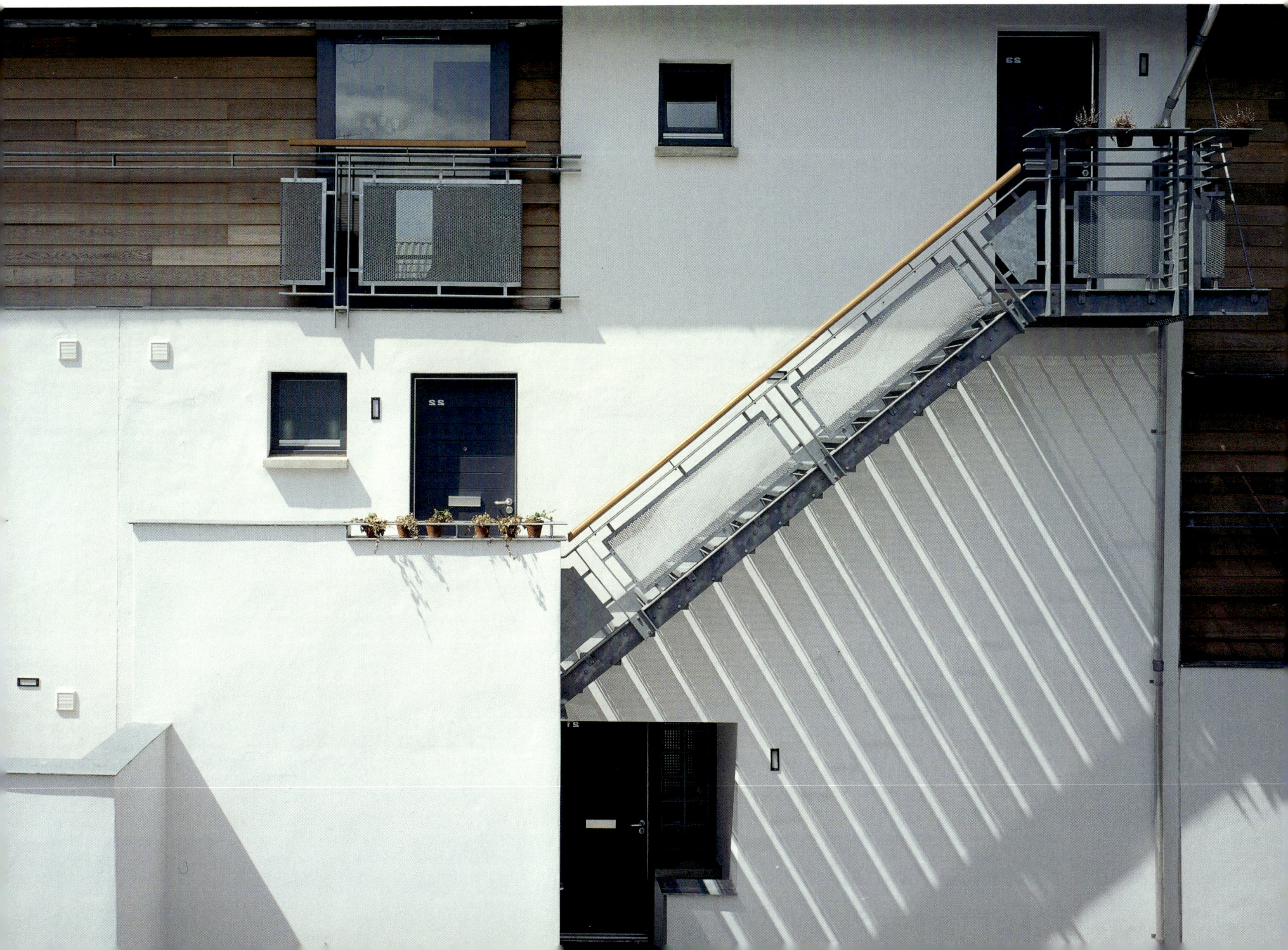

112 Canongate Edinburgh

Completed 1999, for Old Town Housing Association

1   Historic map of the Canongate
2   Original proposal
3   Late Medieval houses, Old Town
4   Brewery arch later demolished to form the site

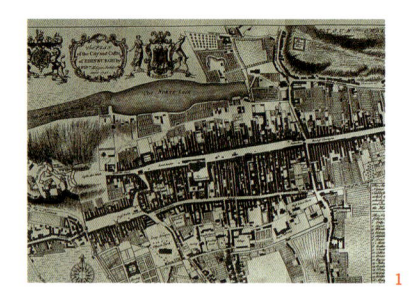

This project was part of the original competition for the masterplan of the former brewery at the foot of the Royal Mile. The original project of nine one-bedroomed flats and a shop envisaged a communal roof garden and greenhouse, but when fire regulations forced the abandonement of this feature the design switched to emphasising an agglomeration of monopitched roofs.

The building sits on the site of the former archway to the Holyrood Brewery on the south side of the Canongate. The design makes reference to buildings of the Old Town which have to a large extent disappeared and been replaced with Georgian and Victorian successors: in particular, colonnades at ground floor level, external staircases, windows frequently arranged as horizontal galleries, and an ad hoc quality to their general appearance. Their upper stories, often cantilevered, were frequently of timber with a roof top profile of 'roofed rooms' (like small independent buildings on the roof line). We have made reference to each of these characteristics in the design, but in a contemporary way.

80 Housing

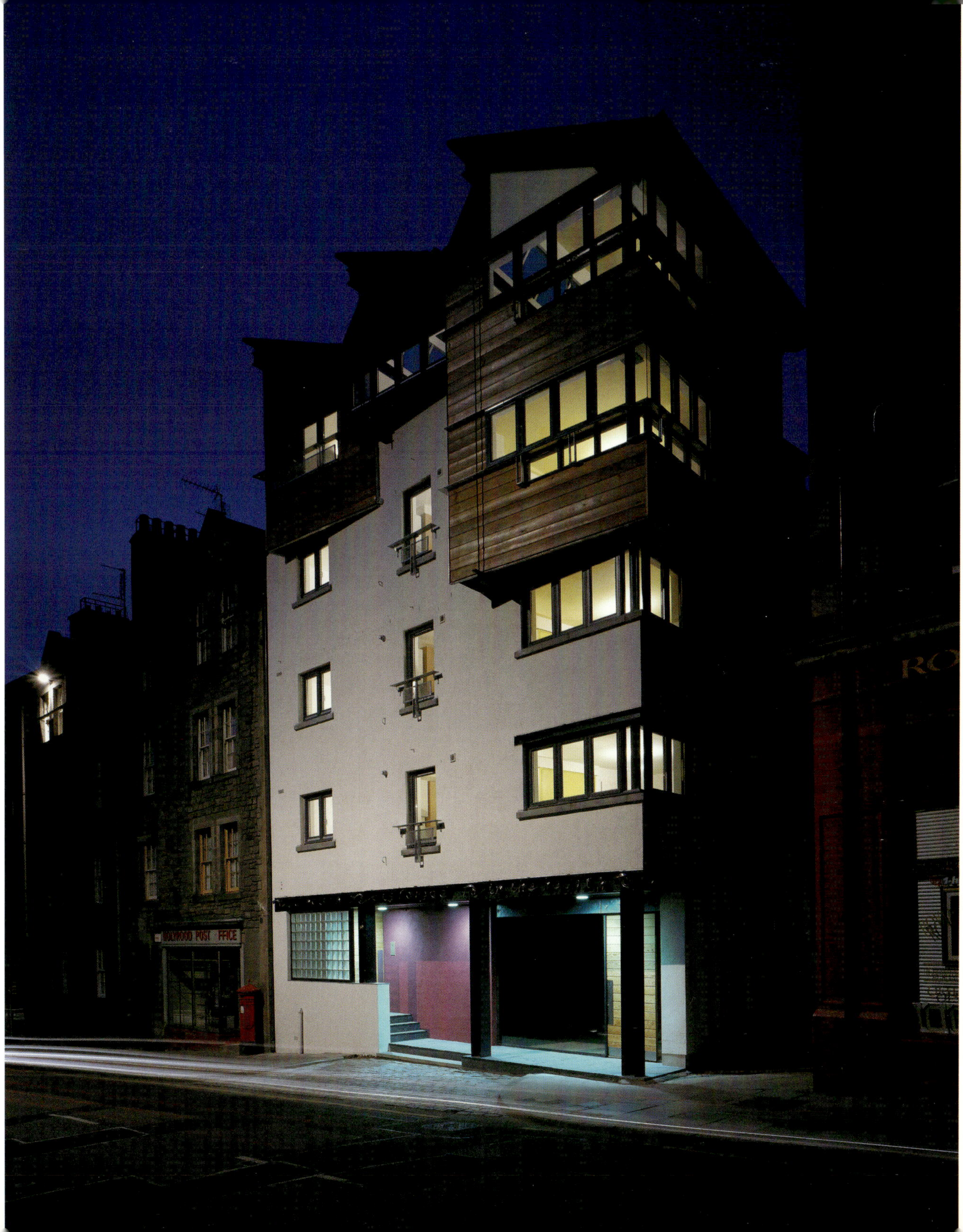

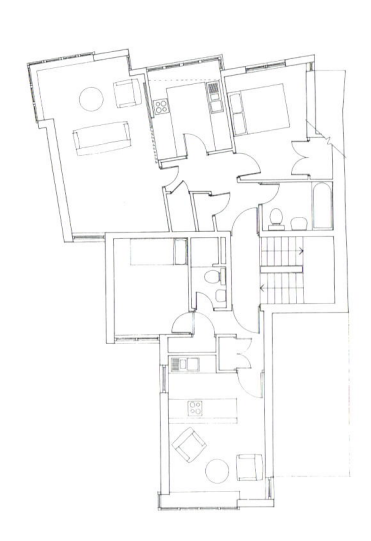

The constraints on the site are the view from the Canongate to the new Scottish Poetry Library, and the need to preserve privacy between the new flats and existing flats to the western side. The opportunities are the stunning views of Salisbury Crags to the south and a chance to make a contemporary addition to the heterogeneous development of the Royal Mile.

The geometry of the plot forms an acute angle between front and side elevations allowing the orthogonal cantilevers to progressively jut onto the street. The top flat with views in all directions and generous roof glazing is particularly spectacular.

50 Graham Square Glasgow

Completed 2000, for Molendinar Housing Association

Near the Gallowgate in eastern Glasgow are the remains of the former Meat Market. Our site consists of the former Market Hotel, where traders lodged, attached to a surviving and impressive market archway. The building was totally derelict but B listed, with the centre section in danger of collapse. We were asked to provide flats and elected to replace the original central block with a new three storey structure set back from the original building line. The two wings to the north and south of the central block were reconstructed to retain their frontages to Graham Square. This arrangement creates a private courtyard with the entrance from Graham Square through the old hotel entrance now remodelled as a gate in the partially demolished front wall of the old central block.

From the courtyard access to the flats is gained either directly – via a pair of external stairs beneath a glazed canopy – or through a new common stair in the larger south wing. The wing itself makes use of split-level dual aspect plans to take full advantage of the building volume, whilst maintaining the important Graham Square frontage.

With the glazed canopy uplit at night the effect is probably more hotel-like than the original. And whilst the architecture might be relatively quiet, the social experiment of replacing the usual tenement 'common stair' with external stairs within a common courtyard has been a great success, with tenants already populating the courtyard with plants and seats. Car parking to the rear (where a traditional back drying green would have been) connects through to the courtyard at the front so that the ambivalence regarding front and back, where greens are similarly converted, is avoided.

The scheme provides a total of 17 one and two bedroom flats.

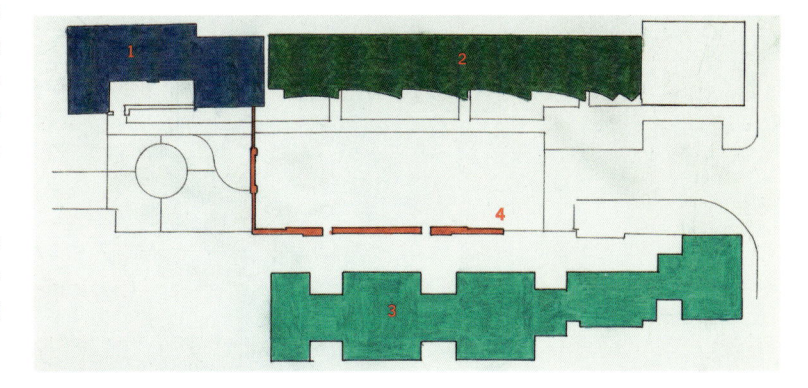

1 Market Hotel conversion
2 New Housing (Page & Park)
3 New Housing (McKeown Alexander)
4 Former Meat Market façade

84 Housing

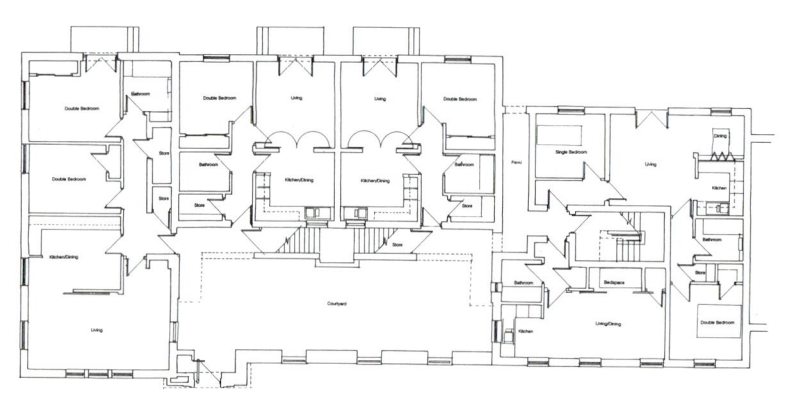

Rob Joiner, Director, Molendinar Housing Association, writes . . .

"In his book *The Architecture of Affordable Housing* Professor Sam Davis affirms: "Housing is not merely shelter, or basic protection from the elements. It must also bestow on its inhabitants a sense of dignity." Much of the affordable (or 'social') housing built in Britain in the last half century has ignored this basic truth.

Molendinar Park Housing Association has consciously pursued a policy, since its inception in 1993, of giving dignity, or a sense of specialness, to its developments. We have sought to achieve this primarily through architectural quality but also, on occasions, by involving artists in the design of elements of a project. We do this for very practical economic reasons. The amount we can spend on each project is limited, and good design not only gives us better buildings for the same money but also makes the houses easier to let and less likely to suffer from a high turnover of tenants. But we also believe that giving people beautiful environments in which to live enriches their lives, and that too is part of our job.

We commissioned Richard Murphy for the Market Hotel project primarily because of his work on house extensions in Edinburgh, and because of his interest in the work of Carlo Scarpa. The Market Hotel, or 50 Graham Square as it is now known, was a B listed building in an appalling state of repair. It required an architect who could maximise the potential of the original building but insert an element of modernity. It was the most difficult of the three projects which made up the Graham Square development – and became more difficult when the demolition of the centre portion resulted in the entire building becoming dangerous and having to be demolished. It is to Richard's credit that having drawn this short straw he was able to produce such a remarkable building. The rather staid Georgian hotel which once provided cheap food and accommodation to drovers bringing cattle to market now has, as a number of residents have commented, the air of a small Mediterranean house. By creating a private courtyard and accessing the upper flats via external staircases a true sense of place and of community has been created.

Raymond Unwin wrote: "The architect . . . should infuse the spirit of the artist into his work because the artist is not content with the least that will do; his desire is for the best, the utmost he can achieve. It is the small margin which makes all the difference between a thing scamped and a thing well done . . . from this margin of welldoing beauty must spring."

Richard Murphy consistently infuses the spirit of the artist into his work. Although no artists, other than the architect, were engaged in the design of 50 Graham Square, three artists have chosen to live in the development, which is itself a tribute to the margin of welldoing which has been achieved."

Old Fishmarket Close Edinburgh

Completion 2002, for Buredi Ltd

This private housing project was won in an invited competition and takes as its starting point and inspiration the famous 1647 aerial map of the Old Town of Edinburgh by James Gordon of Rothiemay. The regular sub division of building fingers of about five metres has been reproduced to create two tall thin parallel buildings on a steeply sloping site in the Old Town tradition. Emphasis has been placed on the roofscape which can be viewed either at eye level from the Royal Mile or at high level from the Cowgate. The traditional 'roofed rooms' which have largely disappeared from the Old Town are echoed here – where the exaggerated roofs house spectacular maisonette flats with double height living spaces. Areas of timber boarding are used at these upper levels echoing the vernacular timber top storeys of the Old Town and lending the buildings scale. The upper gables are largely glazed with a mixture of windows and glass block to give a lantern-like appearance at night.

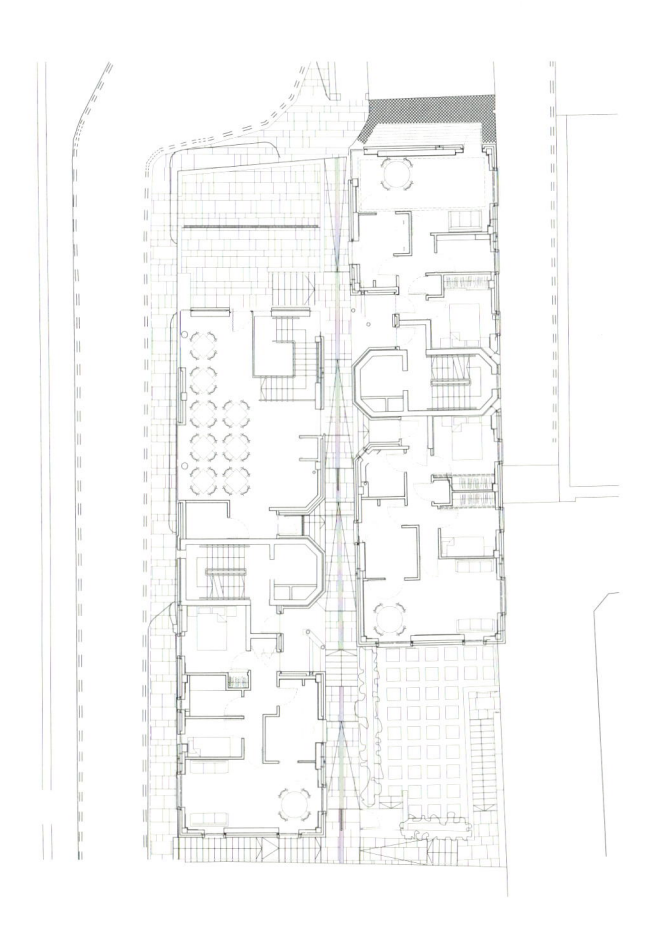

The two new buildings are separated by a short and vertiginous close, which forms an extension of the upper part of Old Fishmarket Close. Both blocks respond to the height of the adjacent Police and Advocates buildings, with the east block book-ending the lower tenement to its north.

At ground level two external spaces are created by the configuration of blocks: public on the north west and private on the south east. The staggering of the two blocks helps to address issues of day lighting and privacy in both the new flats and the existing flats in the north west corner of Tron Square. The public space is a level terrace set against the fall of Old Fishmarket Close, serving a café; a private garden occupies the other.

In the fall of the site offices are also slipped under the housing, but a proposal to serve half of the apartment kitchens with communal dumb waiters from the café kitchen was sadly abandoned by the developer.

Belford Road Edinburgh

Completion 2002, for Buredi Ltd

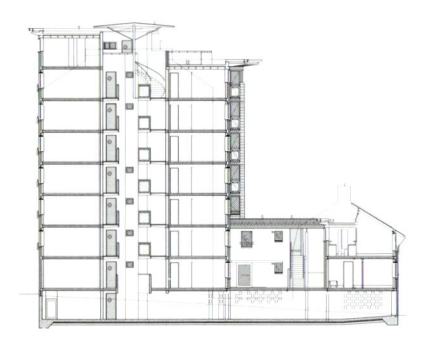

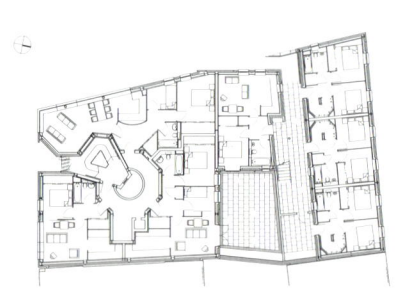

This project for twenty flats and five 'mews houses' is sited at one of Edinburgh's most dramatic topographical moments where a great cliff of tenements hangs over the valley of the Water of Leith. The design continues the pattern of the adjacent building, a tenement to the street and mews to the rear, but celebrates the corner with a stack of sliding corner living room windows topped by a penthouse maisonette. A quirk of the fire regulations has led to unusual internal access arrangements of a circular court open to the sky ringed with steel galleries at every floor.

Housing 89

Cramond Edinburgh

Phased completion 2002/3, for AMA (New Town) Ltd

The development is a joint venture between Bryant Homes and AMA (New Town) Ltd on the site of the former Dunfermline College of Education on the outskirts of Edinburgh. We are responsible for the AMA section of the development.

The site is bounded by existing housing, woodland and a designated archeological site, by the historic tree-lined avenue to Cramond House, and by playing fields. The development consists of both urban and suburban elements: the urban elements are a central crescent reaching to 3.5 storeys and two flatted developments also of 3.5 storeys; the suburban elements are two storey detached houses. In general the strategy for the development of the site is to place the larger urban elements in the centre at a distance from the sensitive boundaries to east and west.

The entrance of the site is marked by an octagonal courtyard of two storey terraced houses. This leads via a walled main road to the central crescent, which is developed by Bryant Homes to the east and AMA in two sections to the west. This crescent is in a tradition of those found in many locations in the Edinburgh New Town, in particular at the west end of the New Town complete with a 'mews lane' to the rear servicing garages for each house.

90 Housing

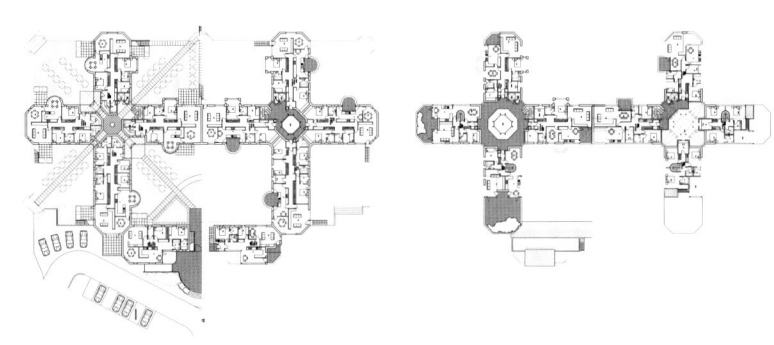

The AMA crescent of town houses has a split section, with each house marked by a one and a half storey window to the living room facing the front and topped by a master bedroom under a monopitch roof. The pattern of monopitch roofs forms a distinctive skyline and each house combines with its neighbour to give the impression of a single building under a split pediment linked to the next house and so on. To the rear, gardens extend out over the garages, which are accessed from sunken lanes. The crescent organises the flow of traffic on the site, and is terminated by the flatted developments for AMA and Bryant. The AMA development consists of two adjacent cruciform blocks of flats around two central internal hallways. These hallways are a stepped terrace design and are accessed by lift and fire escape staircase, which continue below ground floor level to an underground car park which is constructed along the northern perimeter of the site utilising the natural fall in the ground level.

The strategy of the double cruciform, together with perimeter walling, gives the flats a pattern of walled gardens, with four smaller square gardens in each corner and two large gardens in the centre to front and back. The small gardens have gazebos at their corners, whilst the western garden continues out into the landscape over the archeologically reserved area. At the front of the development the eastern walled garden is completed by the construction of two 'gatehouses', each consisting of a ground floor and first floor flat, with their roof continuing across the main entrance.

All flats are organised with external terraces and all the first floor flats also connect via external staircases to their adjacent walled gardens. The roof is a double monopitch arrangement with a central flat roof section and inclined roof glazing giving top light into all the major rooms of the top floor flats. In addition to the 28 flats in the development there are also four maisonettes at second floor level on the east, west and southern arms of the cruciforms. The footprints of the maisonettes do not extend to the extremity of the cruciform arms and thereby offer the possibility of extensive roof-top gardens for these units. This has the effect of both greening the entire development and also reducing its visual impact and massing in the vicinity of the adjacent suburban housing.

The suburban housing on the site is divided into four sections: the north-west and north-east quadrants are developed by AMA, and the south-west and south-east are developed by Bryant Homes. The AMA sections consist of variations of five house types.

The strategy for the AMA suburban housing development is to reverse the pattern of the normal British housing estate, which consists of individual houses surrounded by front, back and side gardens; (in other words object buildings surrounded by space) which are then arranged around suburban roads. At Cramond we have taken our lead from traditional developments such as The Grange or Murrayfield, where roads are bounded by continuous garden walls, and frequently there is an ambiguity between garden wall and building. Peter Aldington's classic three courtyard houses at Haddenham[1] are also a constant inspiration in this respect. At Cramond we have abolished the front garden for each house type, preferring to put all the available space into a private walled garden to the rear. In addition, all the roads are lined with garden walls, each of which engage directly with the walls of the individual houses creating ambiguity between wall and house. Houses are then combined in various formats to form recognisable thresholds and places. For example the smaller houses are paired to form 'gatehouses' to larger house types. L-shaped houses are combined to form private courtyards approached through a relatively narrow threshold. In this way we hope that the experience of suburban housing will be transformed with the creation of distinctive spaces and their thresholds.

The five houses each have common features and materials. These are: low eaves giving an impression of a 1.5 storey house; identical staircase towers which also mark the entrance; and in the case of larger house types, an entrance courtyard of gravel or setts for parking.

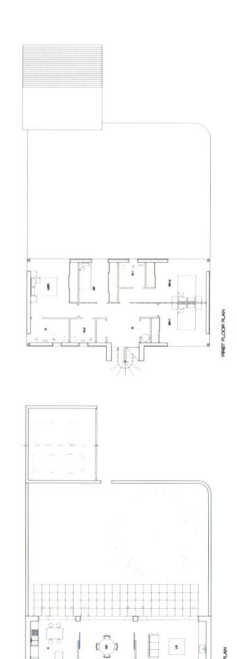

Housing 93

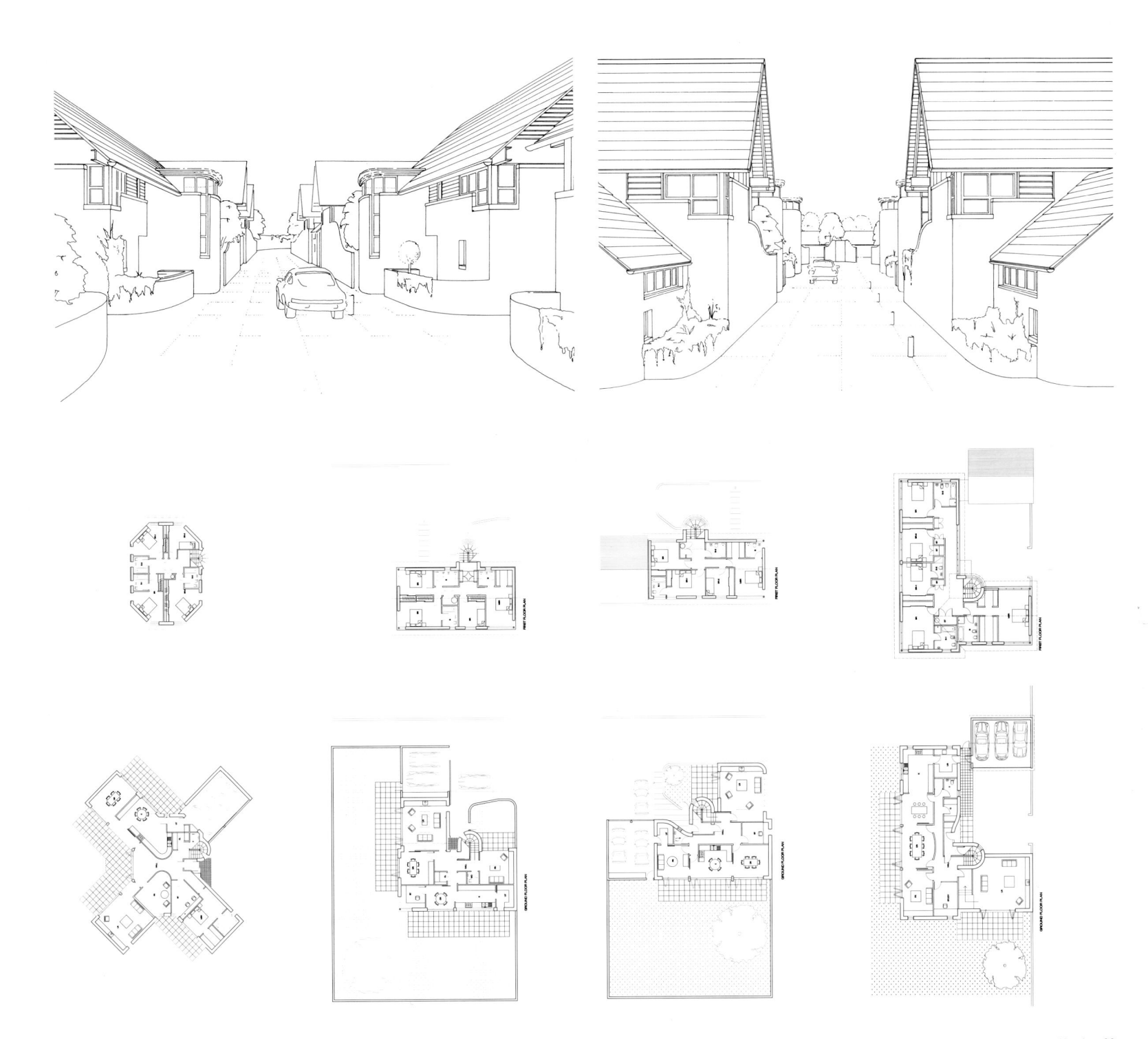

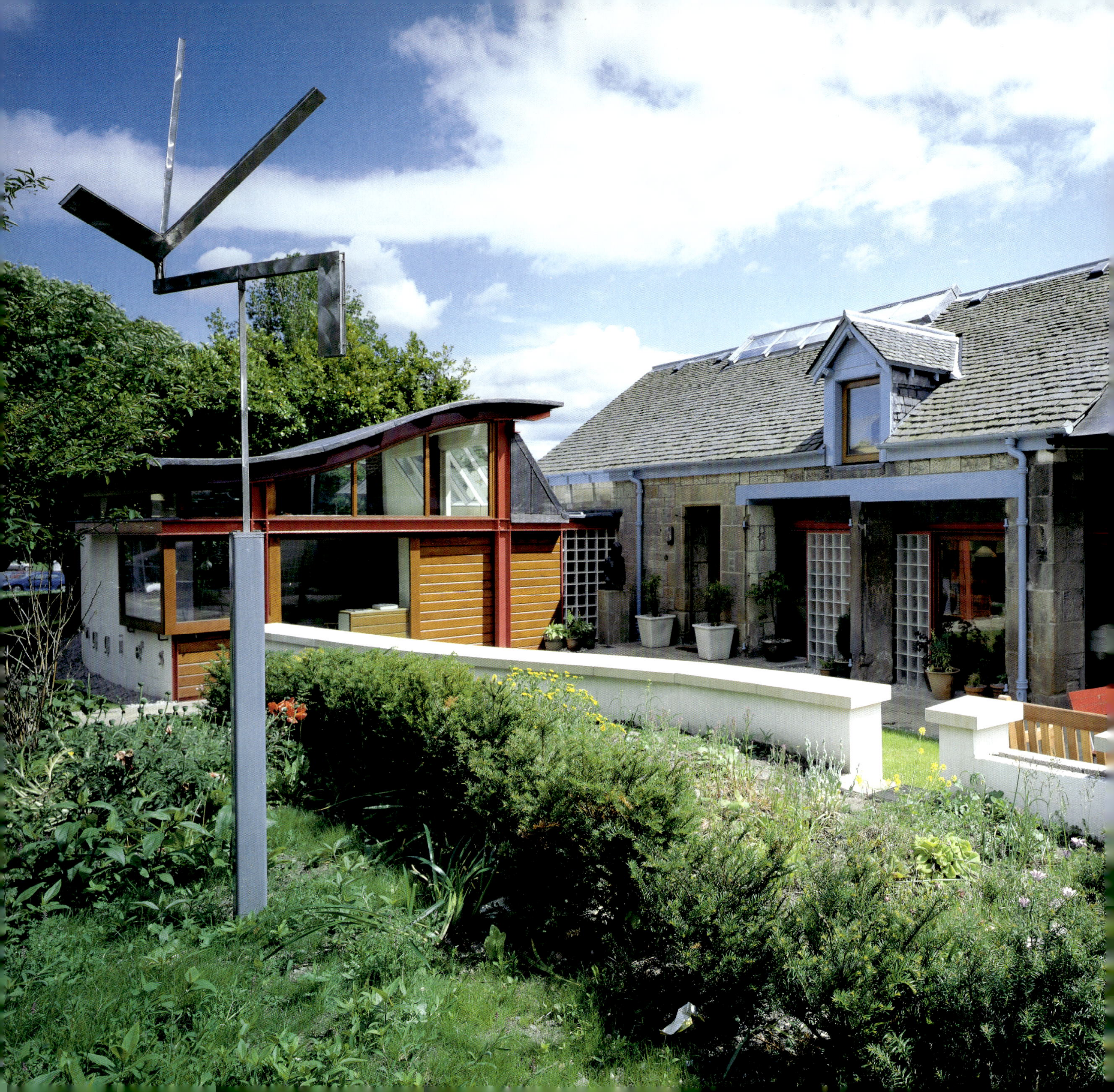

Nine Social Buildings

The common thread uniting this otherwise disparate group of projects is the idea of the potential sociability of strangers and the psychology of the individual in the group. This is a rich mine from which to generate architectural form. In the educational field it has led at Harmeny to the celebration of the individual classrooms and the careful containment of these disturbed children without resort to the architecture of incarceration; at St Andrew's and at Jesus College it is about the deliberate fostering of social groupings amongst postgraduates and undergraduates respectively; and at Napier the genesis of the plan section and roof has been motivated by the objective of breaking down 500 computer users into socially recognisable groupings and providing a number of places to study in what is otherwise a huge single room.

The psychology of the recently diagnosed cancer sufferer guided our work in both phases of work at Maggie's Centre: uppermost in our thoughts were crossing the threshold, having somewhere to sit on your own on the edge of a space; having familiar domestic signs and symbols, and an absence of any institutional characteristics. Happily the many letters and comments received have demonstrated that the Centre has been adopted by its many users irrespective of their background.

The world of work has yet to give us an opportunity but the little competition project at Edinburgh Park was all about making an enjoyable and unusual place to work and, in the context of an out-of-town business park, to address the very real issue of where to go at lunchtime: a hot tub on the roof!

Maggie's Centre Edinburgh

Phase 1 completed 1996, Phase 2 completed 2001

Maggie's Centre at the Western General Hospital is the inspiration of the late Maggie Keswick Jencks whose vision was for a place cancer sufferers could go to get help and solace, as well as access to independent and alternative sources of advice and treatment. Activities range from single and group counselling, beauty therapy, yoga and relaxation, but above all the Centre is a meeting place where experiences can be shared.

The brief was, to a degree, indeterminate, and developed through close liaison with the client. The design aimed to create an atmosphere of domesticity (in contrast to the institutional nature of many National Health Service buildings) and to provide as much flexible accommodation as possible within the limited volume available. The Centre is capable of being combined into a series of progressively larger spaces, or divided into individual rooms.

The building consists of the original conversion of a disused stable building completed in 1996 with later extensions completed in 2001.

Externally the construction is viewed as a building within a building with a new inner language of steel, lead, glass, glass-blocks and timber sliding behind stone. When the extension was commissioned this existing language was continued in both directions.

Social Buildings 97

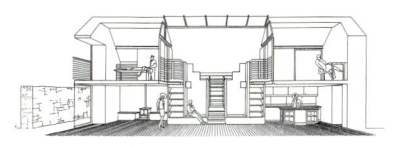

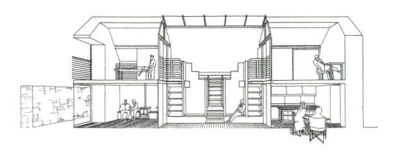

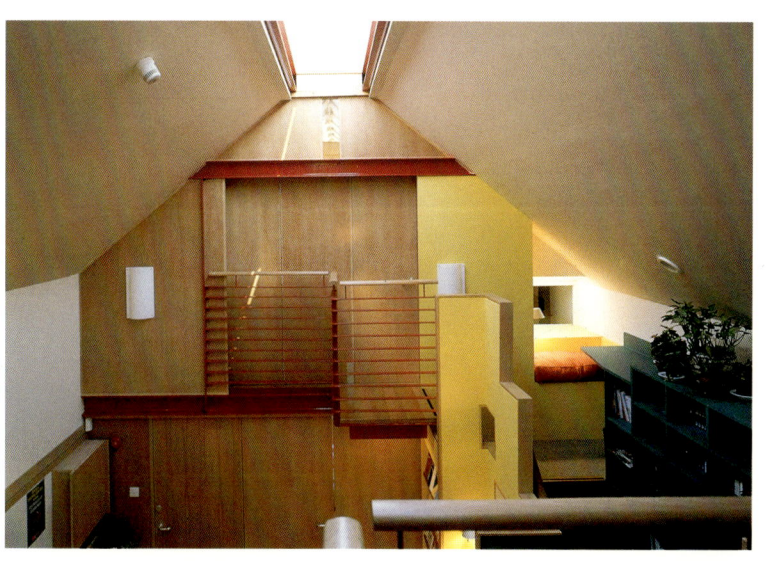

Maggie's Centre, Phase II

Since it opened in November 1997 Maggie's Centre has attracted a large number of visitors and friends and its range of activities has widened considerably. The need has become apparent for a series of meeting rooms for larger groups, or for more strenuous activities.

The additional accommodation required two large meeting rooms, a consulting room for visiting therapists, and a permanent office. While the new extension doubles the floor area of the Centre, it is designed to retain the domestic scale. All the new activities of the new are visible from the original centre space, which still functions as the front door to the Centre.

The extension is in two directions to the west and to the north-east. The western extension is two storey with administration on the top floor and an additional consulting room on the lower floor.

The extension to the north-east is conceived of as an independent but linked building to the original. This is a single volume which can be divided unequally and extends with a rendered retaining wall along its northern boundary to form a terrace on the eastern side and a boundary to the garden on the western side. Again the materials are the same as the other extension with a lead roof, steel framing and Douglas Fir framed windows. The monopitch roof is designed to admit south light into north facing rooms whilst its sinusoidal form deliberately avoids any conversation with the roof pitch of the existing building.

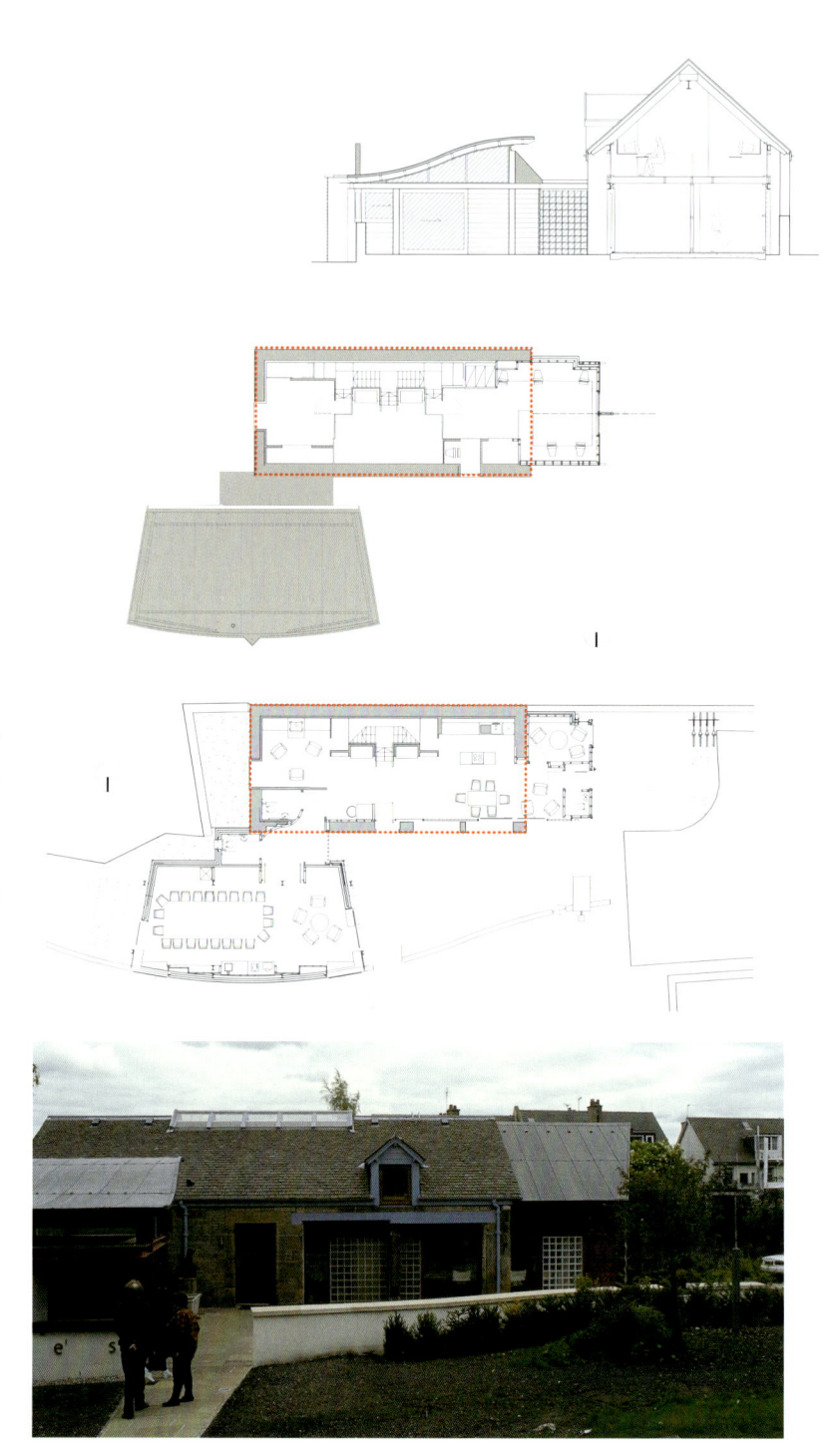

98 Social Buildings

Social Buildings 99

Harmeny School Balerno

Completed 2000

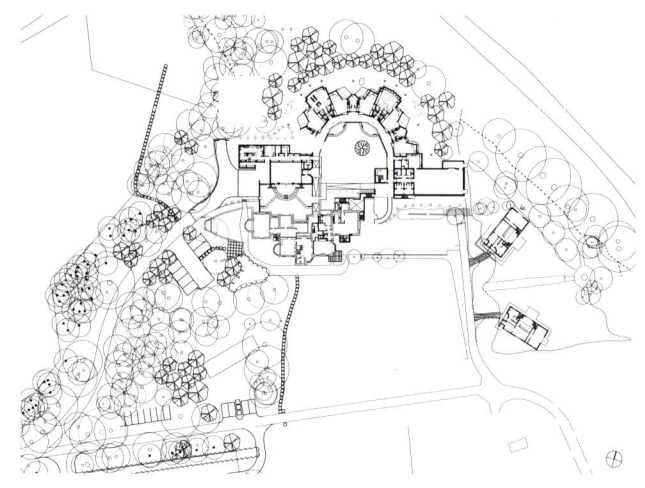

Harmeny School is a residential school for 8-12 year old children with severe emotional and behavioural difficulties. Harmeny Education Trust is an independent charity, and is based in a listed country house built at the turn of the 20th century set in extensive grounds on the outskirts of Balerno near Edinburgh. The house was extensively remodelled by Lorimer in 1910, who added a pitched roof storey, a wing and a tower and reversed the entrance from south to north.

Our involvement with the school resulted in a radical reassessment of the school's brief, emerging as a long term programme of construction to provide two new houses in the grounds for children, a crescent-shaped development of classrooms and specialist teaching rooms, including sports hall and music room, substantial alterations to the existing listed country house, together with the preparation of longer term development and woodland strategies for the whole site.

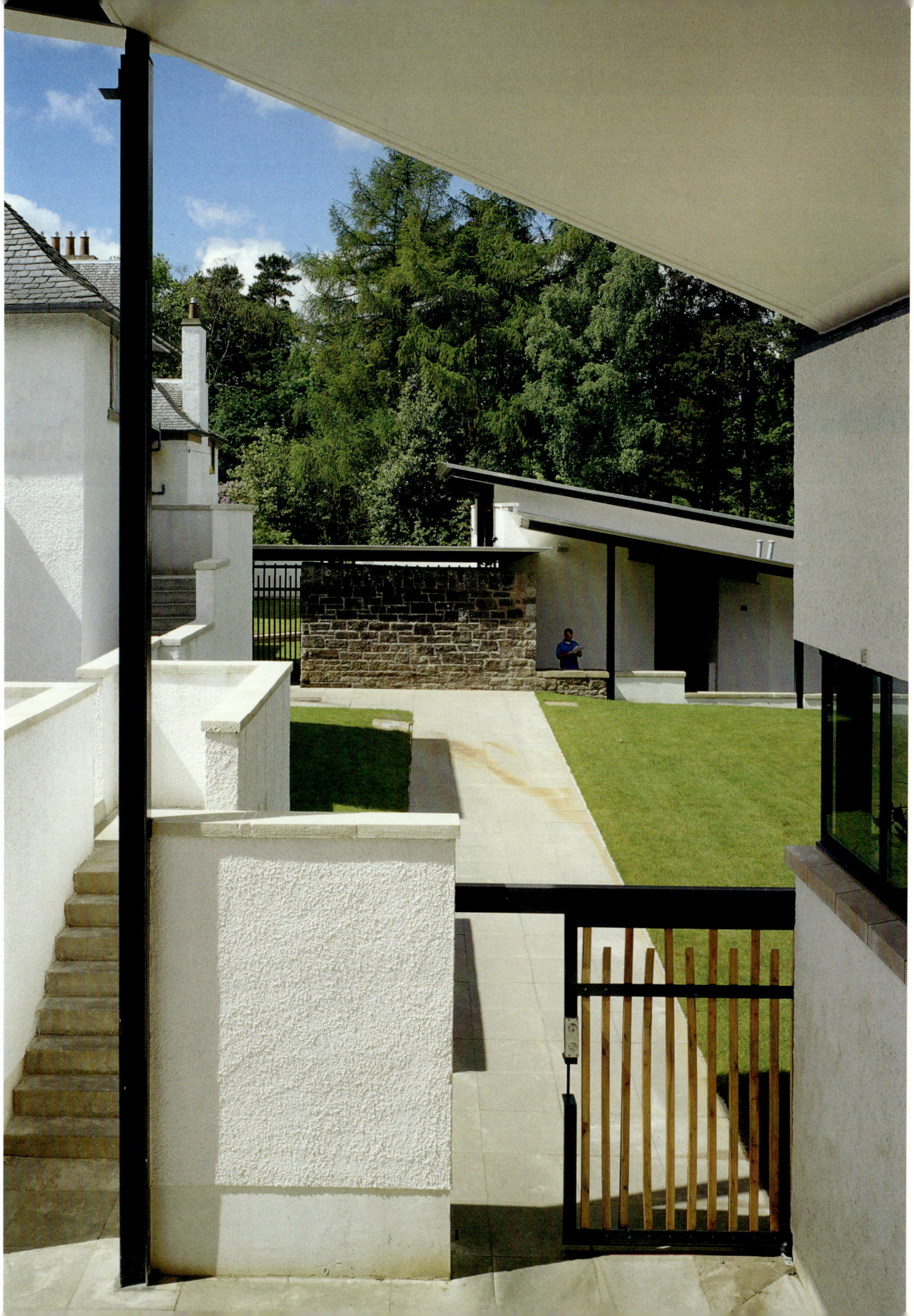

Children are taught in six classes of six, and in the old accommodation could be easily distracted. Now, each of the classrooms looks onto mature woodland but has high silled windows to an interior 'breakout' courtyard. The classrooms themselves are an informal shape with a teaching area, wet area and space for individual study against the window. Observation panels from adjacent staff rooms allow children occasionally to be monitored. Each classroom has its own roof and is surrounded with views of trees.

The crescent is terminated by a gym on one side presenting a 'garden wall' appearance to the formal south front of the house while the other is finished with an assembly/music room, on axis with Lorimer's Tower. Between the two is a second 'quiet courtyard' containing an external auditorium for events staged in the new room.

The two new houses are identical and placed in the old kitchen garden. Each contains six children's rooms in the roof but are architecturally quiet to provide a base of 'normality' for the children's lives. A 1.5 storey living room allows night-time supervision of the children upstairs by a carer situated below.

The project was run on a rolling programme to take account of the client's fund-raising activities, and to allow for the continued functioning of the school throughout construction.

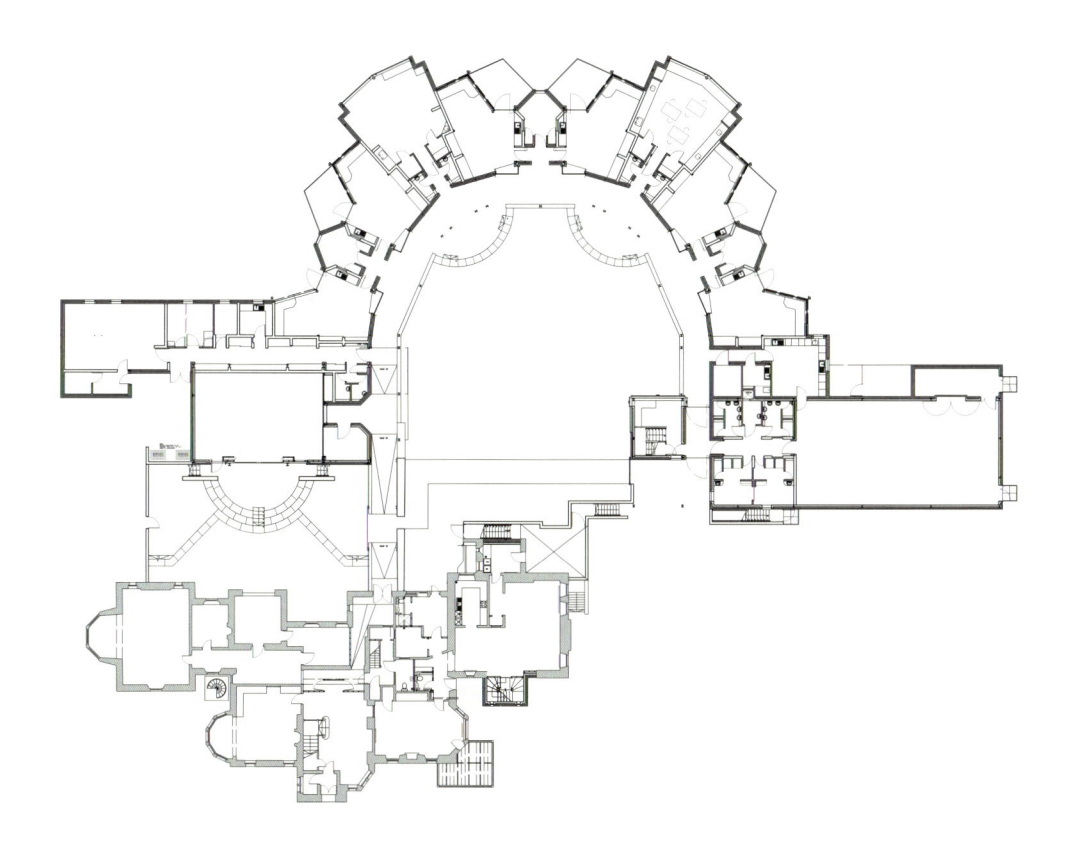

Patrick Webb, Headmaster, writes . . .

"Our new school and residential buildings represented a huge leap forward for Harmeny Education Trust, which educates and provides care for young children with social, emotional, and behavioural difficulties. The whole project was fund-raised by a small but dedicated group of people who did exceptionally well to raise the eventual sum of £3 million.

The story started in 1993 when I was interviewed for the post of Principal and was asked if the organisation was prepared to fund-raise £1 million for badly needed new purpose-built resources . . . the shock and horror gradually became reality in 1995 when a new Chairman – Gavin Reed – took over the helm of the Board of Trustees and supported the idea with action!

We researched many of Richard Murphy's (and other architects') previous works to see how he and the others we were considering interpreted a client's needs. We even toured Hampshire to see modern designs for schools and other establishments. Richard won the mini-competition we then organised: he excelled not only in bringing a distinctive personal touch to the design, but in allowing the client's ideas to shine through as well.

Meeting our needs did not prove easy: 'The brief is like a shopping list which has gone mad', he once remarked. We had been so keen to get all the facilities on our list allocated their own areas that we would have had a building as large as the village if the powers of reason and compromise had not been made to prevail by the Chairman and architect.

Mowlem (Scotland) managed the building of the complex and Richard's highly expressive design took shape. It was very different to the rectangular box I had once imagined. It was even in a different and more apt location. The two architectural awards RMA have won for their design prove how popular it has proved to be, but best of all it works for the purpose.

Educating young people with the kinds of special needs we work with is hard at the best of times, but with poor resources it is quite impossible. It takes special people who have the skills to relate to these needy youngsters, and without them we would not succeed. But linked to the skills of the staff, we now have what must be the best purpose-designed resource in Scotland."

Postgraduate Study Centre Faculty of Divinity, St Andrew's University

Abandoned

The St Andrew's University Faculty of Divinity wished to create a facility for postgraduate student individual study rooms, student social spaces, some collective facilities of seminar rooms, a small CD library and computer facility, and four additional teaching rooms. The current accommodation for the students is in various ad-hoc corners of their existing buildings, often over-crowded with two or three to a room.

The starting point for the design is the observation that post graduates' study of Divinity can often be an individual, indeed solitary affair. The University wished to provide modern, comfortable facilities to attract students to the faculty, whilst at the same time creating the possibilities of social interaction so that they can feel part of a wider community.

The very clear urban pattern of St Andrew's is the familiar 'rigg' system of long backland development separated by narrow alleyways or closes, and this is clear in the immediate vicinity of St Mary's College on South Street, interrupted only by the quadrangle of the college itself. The width of the site for the proposed facility takes up two riggs, each of which have closes which are currently closed to the street. This pattern is the starting point for the design.

Three independent buildings are proposed, each with pitched roofs and arranged in such a way as to form a natural continuation of the rigg system, whilst also forming small gardens or courtyard spaces between them and existing buildings. In this way the development will fit naturally into the overall grain of the town but also present itself as a formal composition to St Mary's College around a small paved courtyard. This is arranged symmetrically around an existing garden gate found in the Sixteenth Century wall separating the former botanical gardens from the quadrangle.

Social Buildings 105

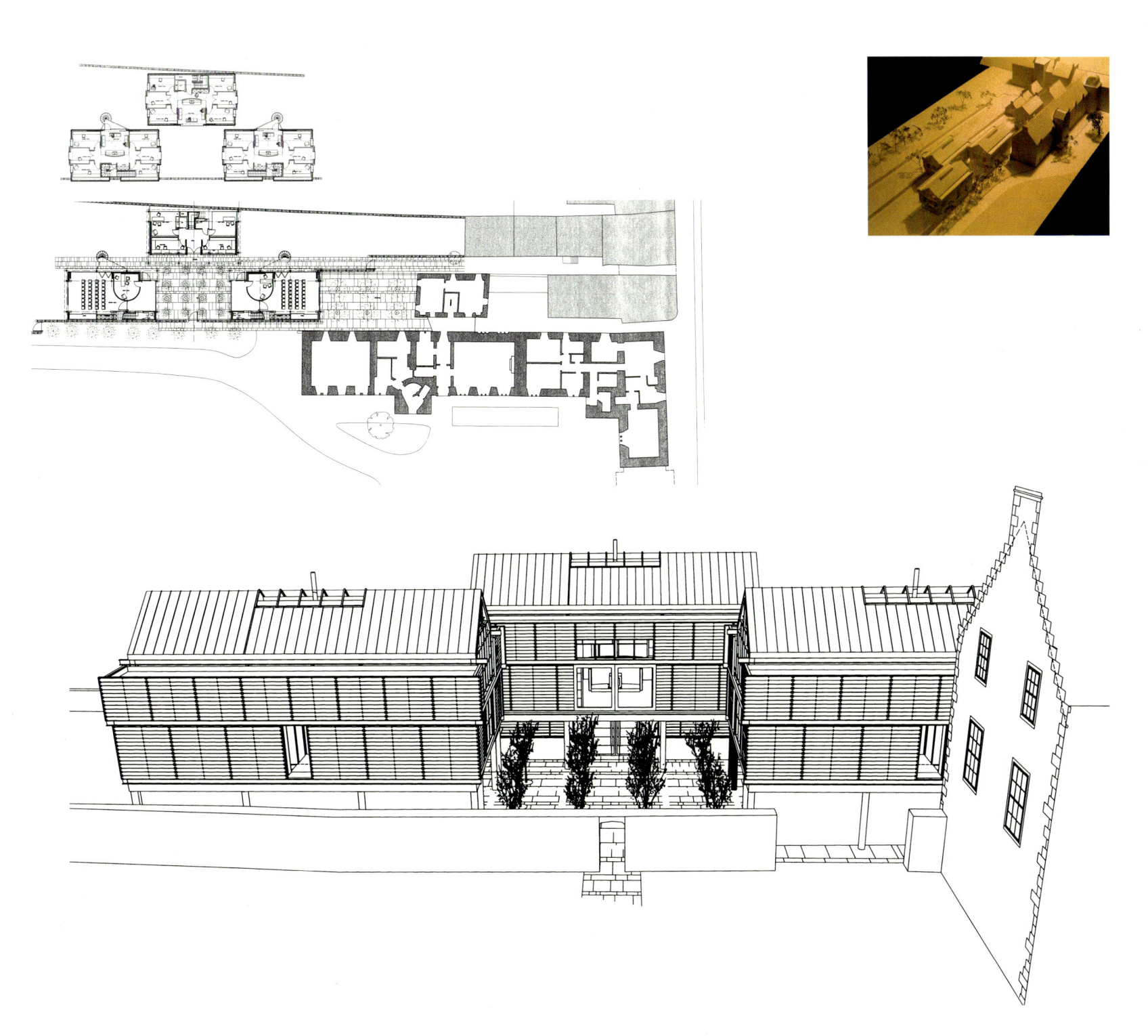

Jesus College Student Residences Cambridge

Invited competition 1997

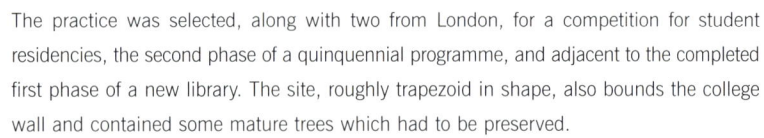

The practice was selected, along with two from London, for a competition for student residencies, the second phase of a quinquennial programme, and adjacent to the completed first phase of a new library. The site, roughly trapezoid in shape, also bounds the college wall and contained some mature trees which had to be preserved.

The college's buildings of brick and stone, whilst charming, are of no extraordinary architectural invention, although the giant chimney breasts to the rear of the Tudor range prompted reinvention as bathrooms in the new design. However, the arrangement of the college accessed via 'the chimney' (a passage way between Fellow's and Master's gardens) is unique. It allowed the original court to be placed in the centre of the college and this led to the subsequent development of three-sided courts facing onto landscape. The new design continues this tradition but places the new rooms in three separate gardens between the new court and the college walls. These south-facing intimate spaces are animated by communal kitchens – one per stair – sitting above each entrance; the latter idea freely inherited from Richard MacCormac's work at both Oxford and Cambridge.

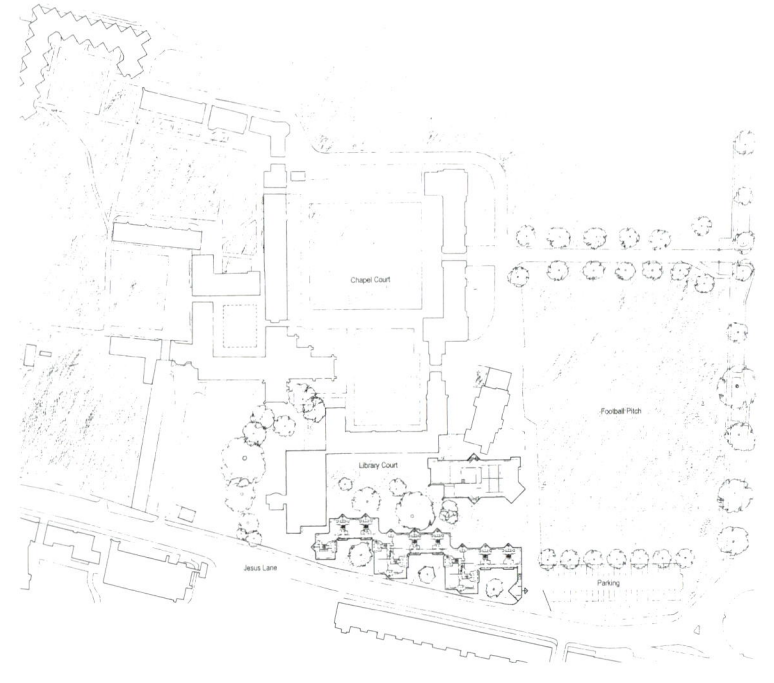

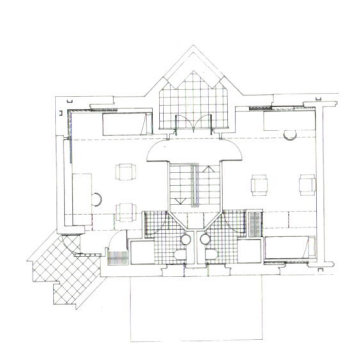

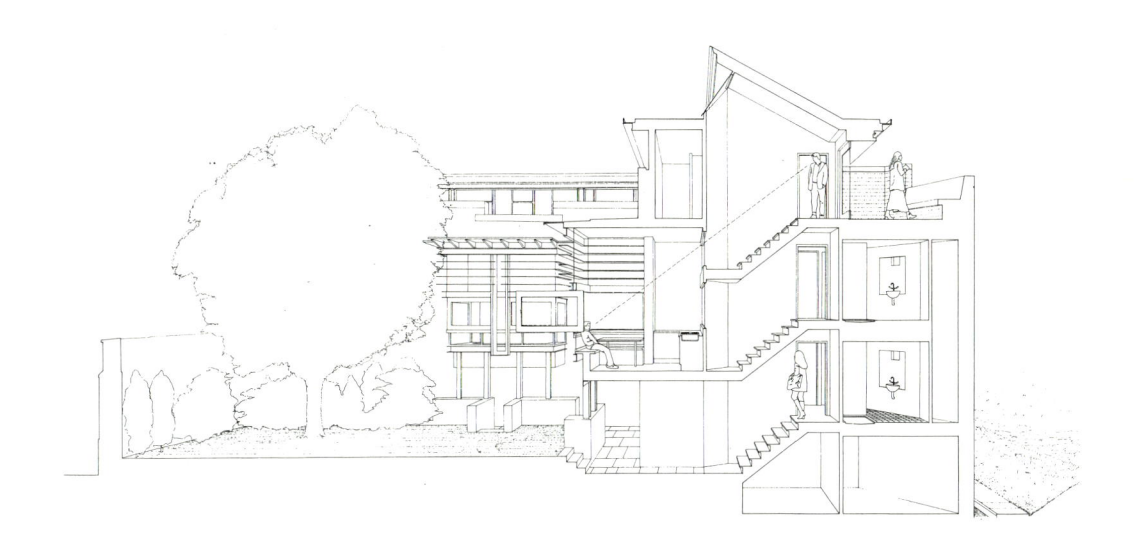

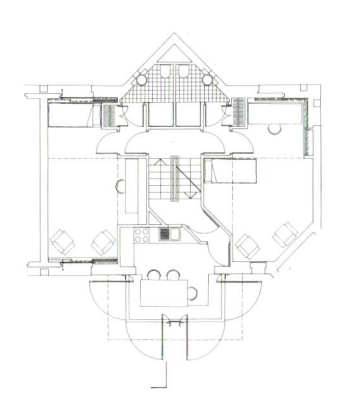

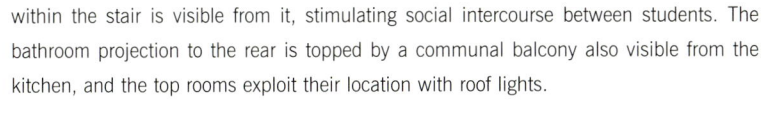

Six students share a stair, and the kitchen is arranged at a half-level so that all movement within the stair is visible from it, stimulating social intercourse between students. The bathroom projection to the rear is topped by a communal balcony also visible from the kitchen, and the top rooms exploit their location with roof lights.

After extensive consultation, the college committee that judged the competition was tied and the project was lost on the casting vote of the Master who favoured the architects of the recently completed library.

Social Buildings 107

Merchiston Campus Computer Library Napier University, Edinburgh

Completed 2001

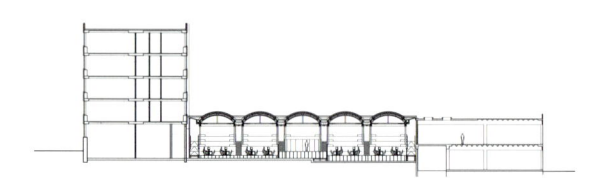

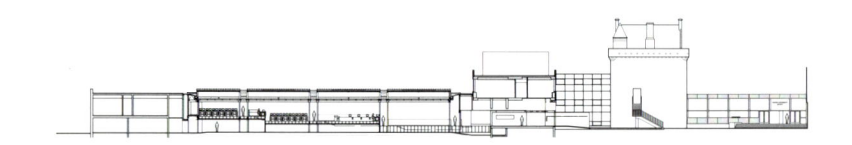

Napier University wished to enhance its present computer teaching facilities with the provision of a new 24 hour access 'computer centre' within its existing campus buildings at Merchiston. It centralises 500 workstations and provides support space for technicians and computer servers together with ancillary accommodation. The new centre is intrinsically linked to the existing university buildings which surround it (there are no elevations), although a separate entrance will give both open access to students 24 hours a day and provide it with a separate, visually identifiable, presence.

The brief was very simple, and yet a room of 500 terminals with no clear subdivision or defined circulation could have been a daunting prospect for its users. We immediately elected to subdivide the plan into a matrix of 5x4 bays defined laterally by five parallel barrel-vaults and longitudinally by a stepped hillside of four terraces. A tartan grid of circulation weaves its way between, under valley gutters in one direction and vaults of light in the other. The whole is supported on clusters of columns and the entire composition is surrounded by light from hidden perimeter roof lights where there are also ramped access routes. The vaults themselves are lit from the sides by sunlight reflected upwards so that sunlight will not fall onto computer screens.

Placed centrally within the matrix is the main support desk, providing the staff there with an overall view of the facility and of the main entrances.

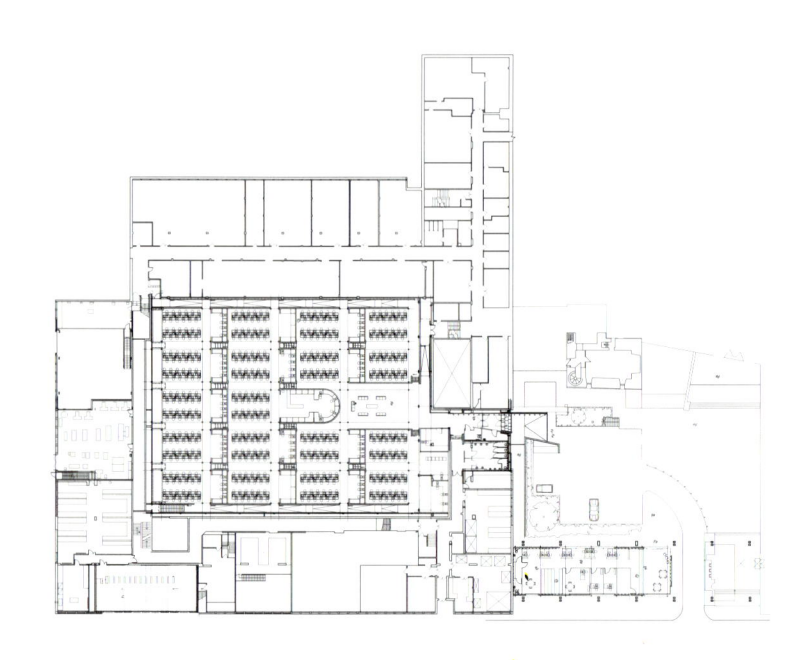

108 Social Buildings

Social Buildings 109

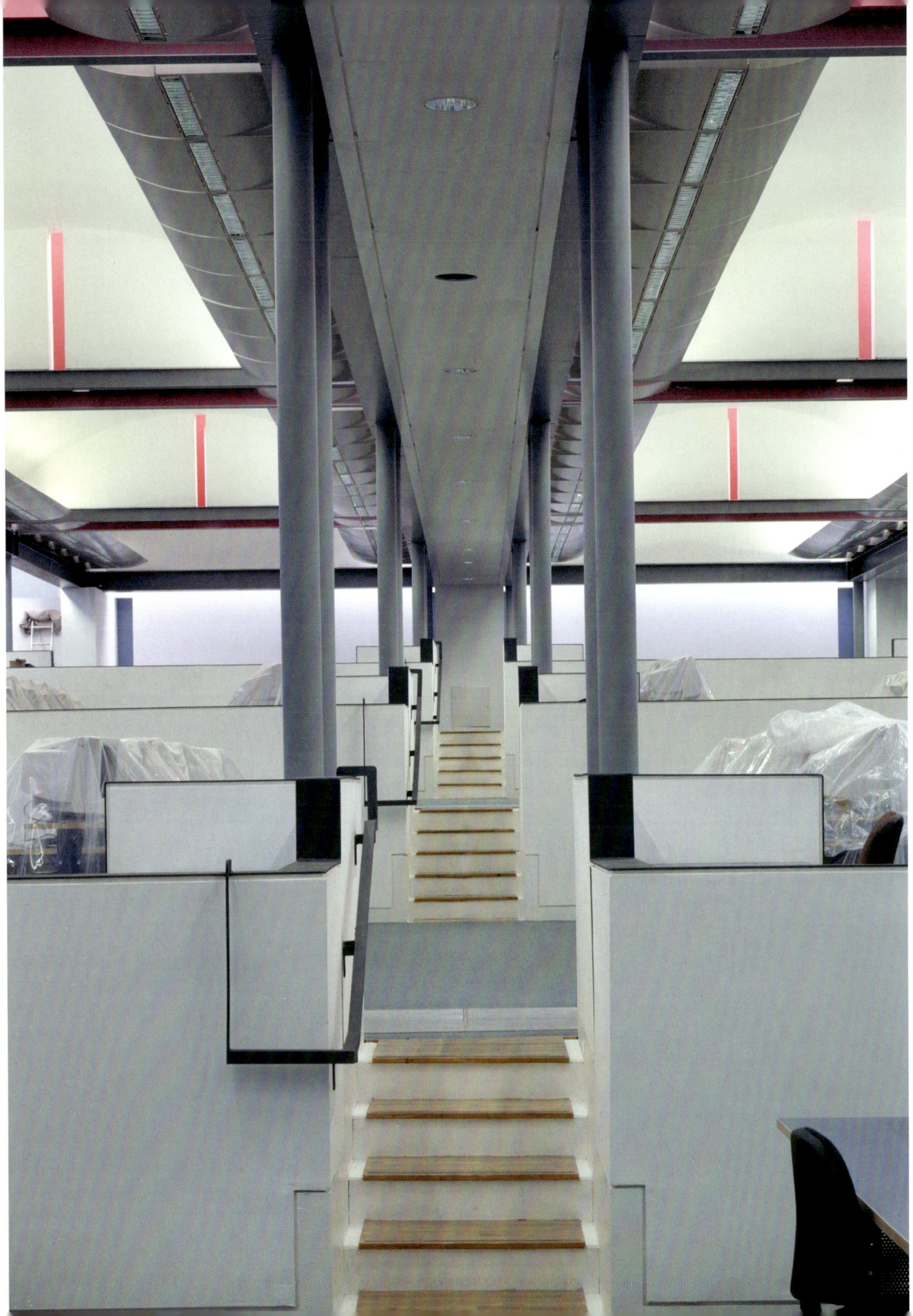

Social Buildings 111

Inverewe Gardens Restaurant Wester Ross, Scottish Highlands

Abandoned 1993

Site

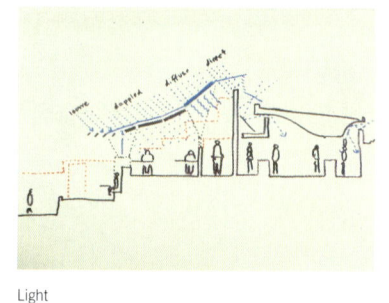

Light

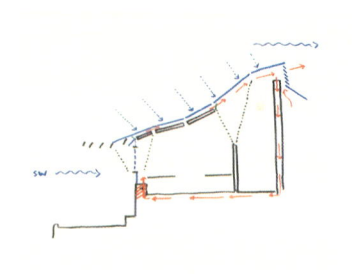

Energy

In the far north-west of Scotland is a remarkable sub-tropical garden begun in the nineteenth century but now in the care of the National Trust for Scotland. We won an open competition for the design of a 200 seat restaurant on a site adjacent to Loch Ewe and also to two extensive existing walled gardens.

Our project divided the restaurant into four cafés of fifty seats each (the size of a bus party) and placed each in its own walled garden. The servery took the form of an underground grotto, and the continuation of the walled garden retaining wall became a thickened 'service wall' penetrated by openings between the grotto and the cafés, the entrance route ramping down on its landward side.

The cafés shelter under a glazed canopy supported by a forest of tree-like steel supports, which also act as the portals from cafés to the terrace, and from the circulation route to the cafés. Cafés can be progressively closed down or opened up to meet the variable demand of the tourist season. The glazed roof, designed to be a continuation of the tradition of walled garden glasshouses, also acts as a solar chimney, with pre-warmed air mechanically circulated down to the cafés. The window wall is capable of completely folding away to transform the cafés into a deep veranda on sunny days.

The project was abandoned one week before construction was due to start on site. An alternative design by a local architect has since been built outside the gardens in the car park.

112 Social Buildings

Social Buildings 113

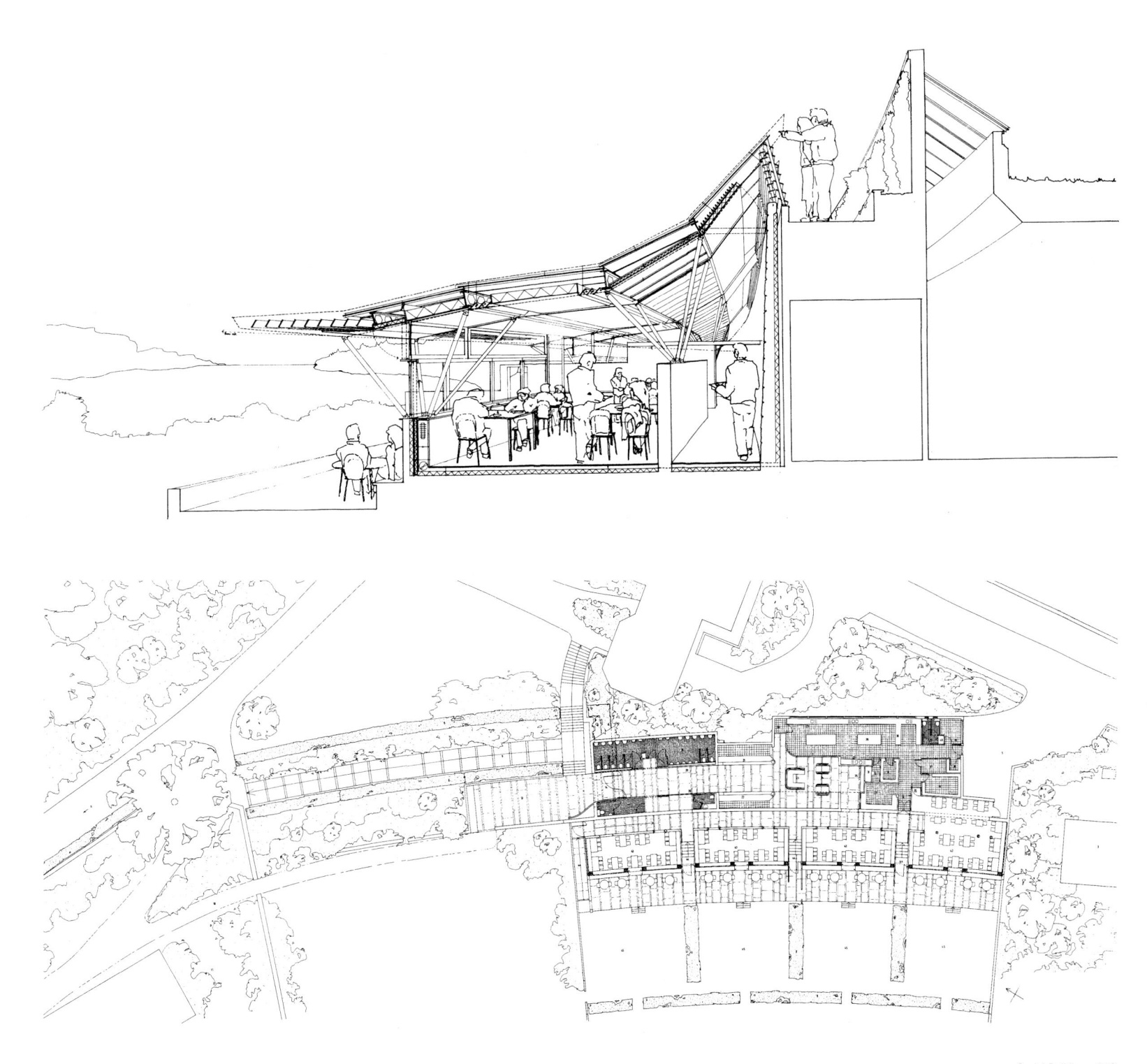

Adult Learning Centre Kirkintilloch, East Dumbartonshire

Completion 2002, for Strathkelvin Development Company

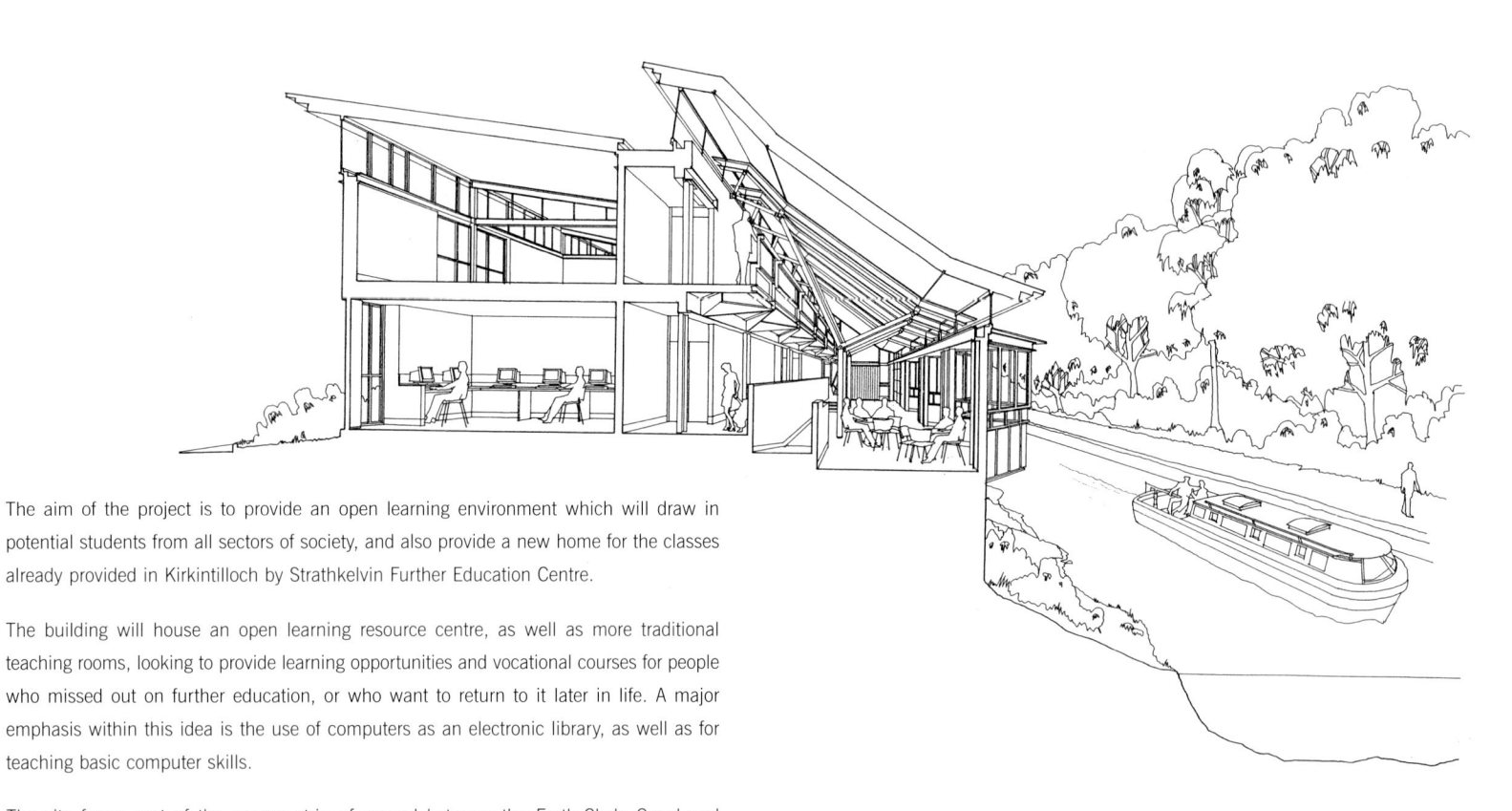

The aim of the project is to provide an open learning environment which will draw in potential students from all sectors of society, and also provide a new home for the classes already provided in Kirkintilloch by Strathkelvin Further Education Centre.

The building will house an open learning resource centre, as well as more traditional teaching rooms, looking to provide learning opportunities and vocational courses for people who missed out on further education, or who want to return to it later in life. A major emphasis within this idea is the use of computers as an electronic library, as well as for teaching basic computer skills.

The site forms part of the narrow strip of ground between the Forth-Clyde Canal and Southbank Road in the centre of Kirkintilloch. The canal bank itself slopes steeply into the water and is presently covered with trees and scrub vegetation.

The building is laid out on a linear plan, with a two storey block to the south side housing classrooms and offices. Against this sits a lean-to structure, which projects out onto the canal bank housing the open learning facilities. The entrance is to the north-east end of this linear plan, facing towards the town centre and accessed from an open terrace space between street and canal. One potential future development is that this space might form the springing point for a new pedestrian bridge across the canal.

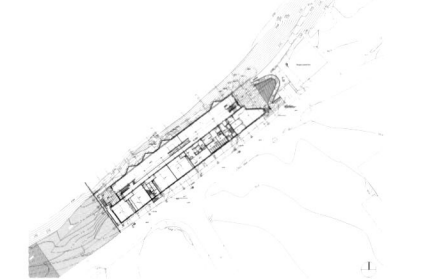

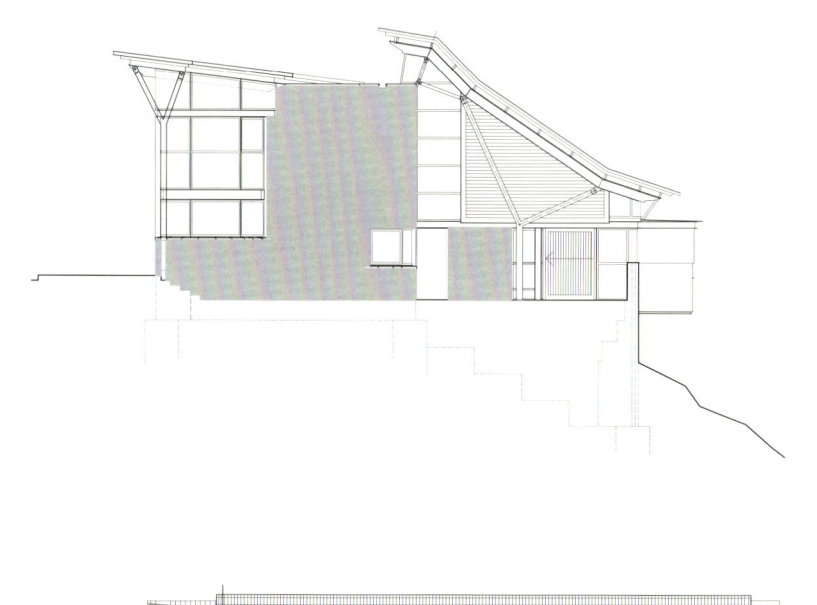

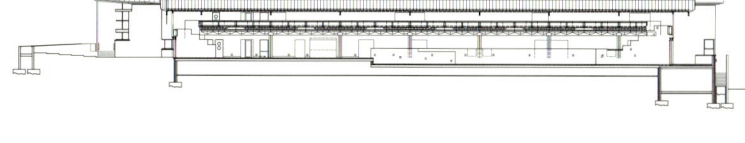

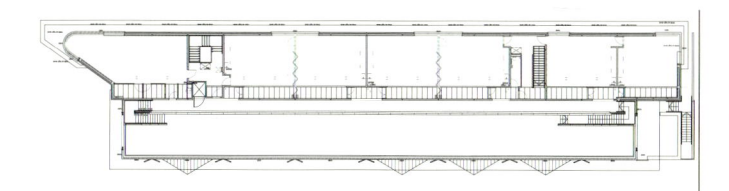

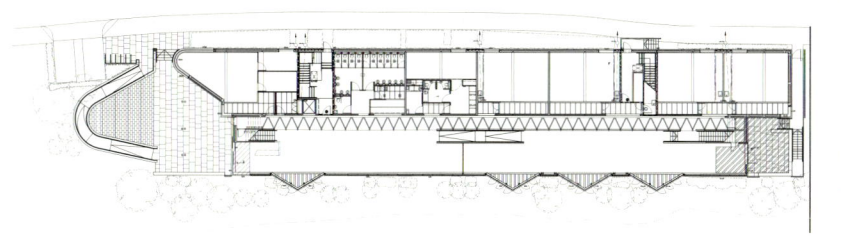

The entrance brings the visitor directly into the open learning space at a reception and guidance area, including a small café space. The aim is to create an instantly legible and welcoming place which is not daunting and allows the new student to understand the layout of the building on their first visit. The open learning space looks over the canal with a series of triangular bays forming workspaces almost among the trees retained on the canal bank. Access to the classrooms and other facilities is from an open gallery on each floor, the aim being that all activities take place in the open learning area except individual classes. The classrooms face out to Southbank Road with the upper level rooms sitting beneath a lightweight roof edge and clerestory windows. The roofs of the lean-to and the classrooms are separated by a continuous roof light which allows sunlight into the main space, controlled by moveable shading systems.

The roofs are intended to form a simple datum from which the planes and levels within the building are arranged to give a dynamic composition to section and façades. The canal bank will be replanted so that the building is amongst trees. This should maintain the wildlife corridor of the canal as it comes into the town centre.

Social Buildings 115

Office Foyer at 225 Bath Street Glasgow

Completed 1998, for West Register Projects Ltd

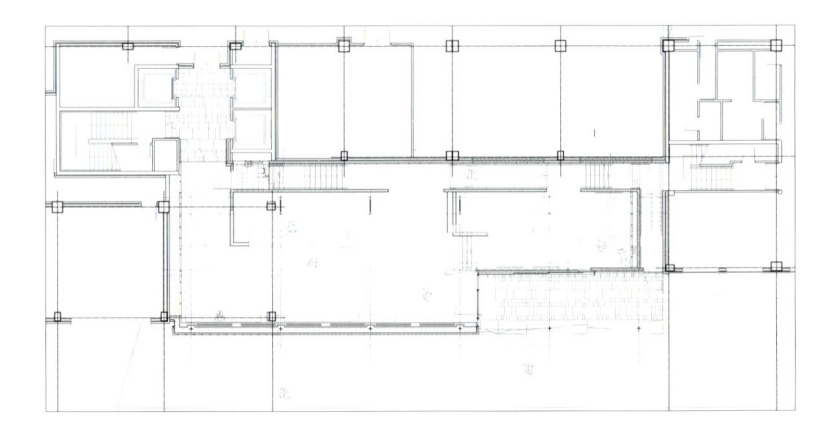

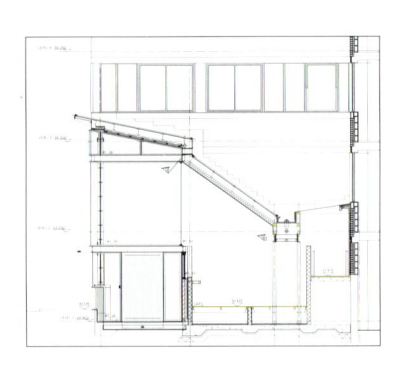

The formation of a new entrance at 225 Bath Street provides a new reception area and lift lobby for the separately refurbished office development, together with a franchised coffee bar.

The design, constructed on the front of a 1970s six storey office building, formerly occupied by the local health board and the local authority, features a cranked steel roof profile that creates the building's distinctive angled soffit planes. These are visible through the large structural glazed façade that steps back in plan to meet the two façades to either side. A route to the first floor runs parallel to the street at the rear and is slipped in behind a hidden rooflight; the whole composition is designed to contrast with and distract from the banality of the surrounding building.

Office at Edinburgh Park Edinburgh

Competition 2001, for Edinburgh Park Ltd

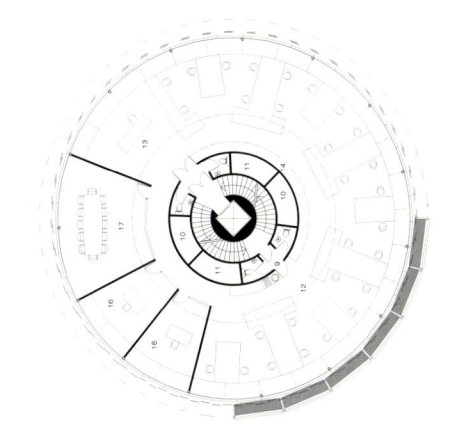

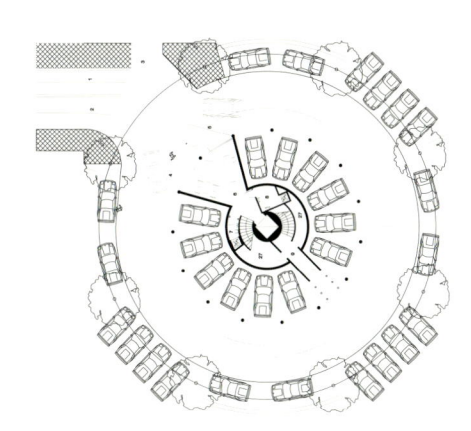

An unsuccessful competition entry for Edinburgh's business park, the design proposed a circular five storey tower with a central core consisting of a double helix of two stairs (access and fire escape), lift, WCs etc. This gave a very high net/gross ratio of 85%. The usual roof plant room was piled up to make a lantern tower liberating most of the roof to be used as a communal garden with hot tub, sauna and picnic facilities. Parking in a semi-excavated ground floor continued the circular theme and the mostly glazed façade was protected by a screen of louvres covering 25% of the facade which would have tracked the sun by continually circumnavigating the building once a day.

Social Buildings

Dundee Contempora
See the world differently
Dundee Contemporary Arts
a bug's life

Eight Buildings for the Arts

Not long after the practice began the National Lottery was launched, with the subsequent explosion of buildings for the arts. Many of these have been commissioned by competition, and all place architectural quality as a precondition for funding, a very welcome development that in all logic should be extended to all publicly funded buildings. Only The Fruitmarket Gallery, converted on a shoestring, is a pre-Lottery project. And whilst there are frequent newspaper stories of 'Lottery turkeys', happily, our completed projects are all Lottery swans; indeed the flagship of the practice, Dundee Contemporary Arts, has had success in terms of visitor numbers beyond the most optimistic predictions.

A decade ago the arts world was shocked by a brash new marketing strategy for the V&A in London: "Ace café with museum attached" ran the poster. Encapsulated in that slogan was a kernal of truth – today arts buildings are social meeting places, agents of urban regeneration and, hopefully, classless in their appeal. Thirty years ago an expedition might have been made to see an exhibition and, if there was time, have a cup of tea. Now the sequence is reversed, and our strategy in all these projects has been to tempt the visitor over the threshold with social devices and glimpses of what's to come, using a social focus as a spring-board from which the art venues can be explored. In such a way art – gallery, cinema and theatre – can become genuinely more socially inclusive and part of everyday life.

The Fruitmarket Gallery Market Street, Edinburgh

Completed 1993

The Fruitmarket Gallery sits in the central valley of Edinburgh adjacent to (and above) Waverley Station. Our original commission to facelift the gallery (itself a 1970s conversion of the old market) was greatly extended to undertake a complete remodelling. This involved the construction of a new roof which flies over the old parapet thus dramatically increasing the hanging height of the upper gallery. In the centre of the roof are large rooflights and under these is a new staircase connecting the two floors and also bringing light down to the lower level. On the ground floor the café and bookshop were relocated to the front facade which was opened to the street as a means of dissolving the threshold and tempting visitors into an intermediate space between street and exhibition.

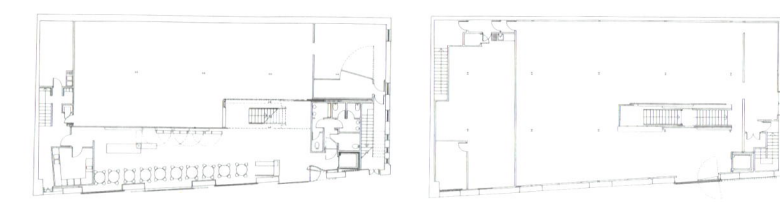

Buildings for the Arts 121

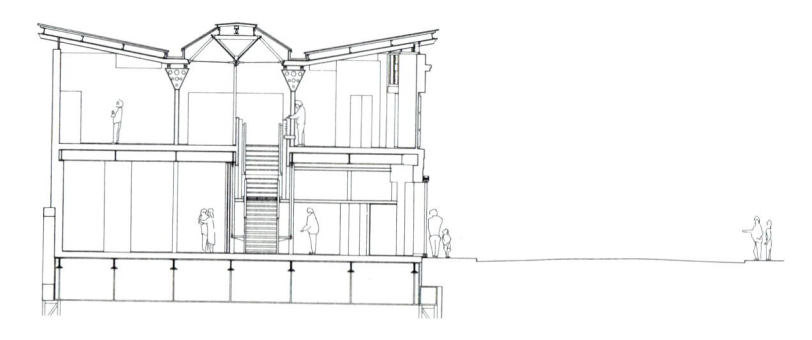

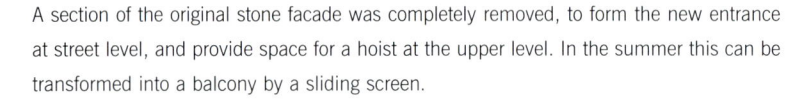

A section of the original stone facade was completely removed, to form the new entrance at street level, and provide space for a hoist at the upper level. In the summer this can be transformed into a balcony by a sliding screen.

From within, the clerestories and new windows give selected vistas of recognisable monuments, both near and far, around the city linking the experience of the interior to the experience of the city; daily life is a background to almost all the exhibitions.

Top light is reflected off a central warm air duct with south light animating one side of the central screen. This appears as a hidden source when seen from the street. The new winged roof springs from tree-like portal frame columns and the staircase is capable of being raised to allow large objects into the lower gallery. The reception desk and café were designed by the office but the bookshop, of which they were an intergral part, was never constructed.

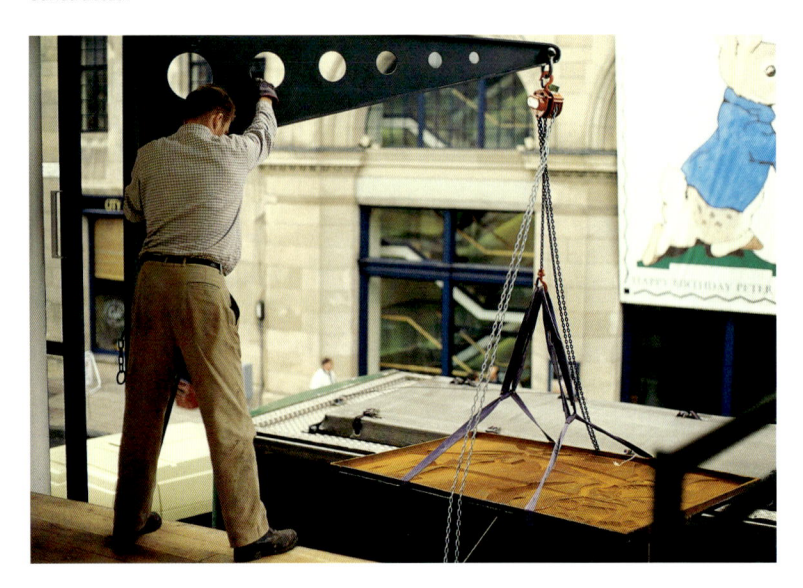

122 Buildings for the Arts

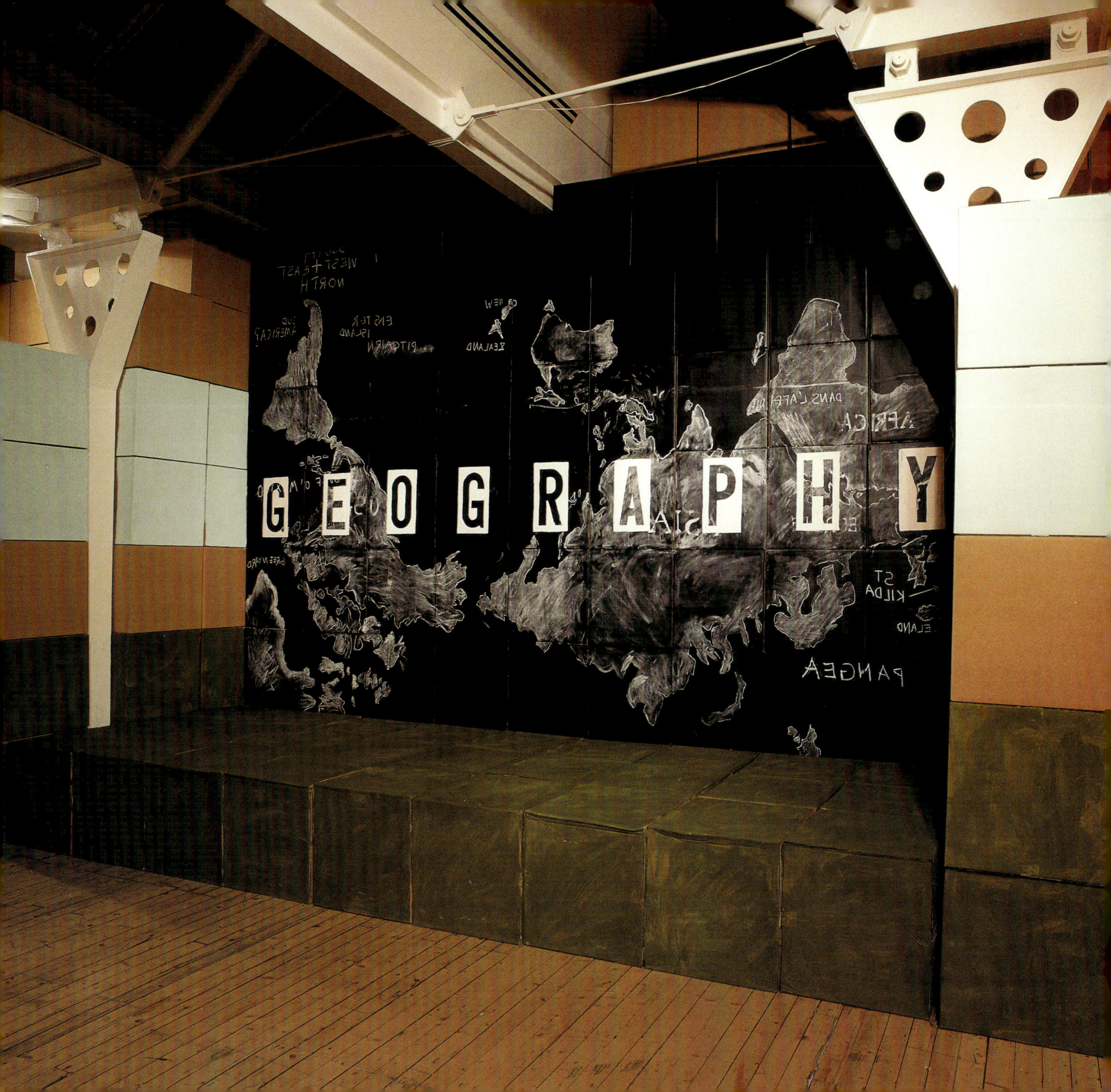
GEOGRAPHY
AFRICA
ST KILDA
PANGEA

124 Buildings for the Arts

Buildings for the Arts 125

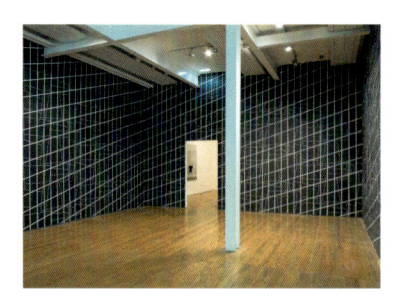

Magnus Linklater, Chairman, Scottish Arts Council 1996–2001, writes . . .

"I first encountered Richard's magic touch in The Fruitmarket Gallery in Edinburgh. No one could reasonably claim that location is this building's strongest point. Hidden away in Market Street, an undistinguished thoroughfare beneath the North Bridge, it funnels passengers into Waverley Station, and vehicles into the New Street car park. Half-way along it, the Fruitmarket had always been a problem building – dark, unwelcoming, and seemingly short on that one prerequisite of a decent gallery, space. Richard had very little room for manoeuvre. It may be a dull street, but this is still Edinburgh, where you alter a stone at your peril. What Richard did, within the restrictions, was little short of miraculous. Essentially, he raised the roof and let in the light. But that, of course, is to oversimplify. Today the Fruitmarket is a proper contemporary gallery – bright, airy, a place transformed, with open spaces on two levels, a café, bookshop, and a large expanse of hanging walls. That work has helped transform the fortunes of the gallery. Hand in hand with architectural change has gone artistic renewal. Audiences and artists alike have warmed to the gallery which has staged a series of ground-breaking exhibitions, including Gerhard Richter, Bill Viola, Northern Lights, Jeff Koons and the Visions for the Future series. Success breeds success, and the Scottish Arts Council, which had had a difficult relationship with The Fruitmarket Gallery down the years, now enjoys a far more comfortable relationship with its flagship gallery.

It was in Dundee, however, that the impact of Richard's work on the cultural scene has been most dramatically felt. Again, the Arts Council was involved, with a £5 million investment in Dundee Contemporary Arts, a major gallery space overlooking the Tay Bridge and Estuary. This was not so much a gallery, more a supreme gesture of confidence by a City determined to transform its fortunes, and looking to the arts to help do it for them. Dundee is not exactly synonymous with contemporary art, nor, hitherto, has it been regarded as a cultural capital. The loss of its major heavy industries had led to a steady drain of people and jobs. Over two decades, however, it set about rebuilding the City's economy around its expertise in science and medicine, creating a reputation for excellence in bio-technology and research at its two universities. The City Council realised, however, that if it was to attract the younger workers and bright graduates it needed, it would have to make it a more attractive place, and it began investing in the arts. DCA was its boldest experiment, and Richard's work its most important component. I remember seeing the building half-complete, and wondering how this former garage and warehouse could ever work. It sat, uneasily, on two levels. Its main entrance would have to be on the Nethergate but its public face was the one that looked out over the harbour.

In the event, Richard created not just one miracle but two. He has made a major contemporary gallery of serious proportions and huge space, and he has made it a place that people want to be. It draws you in off the street – the cinema, the counter and the café all acting as a magnet, the main galleries astonishing for their height and their vastness. Upstairs, the long window overlooking the bay makes the most of its location. You sense that you are on the bridge of on ocean-going liner. Again, the architecture and the artistic renewal has gone hand in hand. Andrew Nairne, DCA's first director, staged a series of shows which have attracted international attention. They have helped put Dundee on the cultural map.

It was, however, an experience one Friday night that convinced me about the role that art can play in energising the life of a city. My wife, daughter and I had been to a performance at the Dundee Rep, and decided to have a quiet cup of coffee in DCA's café. We walked down Tay Street and in through the main door. That was as far as we got. The place was a seething mass – the noise was indescribable. We were the oldest people by far – the place was a heaving mass of young people – DCA, a contemporary art gallery, had become the hub of Dundee's social life. I have no idea how many of those people ever ventured into the exhibitions themselves, but that is not the point. To them a contemporary gallery had become the place to be – it had fulfilled its purpose and become a focus of City life. For that, and for the continuing role that DCA is playing in the transformation of Dundee's fortunes, Richard deserves the highest praise."

Dundee Contemporary Arts Dundee

Completed 1999, for Dundee City Council

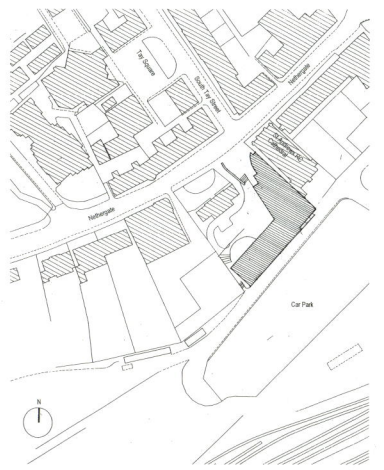

Dundee Contemporary Arts forms a major part of the re-establishment of the cultural identity of the City of Dundee. It has succeeded in making a public arts venue which is inclusive and enticing, and which encourages interaction between the public and many forms of visual art. To quote the Sunday Times (7th March 1999), "It is one of the most satisfying, sublime and stylish public buildings opened in years". To date it is the largest and most complex project that the practice has completed.

The practice won the limited competition in July 1996. From the outset the aim of our scheme was to group all activities – galleries, cinemas, print workshops, shop and research facilities – around a central social space and café. The building partially re-uses the brick warehouse of the former Macleans garage and forms an L-shaped plan on a site which falls three storeys from front to back. The café and foyer sit at the internal corner of this L, and are therefore at the heart of the building in plan and section, and they open out onto a terrace.

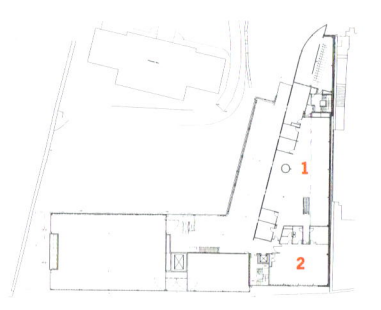

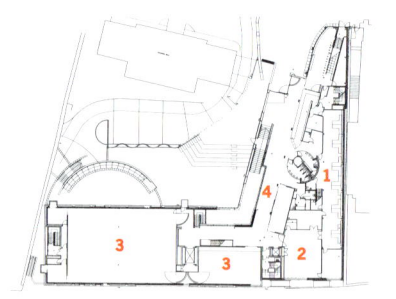

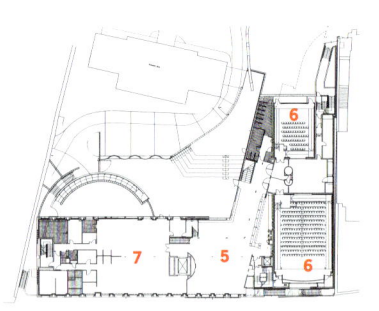

1	Offices
2	Meeting room
3	Gallery
4	Foyer
5	Café bar
6	Cinema
7	Print workshop
8	University gallery/studio
9	University facilities
10	Plant & servicing

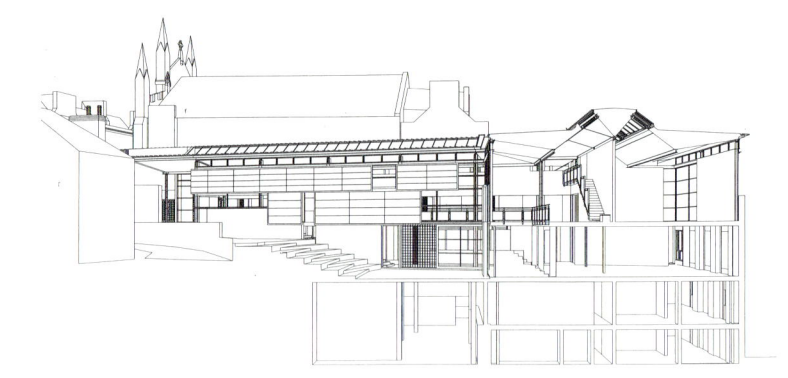

The site has a very narrow street frontage between the Roman Catholic Cathedral and the Georgian house of the Clydesdale Bank. In order to draw visitors into the building we aligned the foyer on the street opposite (Tay Street) so that it might form an extension of that public realm into the building, in effect an internal street. We set the entrance back, below a dramatic canopy, and beside the shop (the commercial face of the arts activities within), to give a breathing space to the street edge and a presence to the approach. Finally we made use of continuous rooflights to cast sunlight and shadow across the internal walls of the foyer, drawing the eye to the farthest part of the plan; a line of light to arouse the curiosity of the visitor on entry.

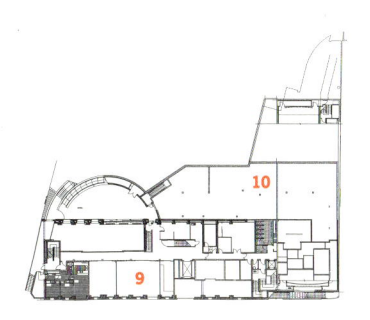

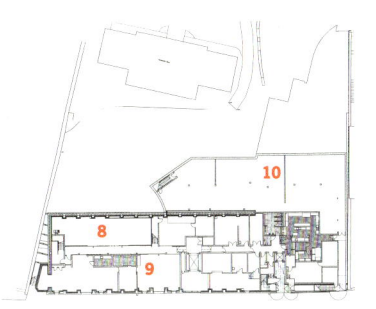

This use of light is continued by windows which give glimpses of the Tay Estuary to the south, and between foyer, café, galleries and cinemas. The aim is to entice the visitor to see an exhibition or a film when they might have come only for a coffee, to draw them in without their feeling the need to specifically come for a show, and to help everyone understand where they are in the building and where everything else is.

Even the main cinema has a large window below the screen allowing the audience to be connected to Dundee before and after the film, and to allow the external world a glimpse of the interior at the same time. This is part of the idea of the building as part of the city as a whole. Everything is visible from either the foyer or the cafe/bar. The internal street is supported by the necessary ancillary facilities, and behind the scenes by a double-height office space.

Buildings for the Arts 129

130 Buildings for the Arts

Buildings for the Arts 131

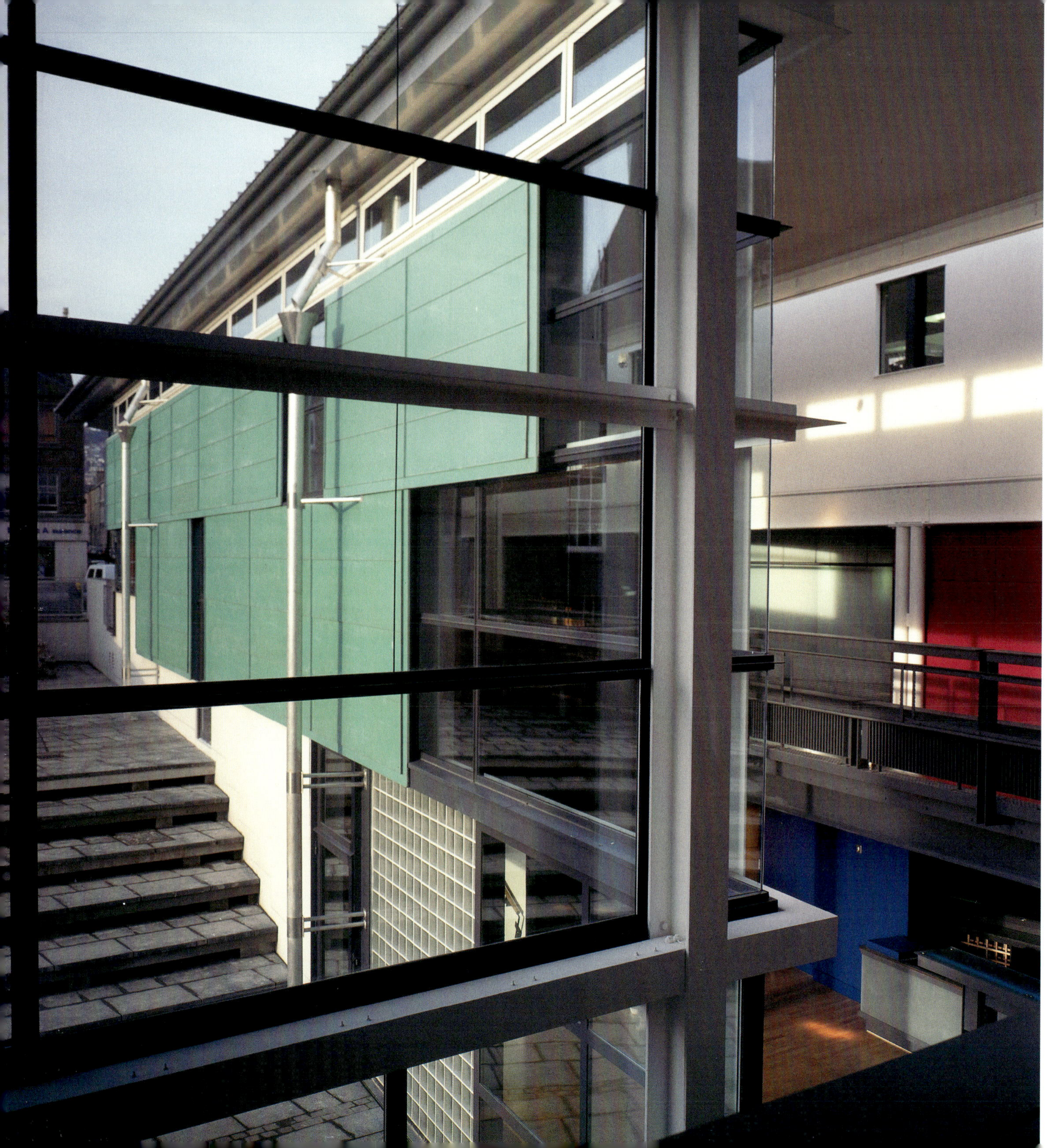

Buildings for the Arts 133

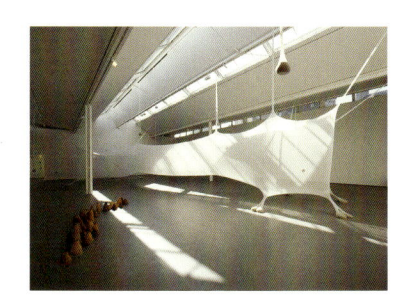

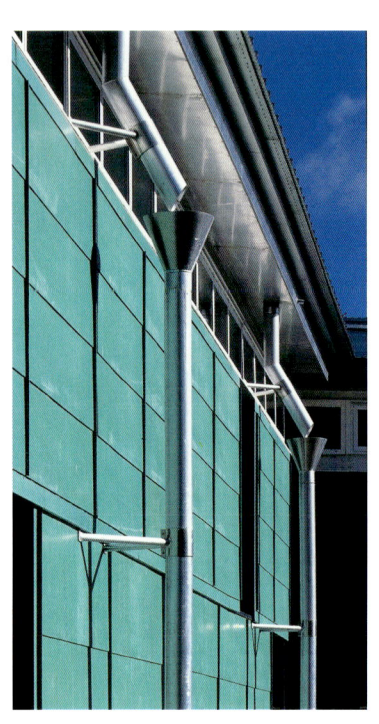

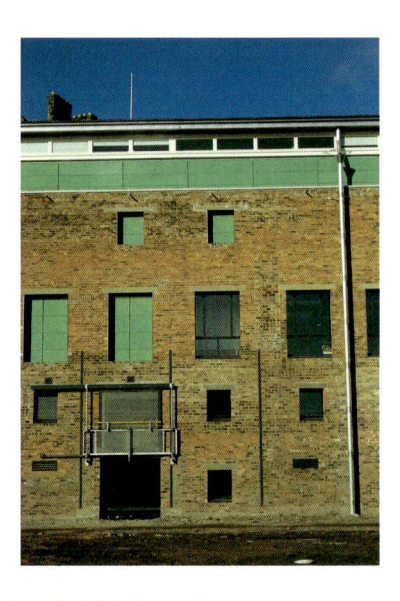

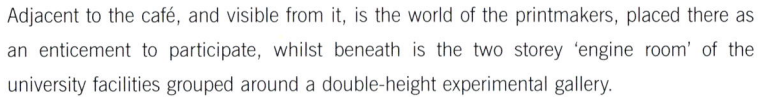

Adjacent to the café, and visible from it, is the world of the printmakers, placed there as an enticement to participate, whilst beneath is the two storey 'engine room' of the university facilities grouped around a double-height experimental gallery.

Finally the language of the building grows out of the idea of inserting the new facilities within the eroded shell of the former brick warehouse. New slips past old in a series of planar elements of copper, glass and steel. This planar language is continued in the new wing beneath a single unifying roof profile and is repeated in sliding doors and walls internally.

Since its official opening in March 1999 the building has been a phenomenal success attracting more than three times the number of visitors expected.

Buildings for the Arts 135

Hamilton Arts Centre Hamilton

Invited competition 1997, for Hamilton Ahead Ltd

The practice was invited to enter a limited competition for a new Arts Centre in the middle of Hamilton. The previous year a competition had been held for the design of a new town square, and The Arts Centre is intended to link this square with the existing town centre. In particular, we were required to retain the façade of the former Phoenix Theatre, a Grade B Listed building on site, due for demolition.

The brief was complex, requiring a new Town Library, a fully functioning theatre space and a series of smaller events rooms along with a major new meeting room which we re-christened the "Town Room".

Our proposal kept the main functions of library, theatre, and Town Room as distinct buildings: the theatre taking on a familiar semi-circular form: the library being a long wall of books on three levels and the Town Room being a townhouse-like building with a large first floor opening onto the Square and a café at ground floor level. These main buildings were linked by an internal atrium space (an alternative Town Square in inclement weather). The Phoenix Theatre façade led to an arcade between the library and the new theatre which opened on to the Town Square. Light was admitted through this arcade, and along its entire length the activities of the library could be viewed, in particular the great wall of books which we proposed to take the form of a town wall against the Clyde Valley landscape.

The entry was unsuccessful but the winning project has not been built.

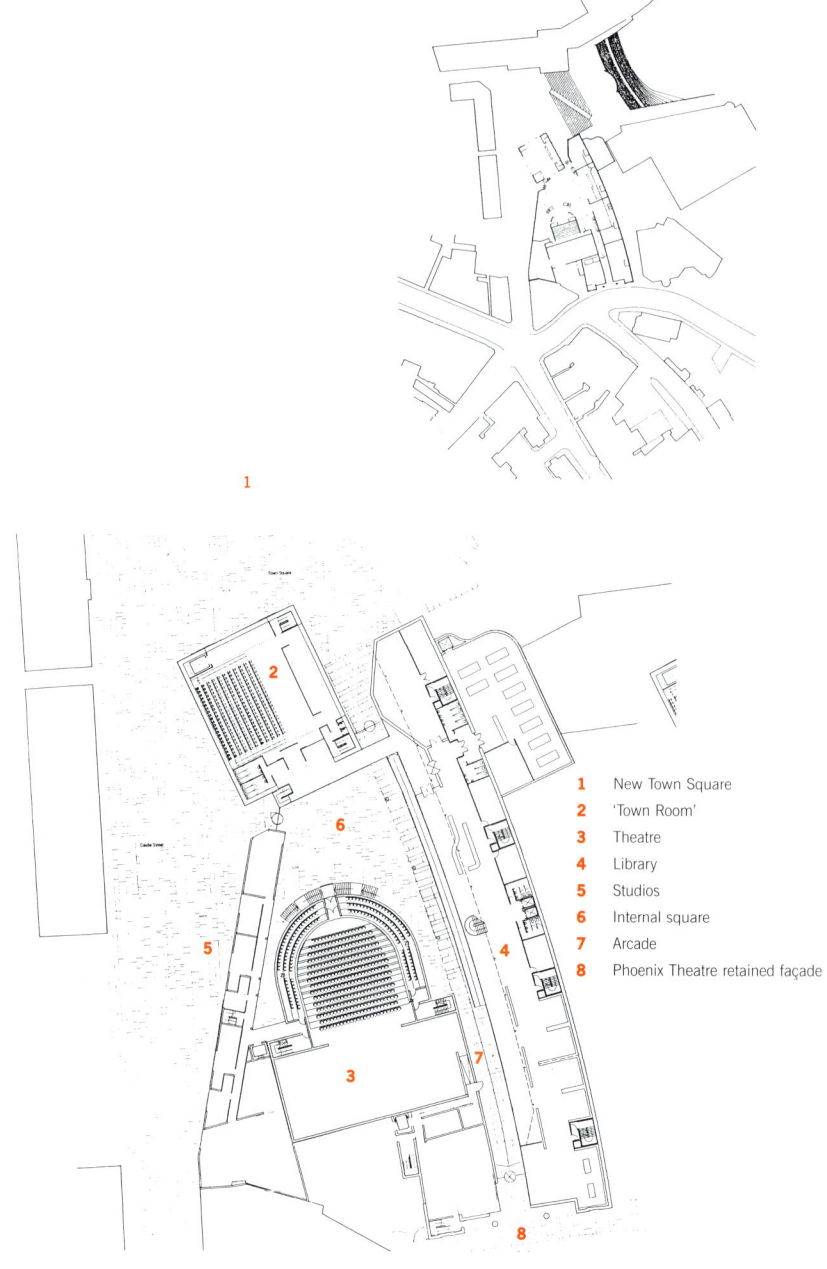

1 New Town Square
2 'Town Room'
3 Theatre
4 Library
5 Studios
6 Internal square
7 Arcade
8 Phoenix Theatre retained façade

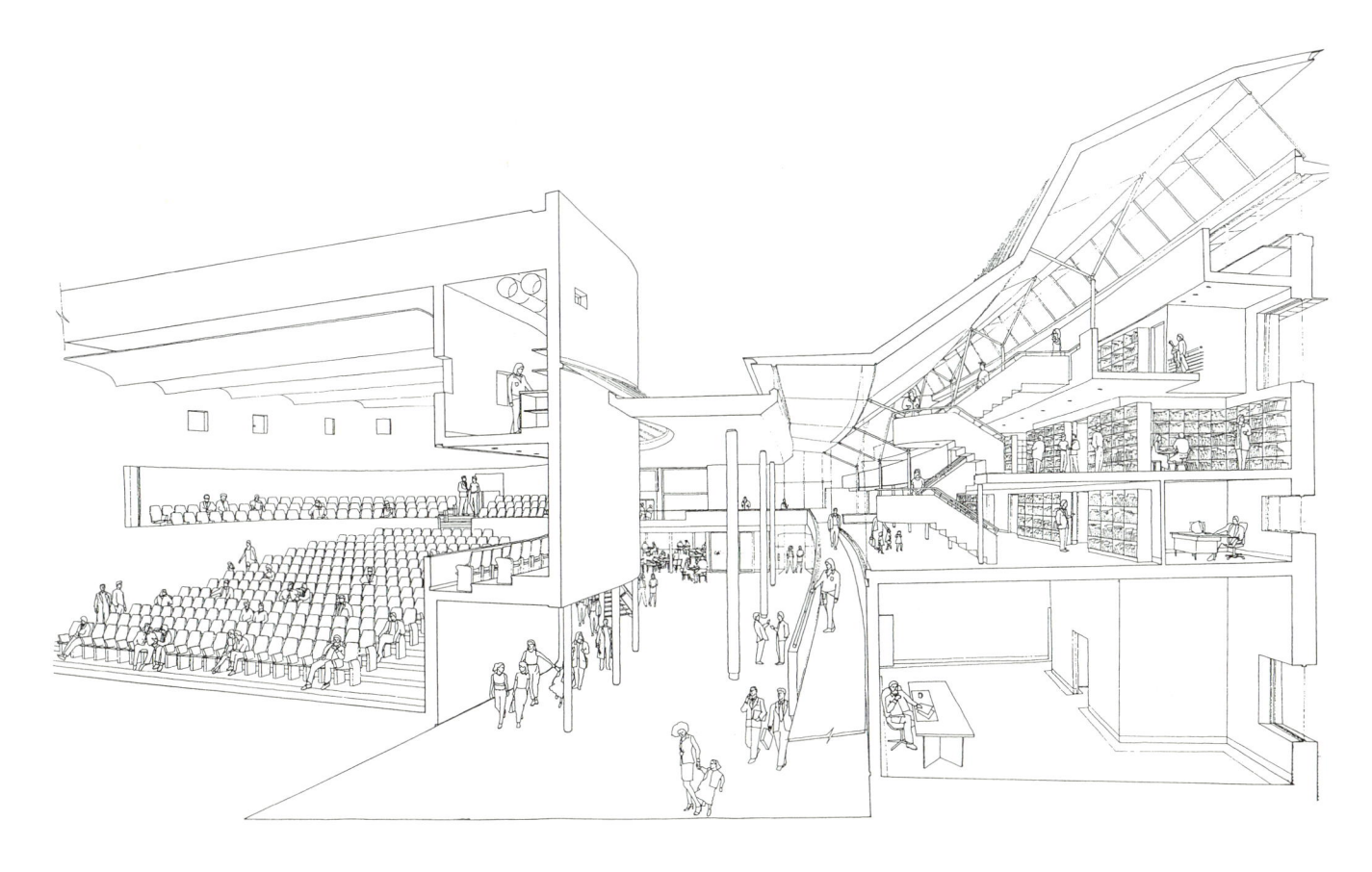

Buildings for the Arts 137

National Gallery of Scottish Art and Design George Square, Glasgow

Invited competition 1996, for the National Galleries of Scotland

The practice was invited to join six others in an international limited competition for the proposed National Gallery of Scottish Art and Design to be situated within the disused Central Post Office in George Square, Glasgow. The existing building, dating in parts from the 1840s, occupies a complete urban block. Three of its elevations are essentially walls of windows while the Ingram Street façade is largely a stone and glass screen wall. The exterior of the building could not be substantially altered but the interior could be completely removed.

Our design attempted to make sense of the existing façades by placing against them all the ancillary accommodation required locating the galleries on the only free elevation – the roof plane. Only in this position could both the varying internal volumes and the admittance of light be freely manipulated. Between the galleries shafts of light where placed so that a large sculpture court below could be lit, in a Piranesian way, from above, and by the Ingram Street façade from the south. Entrance from George Square was by way of a colonnade and then a grand staircase to the sculpture court, which sat above a complete reconstruction of Mackintosh's Ingram Street tearooms. From here escalators direct the visitor to a lantern light and then on upwards to the galleries. These are arranged chronologically horizontally, and by subject matter vertically, allowing cross-referencing between subjects by connecting staircases. The whole composition would act as a gigantic suspended inhabited loft above the sculpture court.

A series of grand formal galleries in the centre is complemented by an upper ring of special rooms designed around individual collections of paintings. The journey to the sky culminated in look-out belvederes over George Square and a summer café terrace above Ingram Street.

The project was unsuccessful and the Post Office site has since been converted into a shopping centre.

138 Buildings for the Arts

Buildings for the Arts 139

Peebles Art Centre Peebles, Borders

Completion 2003, for Borders 1996 Ltd

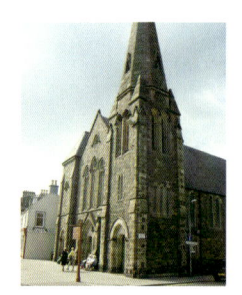

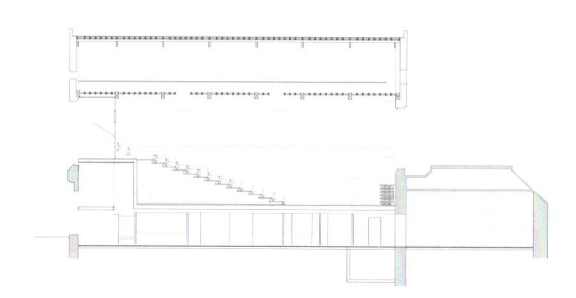

The Arts Centre will occupy a former church building constructed in 1871 in the centre of Peebles. It sits on the corner of a major and minor road, and our design shifts the entrance from the former to the latter.

The brief for the project is to accommodate an arts centre for the town, primarily a 250 seat auditorium, together with a rehearsal room (doubling as an exhibition space), the necessary ancillary accommodation of green room, changing rooms for artists, a small catering facility and café/bar and offices.

The design has been developed in the strong belief that the presence of the theatre should be evident from the exterior rather than simply discovered on the inside of an otherwise unchanged church exterior. The main 'ecclesiastical' gothic façade will remain virtually untouched, however the side elevation will be completely removed and substituted by a new entrance elevation displaying the theatre within. In this way the developing history of the building can be understood, and both eras of its construction can sit in creative juxtaposition with each other.

Internally the theatre sits at first floor and is broadly proscenium with a degree of flexibility. The route to the theatre is visible through the façade, and a fire escape triples as a poster bollard and the support for a new glazed canopy.

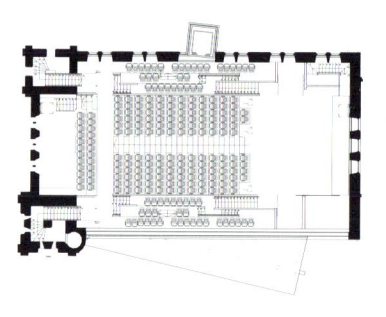

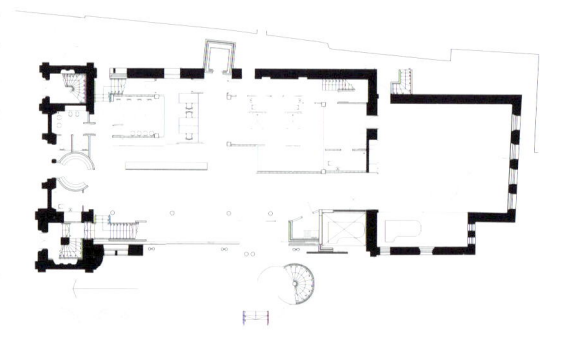

140 Buildings for the Arts

Buildings for the Arts 141

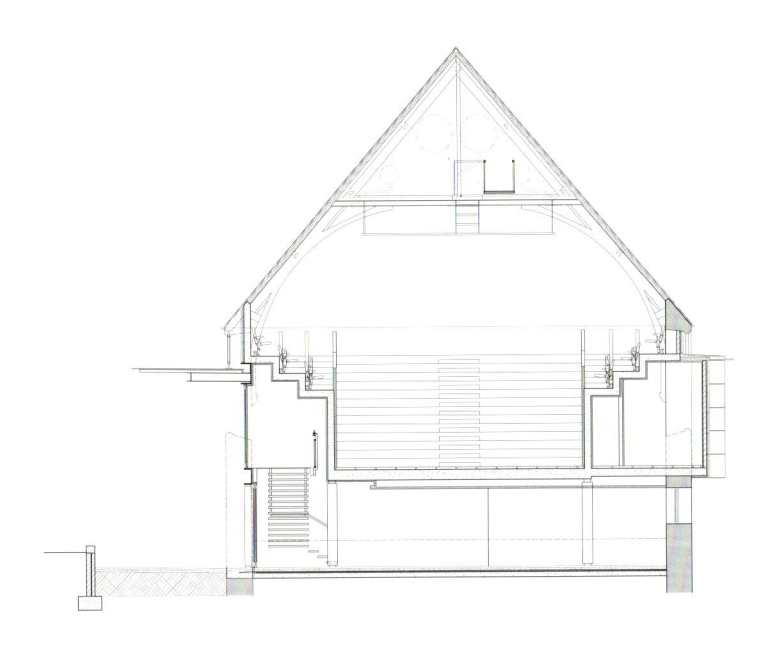

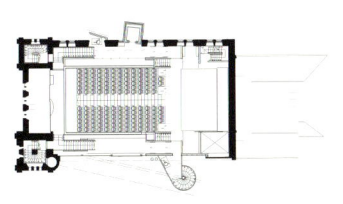

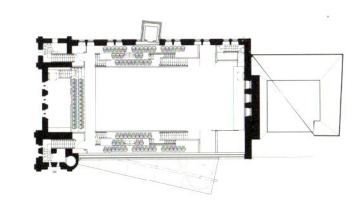

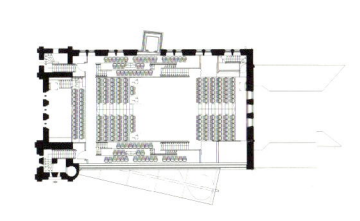

Centre for Contemporary Art and the Natural World Poltimore House, nr Exeter, Devon

Awaiting funding. In association with Simpson and Brown conservation architects.

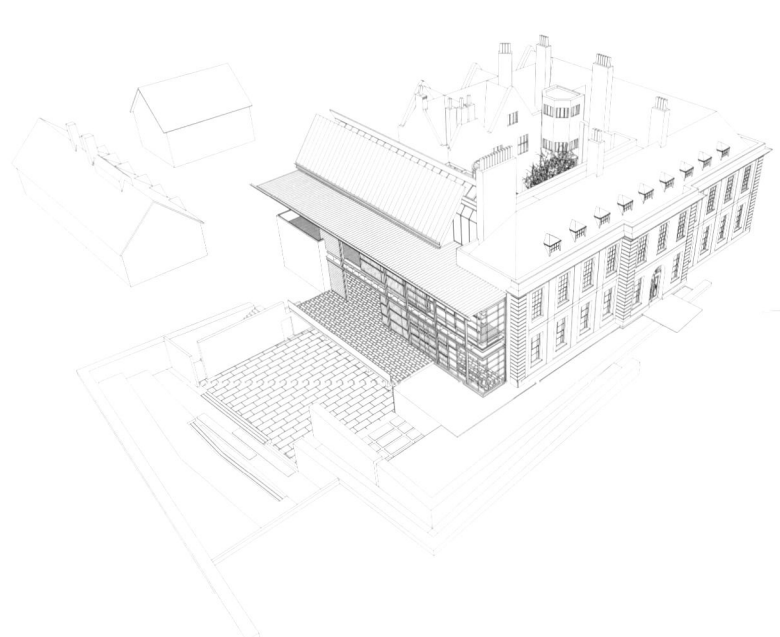

Poltimore House is a Tudor and Eighteenth Century Grade I Listed building now in a very derelict and dilapidated condition. It is an amalgamation of eras of construction, culminating in the downgrading of the Tudor house to servant accommodation, the change of the front of the house from north to south, the creation of a courtyard, and then its obliteration by the construction of a grand staircase. East Devon Council and the Poltimore House Trust commissioned the practice in conjunction with Simpson & Brown Architects, who are responsible for conservation work, to convert the building into a Centre for Contemporary Art and the Natural World. In addition, Gross Max Landscape Architects are collaborating with us on proposals to transform the landscape around the house.

Our project involves a number of radical demolitions, mostly of Nineteenth Century alterations to the house: principally the demolition of an already fire-gutted ballroom wing, the removal of the west wing and the complete removal of a much vandalised grand staircase in the centre of the building. The result will be a courtyard building where elevations of the original Tudor courtyard will be once again visible for the first time in 200 years. The courtyard will act as a focal point and distributer for the whole building.

Buildings for the Arts 143

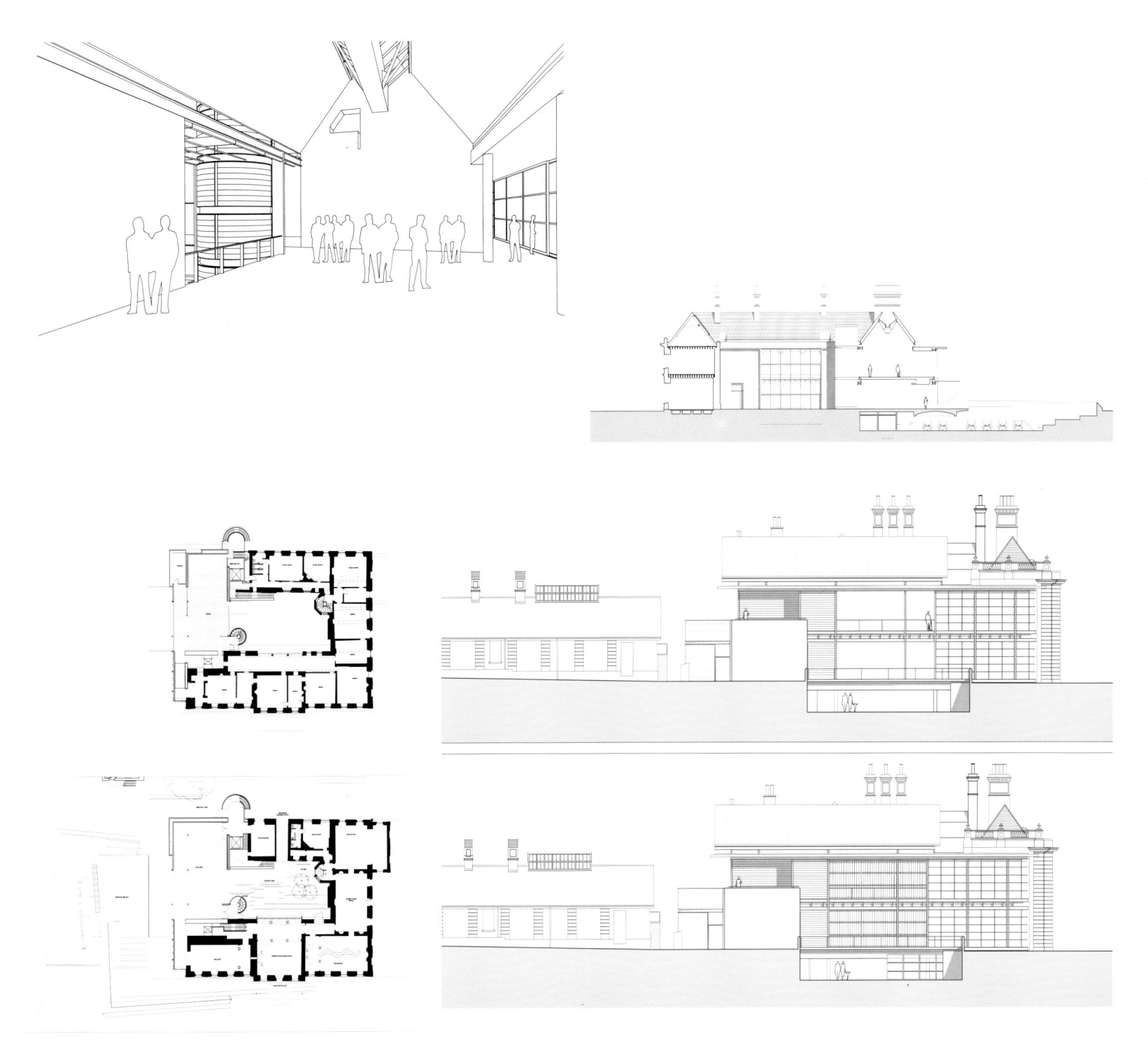

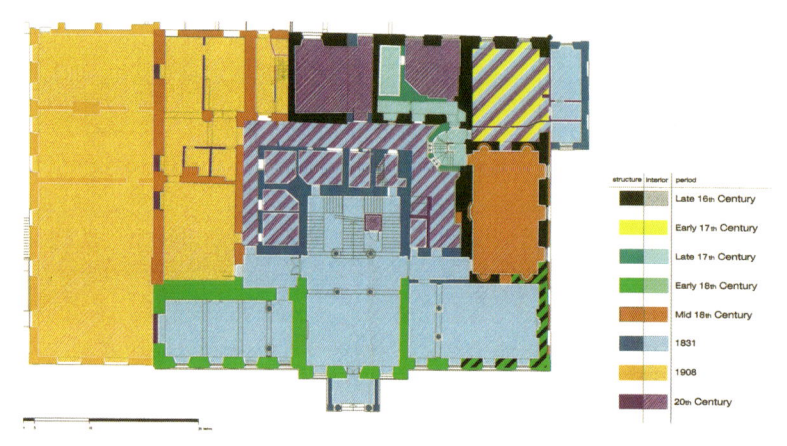

Our major proposal is the construction of a new west wing of galleries on the ground and first floors. These galleries will be large white rooms, characterised by a series of adjacent sliding walls. There will be three sliding surfaces of white plasterboard, translucent glass and clear glass, so that a variety of wall conditions can be selected by the Gallery Curator. Galleries will be able to look into the courtyard, to the landscape, do both or neither, on both ground and first floors.

In the basement a café/restaurant is to be constructed into a lowered garden whilst in the attic space the office accommodation for the building and a caretaker's flat will be inserted. The remainder of the house will be converted into galleries, bookshop, a study centre and education facilities, with the major historic room 'The Queen Anne Room' (described by Pevsner "as one of the finest rooms in Devon") being restored as a small conference facility.

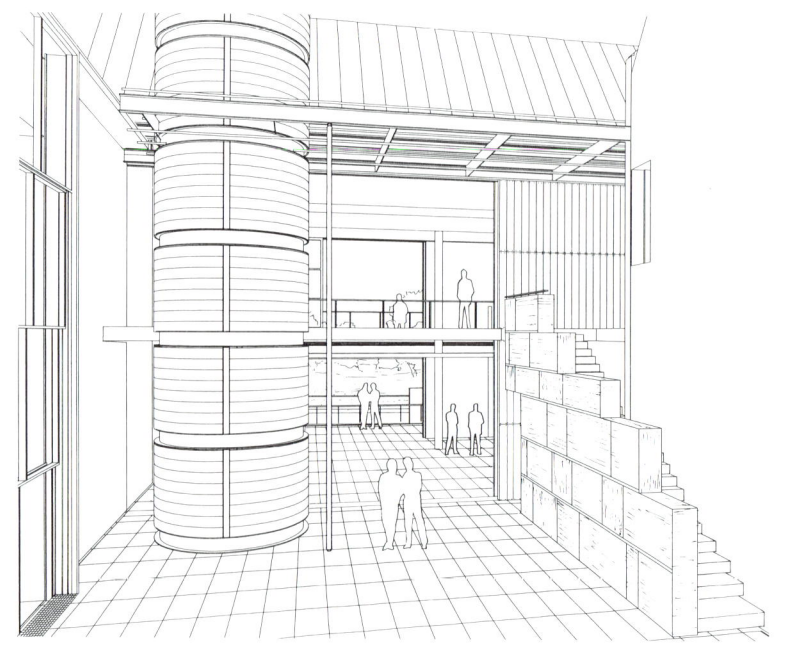

1 The Tudor house
2 The Eighteenth Century façade
3 The Eighteenth Century façade with romantic landscape
4 The classical conversion of one of the tudor façades
5 The entrance façade today
6 The Tudor staircase, as was
7 The Tudor stair today
8 The grand staircase, as was
9 The Queen Anne Room

Buildings for the Arts 145

Creative Enterprise Centre Caernarfon, North Wales

Completion 2003, for Cwmni Tref Caernarfon

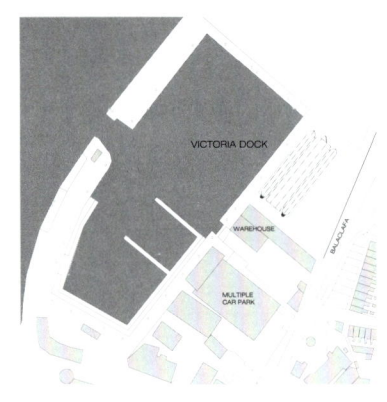

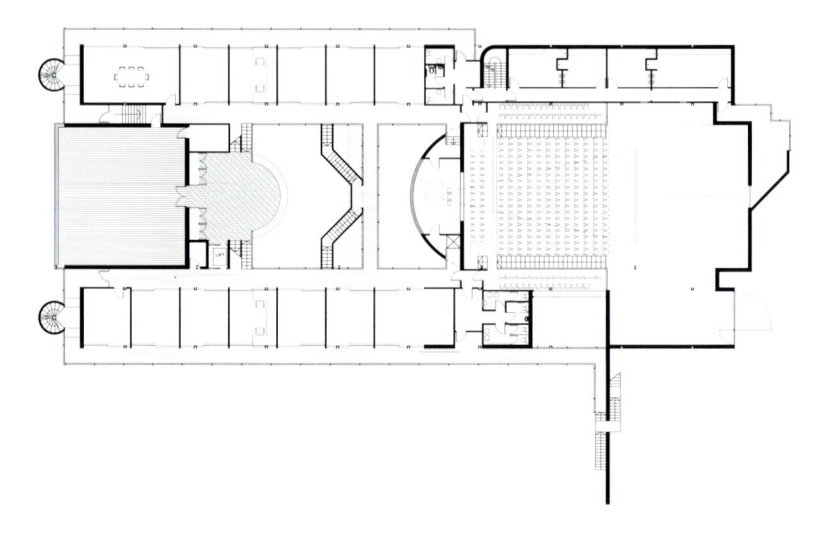

The Creative Enterprise Centre in Caernarfon is a project which has arisen from the resurgence of this area of North Wales as a centre of Welsh Language Creative Industries, together with a perception of the need for a contemporary, flexible and medium-sized performance space in the town. The building is effectively a hybrid between theatre/rehearsal spaces and small office spaces aimed at young creative companies. The essence of the idea is that whilst theatres generally spring to life in the evenings, the office side of the building is a daytime activity, and that putting these two functions together, both of which involve creative people, will ensure a building that can be continually in use. The heart of the idea of the building is communication between those working there and visitors.

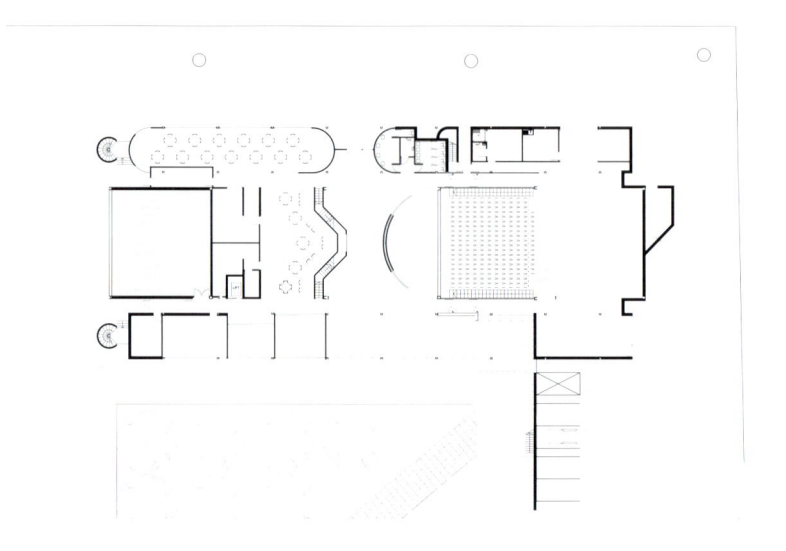

Buildings for the Arts 147

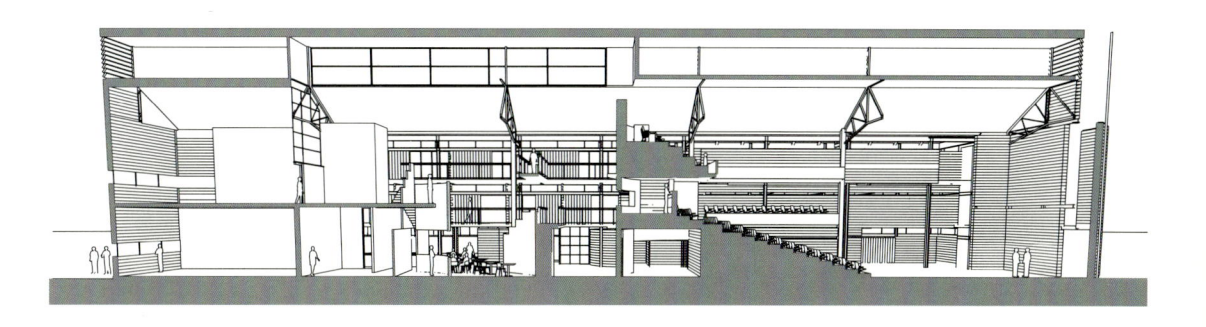

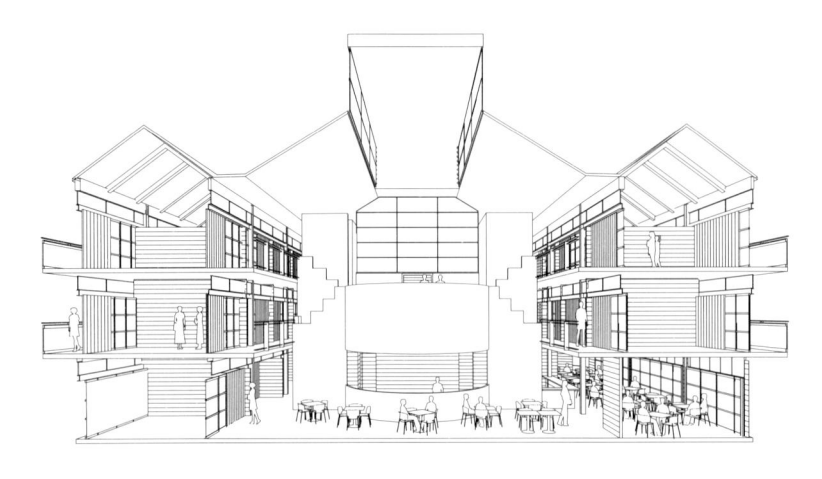

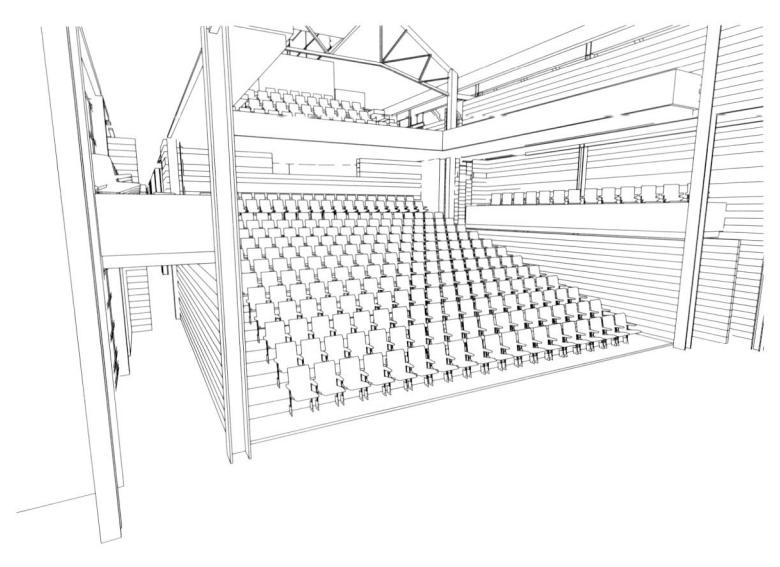

The idea of the building, inspired by its location on the dock, is to make a warehouse-like construction of three parallel sheds, an inner shed containing the large volumes, requiring large span structures, flanked on either side by smaller, more domestic-scaled sheds of individual rooms. The inner shed, which has the theatre at its east end and the rehearsal rooms at its west end, contains within it a large atrium foyer space around which everything circulates. The objective of the design has been to attempt to ensure that most of the office spaces on the first and second floors face directly onto walkways in an atrium space so that their activities and presence are visible to everybody entering the building. The idea of this space is further strengthened by the presence of the theatre and rehearsal rooms as curved objects inserted into the rectangular shape of the building.

The exterior of the building is largely to be formed by a steel frame and green oak boarding. The oak will develop a natural weathered grey patina over the years and forms a rain screen to the building. External walkways will be formed of galvanised steel with lightweight perforated metal decks, while the exterior wall adjacent to the entrance will be formed of board-marked concrete. Windows will generally be aluminium or steel and the interior of the building coloured as a contrast to the relatively monochrome exterior.

Buildings for the Arts

Tolbooth Arts Centre Stirling

Completed 2001, for Stirling Council. In association with Simpson and Brown conservation architects.

A complex of buildings dating from the Seventeenth Century onwards, the Old Tolbooth in Stirling has functioned variously as a Town Hall, a Courthouse and a jail. In 1997 Stirling Council held an invited competition to renovate the Tolbooth as a music-focused Arts venue, opening the building up to the local community and the wider public for performance and participation.

The existing building forms a U-shape with the courthouse occupying the central section and vaults underneath. It sits between the two main streets on the approach to the Castle. As part of the design the connecting street, Jail Wynd, has been closed and pedestrianised, and it is here that we have made a new entrance utilising one of the vault spaces as a passageway.

150 Buildings for the Arts

Buildings for the Arts 151

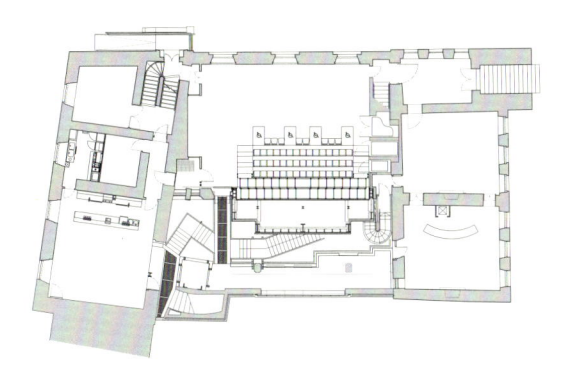

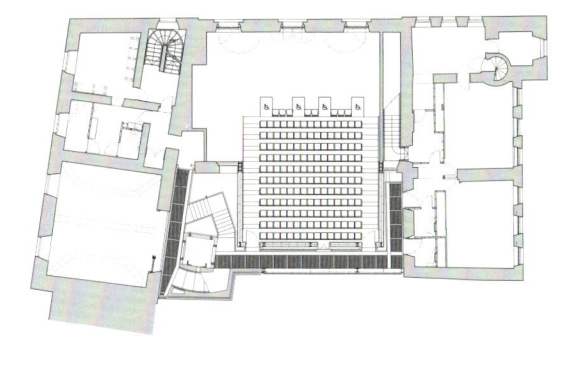

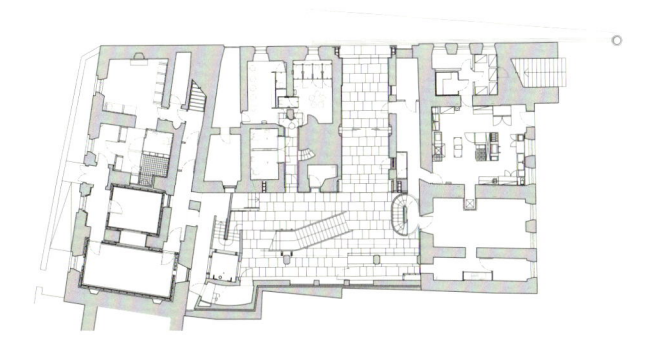

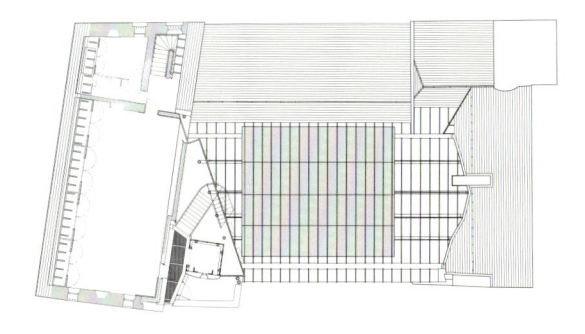

The A Listed existing building has been interfered with as little as possible. The elevations to the public streets and the fine interiors retain their character and can be enjoyed as 'the Old Tolbooth'. Special interiors have been reserved for specific uses within the existing building: the old Courtroom is re-used as the pre-eminent performance space; the robing room as a grand bar; and the old council chamber as a high quality restaurant.

All the major interventions necessary to achieve the above have been located in the only empty space available on this restricted site: the eastern courtyard, where the foyer and circulation system of the building are located. Overhanging it is a lead cassette (known as the 'backpack') containing the extension to the courtroom which creates the auditorium and above it the air handling plant. Using the courtyard as the foyer allows visual and actual access to all the facilities and permits a single lift to reach the many existing floor levels.

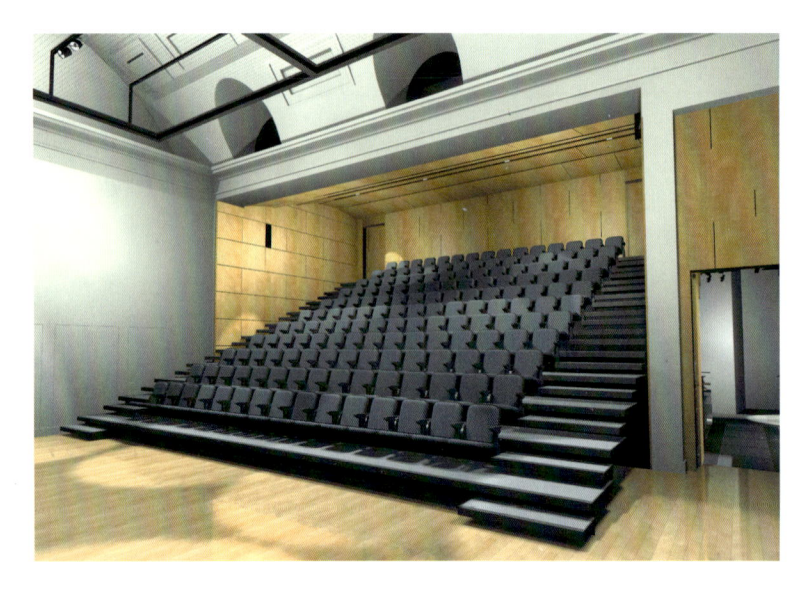

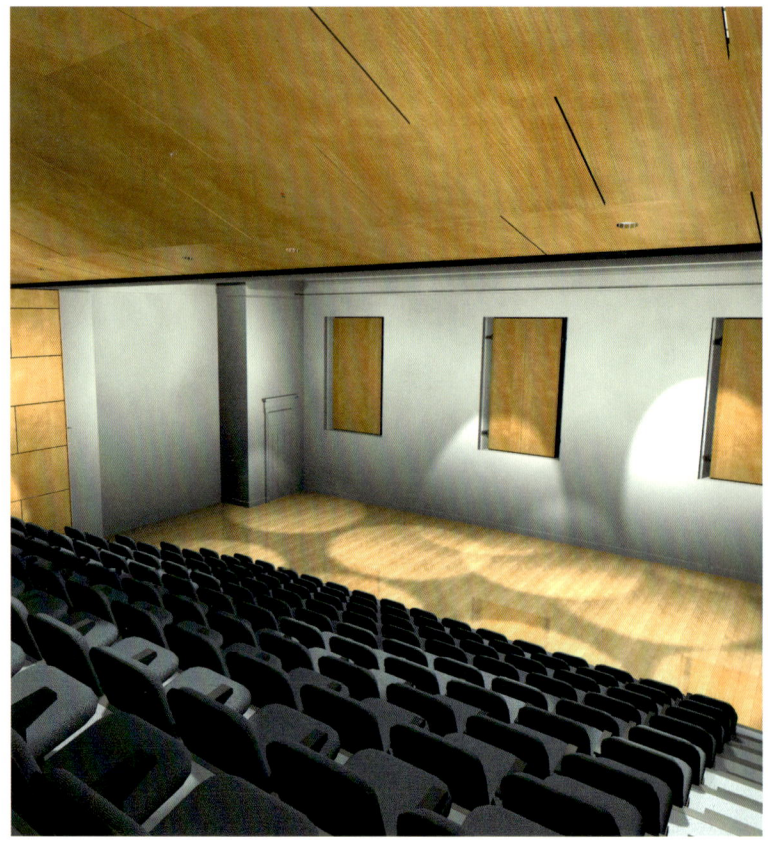

Buildings for the Arts 153

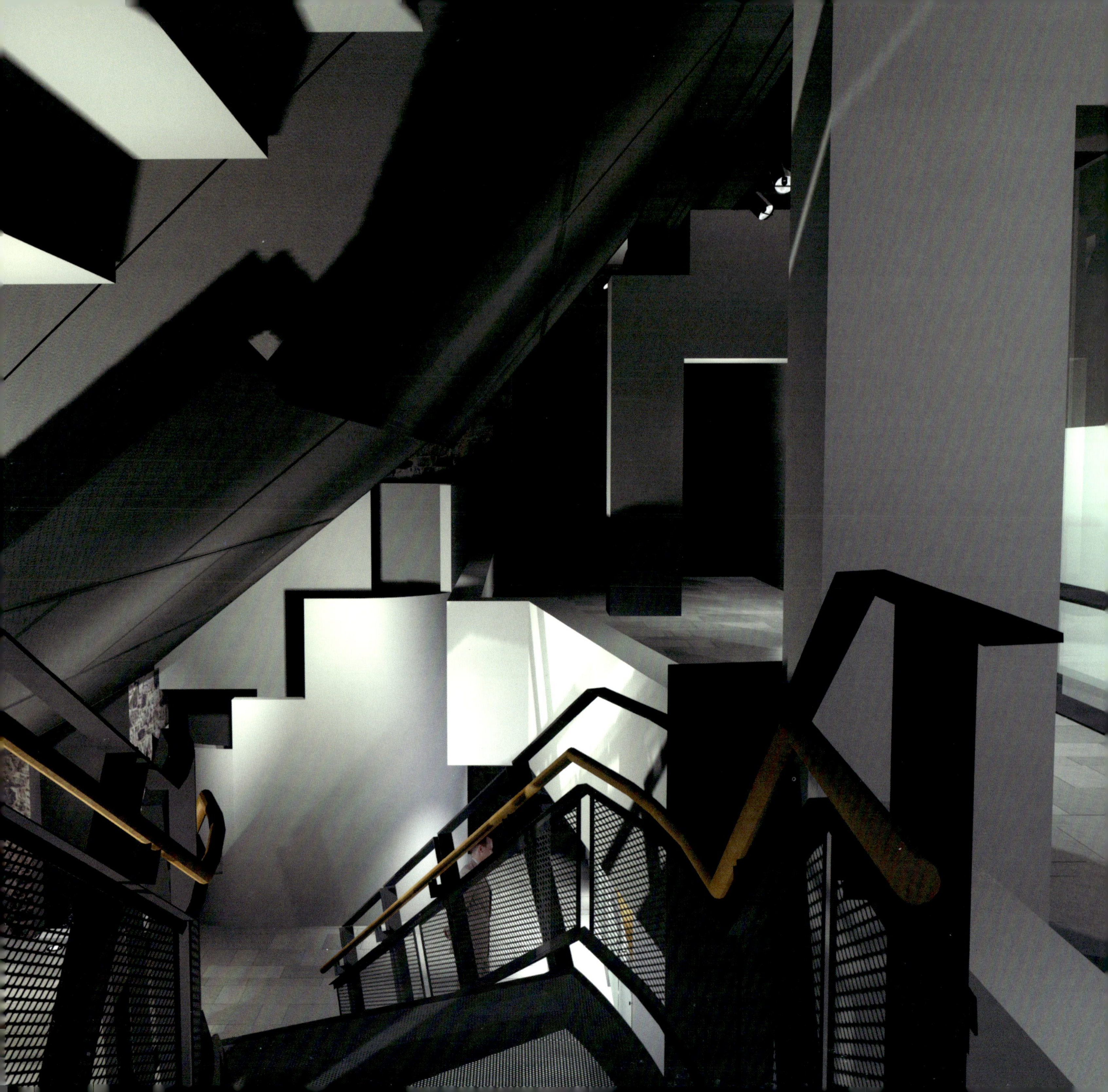

Buildings for the Arts 155

A Moment of Introspection

Richard Murphy

The practice of architecture is well-named, for despite the many influences that pervade our office the best teacher over the past ten years has been the experience of building, and then afterwards, the observation of how buildings have been accepted by their users. Some architects make a rule never to return once a project has been completed fearing, I suppose, the incremental and gradual destruction of their vision. I take the opposite view. The last ten years have convinced me that architecture is primarily a social art and the starting point for all our designs has been to understand the potential for human interaction made possible through architectural space. It gives me the greatest satisfaction to watch how a family inhabits a house, how children populate a classroom, how a stranger explores a public building, how a people-watcher places himself in a café, and so on, and it is no accident that most of the project descriptions in this book are stated in these terms. Unfortunately it seems necessary to make this assertion in contrast to much of the current media reportage, which would have architecture as a branch of the fashion industry. Today the greatest publicity is given to the buildings with the highest shock value or at least those which are the most photogenic. Against this background of what we call 'sound bite architecture', there is probably little in this book that might be termed avant-garde; rather, I hope that the buildings illustrated will be judged to be of their own time yet rooted in the places in which they are built, contributing toward their wider context and having a qualities which outlive the fashionable.

Saying that architecture should be of its own time may be stating the obvious, but my generation was educated in the 70s when the vilification of the architect was at its height. Modern architecture, it was generally agreed, had spoilt the view, and modern architects in the popular imagination were almost another branch of the criminal classes. While Edinburgh had escaped the worst of the calamities wreaked by so-called urban renewal and the ravages of the traffic engineer the reaction in this city had been so complete, and the consequent conservation movement so all-powerful, that for some time it looked like the history of architecture was officially coming to an end. "Edinburgh would shortly be finished" was the comment of a well-known Civic Trust secretary after a particularly notorious hole in the ground was eventually filled. But a city that is finished is most certainly finished in both senses of the word, and today there is a creeping consensus that for a city to be a living organism it must accept the architecture of its own time; to make history for future generations and to enrich rather than disrupt its context. This is no easy task.

Architecture of its own place is an equally perplexing objective. The old connections between local materials or a local way of construction that collectively forms the character of a place have been swept away, and today an architect must look for more subtle connections to the locale. At the urban scale, and particularly with the city under such attack, our projects have been conservative, developing or sometimes resurrecting historic patterns of development for re-use. Scotland is a stone country, a place of thick-walled buildings and at the much more local scale of working with existing buildings, we have enjoyed exploiting this quality by making additions which complement by contrast. To heavy stone bases we have added light thin-walled tectonic constructions and flying floating roofs above expressed structures. Setting up such juxtapositions is not only an enjoyable game of opposites, but has a historical motivation too, since in the traditions of Ruskin and Morris history is always a continuity and cannot be arrested nor should ever be reconstructed. We prefer to leave no opportunity for historical confusion; indeed on most occasions the original buildings have been deliberately 'ruined' to allow the new constructions to act as either revealed inner-linings or as new superstructure growing out of the wreckage.

A major abstract influence of working in Scotland is the quality of light. Changing every day, this phenomenon happily coincides with an architectural interest in a Soanian way of lighting buildings from above. In the particular world of gallery lighting it was a happy accident that we never had the budget at The Fruitmarket Gallery to install all the usual filtering precautions, for now I am convinced that just as so much Scottish Art has been preoccupied with light, this gallery and other subsequent ones come alive by reflecting the dramatic changes of atmosphere evident outside.

For me, the main interest in Scottish light is the dramatic difference in daylight hours between winter and summer which becomes exaggerated the further north you travel. To stand on the most northerly coast on June 21st and watch the sky never get dark is a magical phenomenon. Likewise, and maybe some would say perversely, I also enjoy the feeling of hibernation when the city is dark at 3.30pm in the middle of December and expressed by the physicality of closing Georgian or Victorian shutters against the winter night. These two extremes connect directly to the human psyche of introvert and extrovert, necessarily complementary. Sometimes when lecturing I show a slide of Mies Van de Rohe's Farnsworth house and at the same time read a few lines from *Wind in the Willows* and in particular the evocation of Mole's wonderful womb-like home. Both images, one of a light glassy pavilion and the other a dim, warm, cosy place are equally valid as ideas of inhabitation, but it has to be admitted that the Twentieth Century has been much more successful in the former than with the latter. Interestingly, Scotland's primary architect of that century, Macintosh, understood this winter mood: witness his beautiful white cave for the marriage bed at Hill House or his library in the School of Art in Glasgow. Situated on a corner, this could have been a great light-filled open space, but instead he chose deliberately to make it a place of autumnal gloom where, as Hans Hollein puts it, "books engulf the reader in study". Aldo Van Eyck's observation that a house is both a nest and a cave encapsulates this idea, and there are a number of projects illustrated that have pursued an interest in internal shutters and hinged ceilings that have attempted to transform a single space from one to the other – from a daytime transparent space open to the outside to a night time warm, closed space usually lined in wood. In some instances, the closing ceiling shutters also dramatically reduce and alter the section of the space further adding to the effect. Needless to say, there are also dramatic energy improvements through such moves, although these are not the prime motivation.

An architecture of moving parts is not just confined to the exterior skin. A range of projects have devices which allow the users to adapt their buildings internally in a variety of pre-determined ways. This we have come to call transformability and should not be confused with the concept of flexibility or 'loose fit' which in my mind reduces architecture to the status of a dumb warehouse. Transformability is part of an elemental way of thinking about building construction. A valid criticism in modern architecture has been its banality of detail. While for some this can become a fetish in minimalism, I agree with another of Van Eyck's famous one-liners that "a sign of a bad building is that it only gets bigger as you get closer to it". Much of our work could be described as straightforward and simple in concept – the free-standing houses for example – which only begin to get a degree of complexity when the process of construction and detailing commences. Ted Cullinen called this "the celebration of necessity" and I readily admit a tendency to over-express the constructional, to having a way of thinking about a building as a story line, a process of placing one element on top of another. Inevitably the arbitrary staging post of a set of planning permission drawings we find very frustrating as a design can only crystallise at the scale of 1:50 after the thinking at 1:5 has been completed. Design elaboration never stops even when, indeed particularly when, the building is on site. This can occasionally cause our contractors and clients anxious moments, but working initially on small projects, many of them with the same contractor Steve Evans, has allowed us the luxury of site finesse that larger more legalistic contractual agreements inhibit.

The shift in a relatively short period of time from a practice of three or four working on small works to a group of 20 or so with several multi-million pound projects has been a testing process. One is only too aware of some architects who have attempted the transition, but whose work seems to have the quality of having been put on the photocopier with the enlargement button pressed. Managerially, I believe we have passed this test with flying colours, but what is more interesting is how the architectural language has survived. The reputation of the practice was undoubtedly founded on tiny house extensions, frequently described as 'crafted'; and on works to existing stone buildings or "cannibalisations" as Gordon Benson once memorably described them. With a larger project, the degree of invention per square metre must of course relax, and moments of intense architectural activity need to be counterpointed with areas where nothing extraordinary happens at all. At Dundee Contemporary Arts I believe the balance was well-struck and a large, complex and non-repetitive building is constructed in a highly particular manner without the architecture over-powering the essential functions within. The same I think will be true of our soon-to-be-completed Stirling Tolbooth Arts Centre where we have had an extraordinary opportunity to engage with the complexities of an historic building on a very large scale. We have had less opportunity at this scale to build new constructions: most of it has been housing to date, but even then I believe the architectural language has shifted successfully from the individual statement to the inevitably repetitive with no loss of visual interest. As a pointer to the future, undoubtedly one of the most unusual and intriguing recent projects has been the computer library at Napier University. We have been used to long, highly particular and non-repetitive programmes (more than once we remarked that briefs, especially those for arts-related projects, read like a student project) whereas the brief at Napier could have been written in two sentences. However, a simple brief has been translated into a space of repetitive elements which none-the-less has been constructed to provide a complex experience of movement, structure, light, and place-making. Absent from our portfolio to date has been any significant design projects for the commercial sector, and this project gives a taste of how we might develop a natural complexity from a straightforward brief given an opportunity in that particular area.

This is not the place to discuss the architectural influences on the office – Richard Weston has performed that task admirably. My academic studies of Scarpa have of course tended to overshadow what is a very catholic range of architect heroes. I believe it was Peter Smithson who said to his students at the Architectural Association that they would be very lucky if they had a single original idea in their life. I readily admit to not having had one yet! Architects are, and always have been, the greatest of magpies and I make no apology for stealing ideas from wherever we find them. Critics have observed that there is a distinctive language emerging from the office which I find both flattering and a little worrying. It is natural that an architect should have a recognisable signature that passes from building to building (and those who don't stand accused of a kind of architectural schizophrenia) but the danger is that it becomes a dogmatic style incapable of development and imposed regardless of context. The engagement between this inner driving of the architect and the exigencies of client, programme, and site is after all what make the practice of architecture so endlessly fascinating and I see no reason as the clients and programmes and sites develop why the language should not develop with them.

At our launch 10 years ago, Isi Metstein spoke generously and memorably, "We all know that the boat is sea worthy, but the question tonight is, is the sea boat worthy?". Edinburgh is a tough place to be a modern architect; there is hardly a project in this book which has not produced a torrent of objections from local residents. Resistance to change is massive and all-pervasive, but this is understandable in a city which is so much of a set piece. We have been very lucky with our clients who have been unstinting and dogged in their support through the torturous twists and turns of the process of obtaining planning permission. Not a native of Edinburgh, I am frequently asked why I stay in such an architecturally hostile place. Indeed the apparent disinterest, to date, in our work from any government source or our local authority is further dispiriting, and contrasts with Glasgow where the local authority and enterprise organisations seem to take such an active interest in patronising their own creative talent.

And yet the challenge of continuing the history of such a remarkable place is intoxicating. Morris wrote magical words when he said, "All continuity of history is perpetual change and it is not hard to see that for good and for evil we have changed with a vengeance and established our claim to be the continuers of history". My generation is the one that currently holds that responsibility and, given the opportunity, there is no more challenging or rewarding place in which to work.

The Practice

The practice enjoys or has enjoyed contributions from:

Alex Abbey
Clive Albert
Michael Brookman Amissah
Graeme Armet
Patrick Bankhead
Tim Bayman
Peter Besley
Lorraine Beveridge
Bill Black
Robert Black
Mathew Blair
Adrian Boot
Matt Bremner
Cathy Brick
Edward Burgess
Joe Carnegie
Phil Catchside
Oliver Chapman
Aaron Coates
Robbie Cullen
Lesley Dell
Francesco De Domenico
Alan Dunsmore
Patrick Fallis
Jose Fernandez

Mark Floate
Colin Foster
Steven Fraser
Claire Gaffney
Hamish Ginn
Allan Gray
Lee Hallman
Scott M Harrison
Andre Henkamp
Ed Hollis
John Leach
Matt Loader
Chris Malcolm
James Mason
Manfred Mattersberger
Alistair McAuslan
Andy McAvoy
Wattie McCallum
Calum McDonald
Euan McDonald
Sarah McInenry
Guido McLellan
Ian McMurray
Graeme Mitchell
Graeme Montgomery

Sam Moran
Richard Murphy
James Nelmes
Gareth Pugh
Peter Quinger
Brent Railton
Gerard Reinmuth
Chris Rhodes
Johnathan Riddle
Chris Rogers
Keith Ross
Neil Simpson
Richard Smith
Stewart Stevenson
Ian Strakis
David Stronge
Ryan Sylvester
James Taylor
Marco Terranova
Will Tunnell
Iolanda Veziano
John Walker
Adrian Welch

Awards

RIBA National Awards	Høgel House	1996
	Maggie's Centre	1997
RIBA (Scotland) Awards	Blytheman House	1992
	The Fruitmarket Gallery	1993
	Francis House	1995
	Høgel House	1996
	Maggie's Centre	1997
	Palmer House	1998
	Morrison House	1999
	Dublin Colonies	2000
	Dundee Contemporary Arts	2000
	Harmeny School	2001
RIAI Regional Award	Stoneman House	1999
Edinburgh Architectural Association:		
Silver Medal	Blytheman House	1992
	The Fruitmarket Gallery	1993
	Palmer House	1996
Bronze Medal	Maggie's Centre	1998
	Harrison House	2001
Commendation	Francis House	1994
	Dublin Colonies	2001

RIAS Regeneration of Scotland:		
Supreme Award	Dundee Contemporary Arts	1999
	Graham Square	2000
Award	Høgel House	1996
Royal Scottish Academy:		
Gold Medal	Experimental Energy house	1995
Saltire Award	Canongate	2000
Saltire Commendation	Dublin Colonies	2000
Civic Trust Award	Dundee Contemporary Arts	2000
Civic Trust Commendation	The Fruitmarket Gallery	1993
	Høgel House	1998

Photography credits

Photographers:
- CA — Clive Albert
- JB — John Brouwer
- JC — Joe Carnegie
- RC — Robyn Chapehrka
- DC — David Churchill
- PC — Peter Cook
- AD — Alan Dimmick
- AF — Alan Forbes
- GF — Gavin Fraser
- CG — Catriona Grant
- KH — Keith Hunter
- ML — Matthew Loader
- SM — Simon Morrison
- RM — Richard Murphy
- VN — Vanessa Nicholson
- CR — Colin Ruscoe
- JR — John Richards
- MT — Malcolm J Thomson, studio M
- DV — Dick Verton
- RW — Richard Weston
- DW — David Williams

Electronic images are from Richard Murphy Architects.

Photographs are credited on page numbers shown, clockwise from top left.

Front cover:	DC
Back cover:	MT
2	DC
8	AF
9	RM, CA
10	AF
11	JR, AF, AF, AF
12	MT
13	RM, RW, AF
14	DC
15	AF, AF, RW
16	RM
17	RM, ML, AF
18	AF, DC
19	KH, RM, RM
20	all DC
21	AD
22	RW, RM
23	KH
24	RM
25	AF
26	RM
28/9	AF
30	RM, RM, CA
31	all CA
32	RM, GF, GF
33	AF
34	AF, RM
35	RM, AF, AF
36	all AF
37	AF
38	RM, SM, SM, SM
39	all SM
42/3	MT
44	all RM
45	VN, VN, RM
46	VN
48	DV
49	DV
50	DV, JB, RM, DV
51	DV
52	RM, RM, MT
53	all MT
54	RM, MT
55	all MT
57	all AF
58	RM, AF, AF
59	AF
60	AF
64	AF
66	RM, RM, AF
67	AF
68	RM, AF, AF
69	JC
70	RM, JC, JC, DC, AF
71	DC
72	all DC
73	all JC
74/5	DC
76	RM, DC
77	all DC
78	ML, ML, DC, DC, DC
79	DC
80	KH, RM, RM
81	KH
82	all KH
83	RM, AD, AD
84	all AD
85	RM
92	RM
94/5	AF
96	RM, AF, AF, AF
97	all AF
98	all AF
99	AF
100	anon, DC
101	DC
102	all DC
103	RM, DC
108	RM, AF

Exhibition credits

109	all AF
110	AF
111	all AF
112	RM, AF, AF
116	all RM
118/9	DC
120	RM, RM, AF, AF, RM
121	CG, PC, CG, CG
122	PC, RM, RM, RM
123	AD
124	AF, PC, RC
125	PC, ML
126	AD, AD, CG, ML
127	RM, DC
128	DC
129	RM, RM, AD
130	all DC
131	all KH
132	DC
133	CR, DC, CR, DC
134	RM, DC, RM, RM, DC
135	RM, RW, RM, KH
141	AF
146	DW
159	AF

Exhibitions are credited on page numbers shown, clockwise from top left.

17	Jeff Koons
22	Richard Wentworth
120	Gerald Laing
121	*Tales of the Sands*
	Sol Lewitt
	Tales of the Sands
	Tales of the Sands
122	Sol Lewitt
123	Ross Sinclair VFTF
124	bottom left:
	Northern Lights Peter Fink
125	Sol Lewitt
	Jeff Koons
126	Martin Boyce VFTF
	Yoko Ono
	Jeff Koons
133	Ernesto Neto
	Olafur Eliasson
	Prime

Photography & Exhibition credits 163

Colophon

Book published to accompany the exhibition
'Richard Murphy Architects: Ten Years of Practice'
at The Fruitmarket Gallery, Edinburgh, from 29 September to 17 November 2001.

Exhibition funded by The Dunard Fund and Creative Edinburgh.
Additional support from Hillaldam Coburn and Apotheek van Hulten.

Publication designed by Lucy Richards, Edinburgh.

Published by:
The Fruitmarket Gallery
45 Market Street
Edinburgh EH1 1DF
Tel: 0131-225 2383
Fax: 0131-220 3130
Web: www.fruitmarket.co.uk

The Fruitmarket Gallery is subsidised by the Scottish Arts Council.
Scottish Charity No. SC 005576.

Catalogue printed in an edition of 3,000 copies by specialblue, London. Printed in the UK.

ISBN 0 947912 03 7

All rights reserved. No part of the book may be reproduced in any form, by any means, electronic, mechanical or otherwise, without prior permission in writing from the publisher.

© The Fruitmarket Gallery, the artists, photographers and authors, 2001.
www.richardmurphyarchitects.com

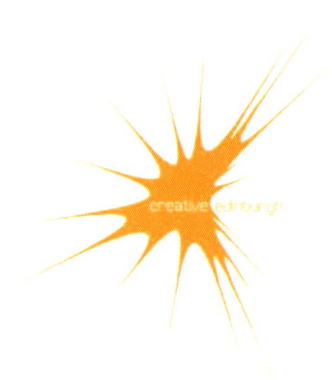

www.creative-edinburgh.com